NOVELIST'S BOOT CAMP

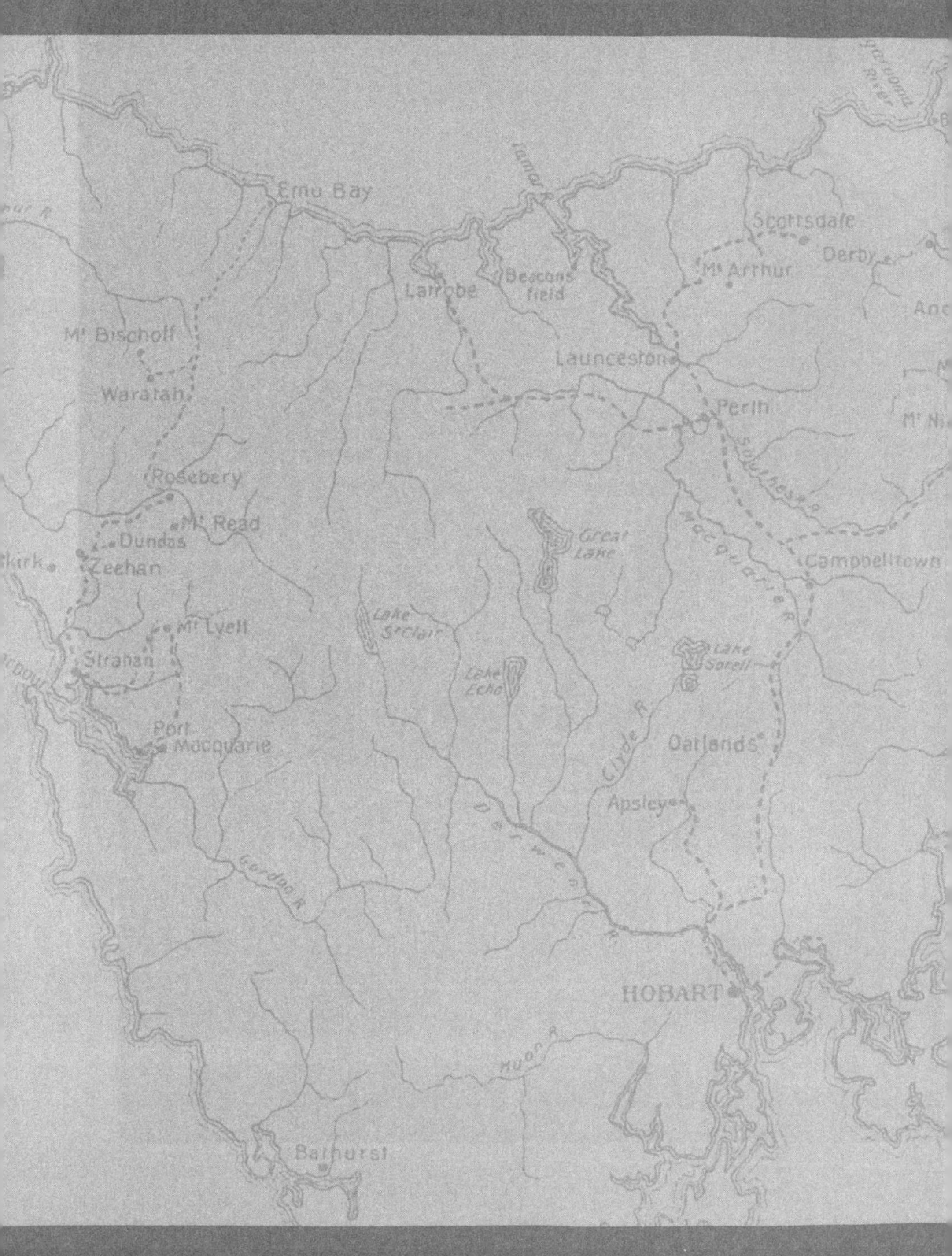

Emu Bay
Tamar R
Scottsdale
Derby
Mt Arthur
Latrobe
Beacons
field
Mt Bischoff
Launceston
Waratah
Perth
Rosebery
South Esk R
Mt Read
Great
Lake
Dundas
Zeehan
Macquarie R
Campbelltown
Lake
St Clair
Mt Lyell
Lake
Sorell
Strahan
Lake
Echo
Clyde R
Port
Macquarie
Oatlands
Apsley
Derwent R
Gordon R
HOBART
Huon R
Bathurst

TODD A. STONE

NOVELIST'S BOOT CAMP

101 WAYS TO TAKE YOUR BOOK FROM BORING TO BESTSELLER

W

WRITER'S DIGEST BOOKS
Cincinnati, Ohio
www.writersdigest.com

 Published by Writer's Digest Books, an imprint of F+W Publications, Inc., 4700 East Galbraith Road, Cincinnati, OH 45236. (800) 289-0963. First edition.

Distributed in Canada by Fraser Direct, 100 Armstrong Avenue, Georgetown, ON, Canada L7G 5S4, Tel: (905) 877-4411. Distributed in the U.K. and Europe by David & Charles, Brunel House, Newton Abbot, Devon, TQ12 4PU, England, Tel: (+44) 1626 323200, Fax: (+44) 1626 323319, E-mail: mail@davidandcharles.co.uk. Distributed in Australia by Capricorn Link, P.O. Box 704, Windsor, NSW 2756 Australia, Tel: (02) 4577-3555.

10 09 08 07 06   5 4 3 2 1

Library of Congress Cataloging-in-Publication Data

Stone, Todd

Novelist's boot camp : 101 ways to take your book from boring to bestseller / Todd A. Stone.

p. cm.

Includes index.

ISBN-13: 978-1-58297-360-9 (hardcover : alk. paper)

ISBN-10: 1-58297-360-1

1. Fiction--Authorship. I. Title.

PN3365.S85 2006   2005029720

808.3–dc22

Edited by KELLY NICKELL

Designed by GRACE RING

Production coordinated by ROBIN RICHIE

DEDICATION

For all my children

ACKNOWLEDGMENTS

The author salutes and wishes to make grateful acknowledgment to Ms. Jane Friedman, for determination to accomplish a mission; Ms. Kelly Nickell for coolness under fire; Mr. Peter Rubie of the Peter Rubie Agency for the ability to navigate in treacherous terrain; Mr. Evan Marshall for setting the example; Ms. Hanley Kanar for success in long-term campaigns, and former U.S. Army Major Teresa V.M. Stone, for the support, motivation, and dedication that made this book possible.

TABLE OF CONTENTS

INTRODUCTION: WRITERS, ATTENNNNN-TION! 001

BATTLE PLAN ALPHA: MENTAL PREPARATION AND MISSION PLANNING 003

Draw your ammunition: disciplined creativity, control of your calendar, and a word-warrior's mind-set.

MISSION I: GET YOUR IMAGINATION IN FORMATION 004

BATTLE PLAN BRAVO: INVENTION 039

Adjust fire on your genre, story idea, main character, and setting.

MISSION II: INVENT YOUR COMPREHENSIVE CONCEPT 040

BATTLE PLAN CHARLIE: DEVELOPMENT 071

Deploy your characters, casual event, story line, and critical development tools.

MISSION III: ENLIST YOUR NEW RECRUITS 073

MISSION IV: DEVISE YOUR OPERATIONS ORDER .. 118

BATTLE PLAN DELTA: DRAFTING 141
Advance aggressively toward a quality first draft.

MISSION V: CROSS THE LINE OF DEPARTURE 143
MISSION VI: COMMIT YOUR RESERVES 169
MISSION VII: SOUND OFF! 187
MISSION VIII: EXECUTE SHOCK AND AWE 214
MISSION IX: UTILIZE STEALTH TECHNIQUES ... 220

BATTLE PLAN ECHO: REVISION AND REWRITING 246
Breach the obstacles to a fully revised draft
with passes of creative firepower.

MISSION X: ADVANCE TO CONTACT 247

BATTLE PLAN FOXTROT: EDITING AND PROOFREADING .. 282
Prepare your draft for command inspection.

MISSION XI: GIVE YOUR PROSE A SPIT SHINE .. 283

BATTLE PLAN GOLF: STAYING BATTLE READY 293
Continue the mission into new terrain.

MISSION XII: GO BEYOND BOOT CAMP 294

APPENDIX: TWELVE-WEEK NOVELIST'S BOOT CAMP ... 303
INDEX 307

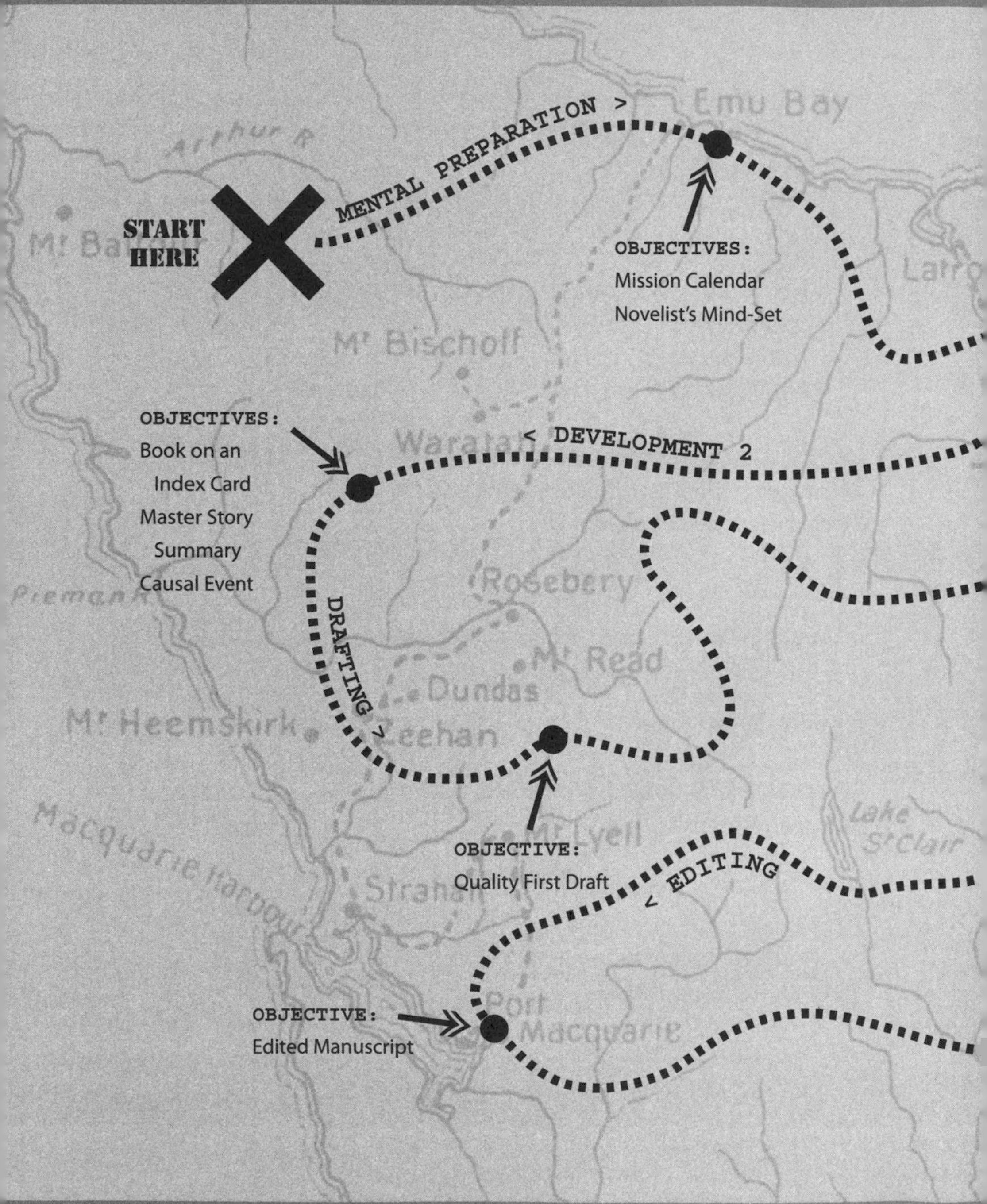
START HERE
MENTAL PREPARATION >
OBJECTIVES:
Mission Calendar
Novelist's Mind-Set
< DEVELOPMENT 2
OBJECTIVES:
Book on an Index Card
Master Story Summary
Causal Event
DRAFTING >
OBJECTIVE:
Quality First Draft
< EDITING
OBJECTIVE:
Edited Manuscript
Emu Bay
Arthur R
Mt Bischoff
Waratah
Rosebery
Mt Read
Dundas
Mt Heemskirk
Zeehan
Mt Lyell
Strahan
Macquarie Harbour
Port Macquarie
Lake St Clair

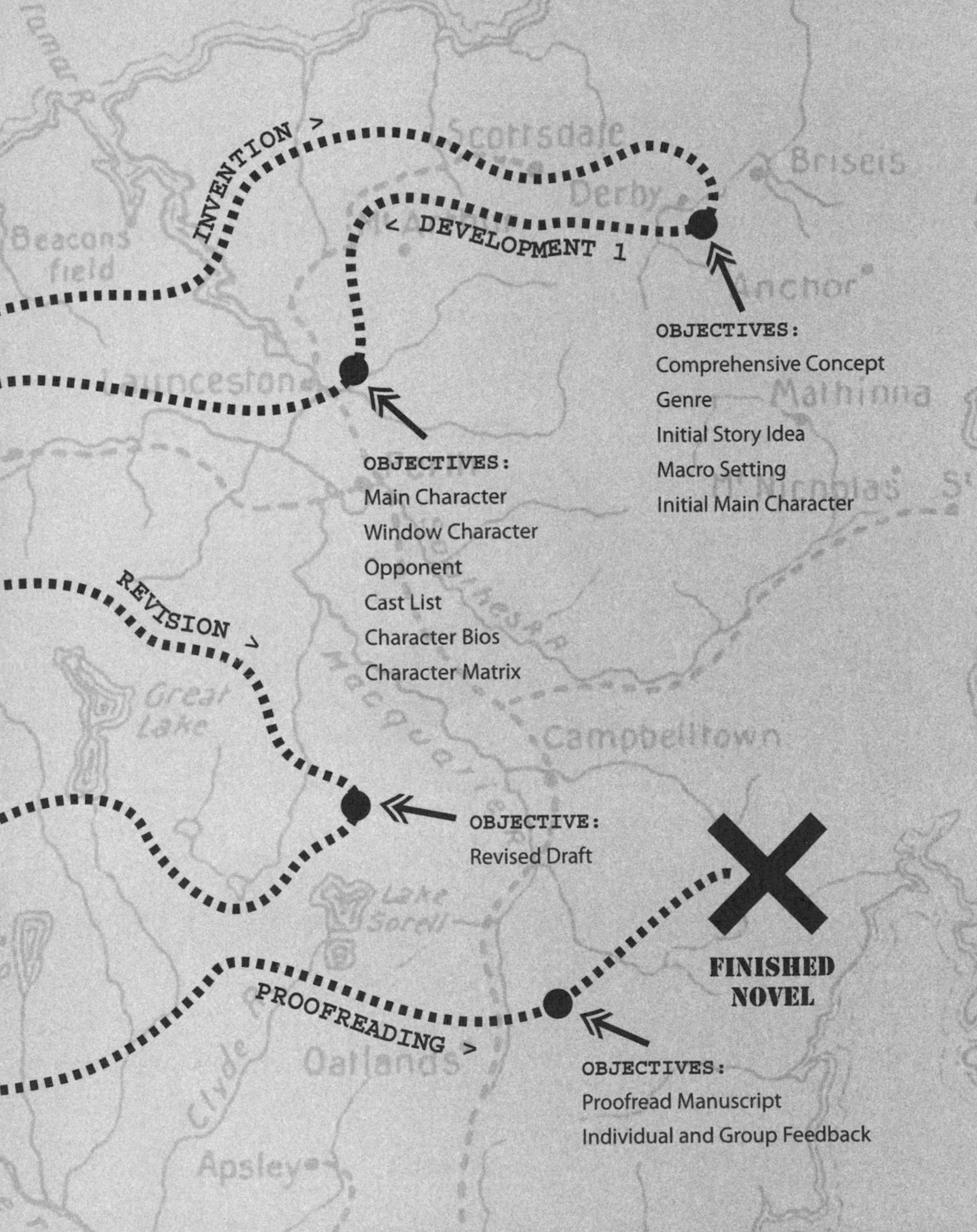
INVENTION >
< DEVELOPMENT 1
OBJECTIVES:
Comprehensive Concept
Genre
Initial Story Idea
Macro Setting
Initial Main Character
OBJECTIVES:
Main Character
Window Character
Opponent
Cast List
Character Bios
Character Matrix
REVISION >
OBJECTIVE:
Revised Draft
FINISHED NOVEL
PROOFREADING >
OBJECTIVES:
Proofread Manuscript
Individual and Group Feedback

INTRODUCTION

WRITERS, ATTENNNNN-TION!

Welcome, new recruit, to your very own novelist's boot camp.

Now drop and give me twenty.

Everyone knows that military life is different from civilian life, so you can expect this book—modeled on the boot camp that makes soldiers out of everyday men and women—to be different from ordinary how-to books. And it is.

You will see and do things differently. And you will do push-ups.

In the modern armed forces, new recruits receive several weeks—sometimes many months—of training in the essential skills, techniques, and attitudes necessary to enable them to both survive in combat and do their duty in the most effective and efficient manner possible. This basic training, also known as boot camp, is physically, mentally, and emotionally demanding. Completion of the training leads to a significant increase in competence, confidence, and maturity in the young men and women who complete it.

Boot camp is also essential because, while successful completion cannot guarantee success on the battlefield, failure to complete the training almost guarantees an inability to survive the deadly environment of modern conflict. In short order, he or she will be no more than cannon fodder—an ineffective statistic waiting to happen. After more than thirty years of writing for publication, teaching writing, and training and leading soldiers, it has become clear to me that today's novelists need the same kind of focused training—a *novelist's* boot camp that equips would-be writers with the skills and techniques they need to successfully complete a strong piece of book-length fiction.

Military boot camp changes how recruits see themselves, their military duty, and the world around them. Today's novelists need this same kind of transformation in how they think about and view their writing. And, like those who don a military uniform, writers may sometimes need a kick-start—or a good swift kick—to begin, pursue, and complete their projects.

Novelist's Boot Camp provides you with proven techniques for succeeding in all phases of writing a novel, and with insights, tools, and instruction for making the most of your writing time and energy—so that you can complete your writing project while meeting your other commitments (to your family and your day job, for instance).

The discipline needed to be successful in the military and the creativity needed to be successful as a novelist are by no means incompatible. In fact, it is only by applying discipline to your creativity that you can be successful. It is discipline that helps a soldier attain an objective. It is discipline that will allow you to exercise your creativity and *your* objective—a finished, polished manuscript.

There are many ways to write a novel—countless techniques and variations. There is no one right answer or one right way to write a book; practices that work well for one writer may not fit at all with another novelist's temperament. Your job is to find what works best for you, what helps you to accomplish your goals.

So make the commitment and join up—start your training today. You just might find something in yourself you didn't know you had.

Now do some more push-ups—then go report for duty.

BATTLE PLAN ALPHA

MENTAL PREPARATION AND MISSION PLANNING

MISSION I: GET YOUR IMAGINATION IN FORMATION 004

Drill 1: Make It Your Mission 005

Drill 2: Adopt a Principled Approach 007

Drill 3: No Sniveling Allowed 011

Drill 4: Control Your Calendar 013

Drill 5: See Your Target 016

Drill 6: Toss Out Your Civilian Clothes 019

Drill 7: Drill Your Way to Success 021

Drill 8: Forget About Reading for Enjoyment 023

Drill 9: Dodge the Land Mines 026

Drill 10: Write What You Must 029

Drill 11: Write in the Right Place 032

Drill 12: Make Peace With the Publishing Industry 034

Drill 13: Be More Successful 037

MISSION I

GET YOUR IMAGINATION IN FORMATION

Your first challenge is to get your imagination in formation and make a mission plan for your success, as well as for the success of your novel. Any boot camp drill sergeant will tell you that 99 percent of success in military boot camp is mental. Mental preparation is also the key to finding success as a novelist. To succeed in novelist's boot camp and in the mental combat of writing your novel, to prepare yourself for a challenging and demanding process, you need to drill. Like the recruit, you will become mentally and physically tired, but you must continue to push. More importantly, just like the recruit, you must learn a new way of thinking. You must develop a specific mental discipline—you must discipline your creativity.

Or do as recruits in boot camp do when their discipline slips—do push-ups.

One aspect of discipline is focus. As of right now, you and your creativity are in a kind of basic training for book-length works of fiction—a novelist's boot camp. Your creativity will no longer lollygag and go anywhere it wants. You will no longer wander around going from one idea, page, character, scene, or sentence to the next. You will create a master battle plan, you will plot out specific missions, and you will perform mental drills to prepare yourself for success. Mental preparation and mission planning get you in the right frame of mind and help you organize your most precious resources—time and energy—and build a strong base for executing the next stages of your battle plan. As you move through each phase of your battle plan and through mission after mission and drill after drill, you will discipline your creativity and build your novel.

And you will succeed. Now turn the page and move out!

DRILL 1

MAKE IT YOUR MISSION

To get your novel written and get it written well, you must leave behind your civilian ways of thinking about the craft.

In the civilian world, the budding novelist thinks of writing her novel as something almost mystic. She sits around and waits for some faceless muse to call. The would-be author performs countless unfocused free-writing exercises, or engages in hours or days of general research while waiting for the words to flow.

Maybe tomorrow, the wannabe novelist dreams, *I'll feel what genre I want to write in. Maybe tomorrow my character will reveal himself to me. Maybe tomorrow my story will make itself clear.*

It's time to start thinking of writing your novel as a mission. A good novel isn't something that just happens—it's a mission you accomplish. You're in charge. You're responsible. There are no maybes and no tomorrows. You don't wait for inspiration. Instead, you make a long-term battle plan for accomplishing the drills and tasks in this book. Then, each day, you do a bit more. You make steady, quality progress toward accomplishing your mission—writing a novel.

No one would expect soldiers to sit around and wait to feel the flow before they went into battle, or to attack a hill with no strategy. A successful attack depends on a strong plan and disciplined execution.

Writing your novel works the same way. Instead of waiting around for the muse to call and being frustrated when she doesn't, instead of getting ten, twenty, or thirty pages into a work and then feeling it die out, think of your novel as a project or mission. Carefully plan for its success, then execute small tasks each day.

You must allocate time for planning, preparation, drafting, revising, editing, and proofreading, so make a mission calendar for your novel-length writing project. Set tentative dates for completion of each of these major phases, and then break down the tasks in these phases and assign dates for those, too. (Refer to drill 4 to get started.) Your novel's mission calendar should have some give in it so you can coordinate your writing tasks with the other priorities and events in your life. This preplanning gives you both the discipline to see that you meet key dates (and get something done each day) and the flexibility to make changes as they're required.

Many people dream of writing a novel, but that's all they do—dream. The way to turn your dream into reality is to change the way you think about writing a novel. Don't think of your novel as some magical creative thing that will just happen—or it just won't happen. Make it a campaign, a mission, a long-term project. Devise a plan, make a calendar, expect both hard work and moments of deep satisfaction, and discipline yourself to see it through by making progress each day. You'll be justifiably proud of the results, and of yourself.

RELATED DRILLS

Drill 3: No Sniveling Allowed
Drill 10: Write What You Must
Drill 49: Know the Unwritten Rules for Quality Drafting

DRILL 2

ADOPT A PRINCIPLED APPROACH

Successful military projects follow proven principles of war, such as:

- **Mass:** Concentrate combat power at a strategic place and time.
- **Objective:** Direct every military operation toward a clearly defined and attainable objective.
- **Offensive:** Seize, retain, and exploit the initiative.

A successful fiction-writing project is also built around carefully identified principles.

1. Trust the process. The sheer size of the task of writing a novel, not to mention all the details that must be mastered in the writing process, can be intimidating. Military tacticians face the same kind of intimidation and challenge when planning and executing complex operations. Those tacticians follow proven processes to plan and execute projects when lives—not pages—are at stake. They know that moving methodically, from one step in the process to the next, is the most efficient and effective method to get the mission accomplished.

When you follow a process, that process helps bring order, simplicity, focus, and confidence to a large, complicated, chaotic, and intimidating project, whether you are planning and executing an invasion or a category romance. Don't worry about what comes next while you're trying to develop powerful dialogue for the scene in which your protagonist confronts her pursuer. Instead, trust the process and concentrate on one task at a time, building upon each step in the process.

2. Use the tools. No commander would think of attacking a hill, defending a piece of key terrain, or conducting an armed rescue mission without using every tool—every tank, cannon, weapon, aircraft, and surveillance radar—at his disposal.

To accomplish your mission and get the best results in your writing project, you also need to use tools. The tools in this book will both simplify your creative tasks and help to ensure that you get the results you want—from more realistic characters to more complex and entertaining story lines. Other tools, such as writers' groups, books and articles on the craft of fiction, and writing classes and seminars can also contribute. Writing is not, as civilian wisdom says, a solitary process. You have a whole network of others to help you, present in the form of their books, tools, and instruction.

3. Start with a seed, build a forest. From the seed of an idea or concept comes a unified and integrated forest of detailed plans and orders, each connected to and building on the others. Military planners like to use the term *centralized planning, decentralized execution.* Those planners begin with a central idea (defend this hill), develop an overarching concept of the operation, then prepare detailed operations orders. Those orders then cascade through the military units, and each unit issues and executes its own more developed, more specific plan.

You can apply this same principle as you move from conceptualizing to drafting to proofreading. In other words, start with your main idea and build to a much larger outline—you start with a seed and build up to a forest. You'll then draft, revise, edit, and proofread your novel in discrete steps, but always based on that concept. Because each step and action builds on the one before it, you'll develop an integrated, unified, and cohesive manuscript as you go.

4. Never fight fair. Military strategists believe in mass, in concentrating overwhelming combat power at a strategic place and time. Such overwhelming mass helps to ensure victory. As a novelist, you can follow this principle by breaking your writing tasks into discrete, easily accomplishable goals. Then bring all your energy to bear on each individual goal in turn. Don't painfully stretch to meet goals; instead, shrink them so you can easily concentrate your combat power—your creative energy—on them. Before you start, cut down any goal that is big enough to even hint at possible failure. Can't write five full scenes in a day? How about two? How about one? How about expanding the first sentence of one?

5. Get your calendar on your side. Military strategists seek to seize and maintain the advantage by staying on the offensive. They look for opportunities for movement toward their objectives, and they have a mind-set and outlook that each day brings not a series of requirements, but a chance to get one step closer to victory.

Many writers have felt the horrible sensation of time slipping away while their projects remained at a standstill. Your calendar is the key to your success and your mental well-being. Think like military strategists, who see opportunities instead of requirements. Don't think of the time you've set aside tomorrow as time when you *must* draft ten pages. Instead, think of tomorrow's writing time as an opportunity to be creative, to do what you love, and to make progress toward your ultimate writing goal.

6. Discipline yourself first, your work second. Military strategists know that victory begins inside the individual soldier. Disciplined soldiers come from disciplined units, and disciplined units achieve victory.

Your novel's success begins with you. A disciplined novelist produces a disciplined, quality work. Discipline requires self-control and dedication and is developed through measured daily practice. Discipline yourself by incorporating these principles into your writing, because the principles will enable you to faithfully execute the tasks and meet the goals you've set for yourself and for your work. You'll find that your writing will improve as a result of the discipline you apply to it.

7. Celebrate successes. Military leaders have two guiding concepts: Accomplish the mission and take care of the troops. Those planners know that better morale means more energy and enthusiasm and so a better likelihood of mission success. Just as the military takes steps to keep up morale, you need to maintain your personal morale by celebrating successes as they occur. It takes a long time to complete a book-length work of fiction, and delaying your celebration until your final draft is proofread means waiting a long time for a little bit of happiness.

These seven principles for more successful writing provide you with guidance on how to more efficiently and effectively complete your work of fiction, and how to feel better while you're completing it. Integrate these principles into the way you write and the way you think about writing, and you'll have a more enjoyable, more successful writing experience. And no whining! Why? Do twenty push-ups and turn the page.

RELATED DRILLS

Drill 4: Control Your Calendar
Drill 6: Toss Out Your Civilian Clothes
Drill 13: Be More Successful
Drill 49: Know the Unwritten Rules for Quality Drafting

DRILL 3

NO SNIVELING ALLOWED

Part of boot camp training is learning to follow directives. Drill sergeants instruct trainees to *do it this way*, and they don't bother to explain the exceptions or entertain the quibbles. There may well be 1,001 ways to fire a rifle—but in boot camp there is only one way. No drill sergeant in her right mind would tolerate a trainee whining, "You mean we always do it that way? Isn't there an easier way? How come other people say there's a different way to do it?" A trainee who sniveled in that manner would find herself doing enough push-ups to move Georgia a mile closer to the Gulf of Mexico.

Sniveling is not permitted in novelist's boot camp, either. Getting a novel written consists not of joyous creative rapture but of applying your bottom to the chair and your fingers to the keyboard and grinding things out word by word, sentence by sentence. You can whine or you can write, but you can't do both.

Your battle plan for writing your novel will involve specific drills to follow. Within those drills, you'll receive specific advice and direction on how to accomplish certain tasks. Your job is to execute the instructions in that drill to the best of your creative ability. For example, you'll learn that you don't use dialogue for the sole purpose of showing the reader some aspect of a character's personality or for revealing backstory.

Never?

Never. As you'll learn in the dialogue drills, your characters should use words as tools or weapons to fight for and get what they want, both within a given scene and within the overall story.

I can't use it to convey information to the reader?

If that information comes out as part of a confrontation in which your characters are fighting to get what they want, then yes. Otherwise, no.

Never? Other how-to books say you can.

Can you read? No sniveling! This is not *other* how-to books. This is boot camp. We're not going to qualify every instruction with *normally, usually, most of the time, as a general rule, based on genre considerations, with some exceptions, try your best to*, or *in most cases.*

But best-selling and acclaimed authors break the rules all the time.

Are you a best-selling or acclaimed author? No. You don't even have a book yet. After you've written and published your third, fifth, or tenth book, you can break all the rules you want. Until then, to get your idea on paper, to produce a complete book-length work of fiction, just to get the darn thing written and get it done and done well, do as you're told.

But it's so hard.

Quit whining. Writing a novel is very challenging, very demanding, and very difficult. It's much easier to fall back on the civilian ways of writing and thinking that you've learned over the years. But those ways of thinking haven't produced the book you want to write, have they?

Well, no, but—

No more *buts*! Do it the *Novelist's Boot Camp* way. If that doesn't work for you, you're free to find another method. Until then, knock off the sniveling and get busy. Or do some push-ups.

I'm not very good at push-ups.

Then maybe you'd better button your yap and move on to the next drill.

RELATED DRILLS

Drill 6: Toss Out Your Civilian Clothes
Drill 7: Drill Your Way to Success
Drill 32: Discharge the Wimps
Drill 49: Know the Unwritten Rules for Quality Drafting

DRILL 4

CONTROL YOUR CALENDAR

Principles and strategies are great for planning large military campaigns, but when it comes to the nitty-gritty of small-unit combat, proven techniques let soldiers devise a plan that will keep them alive and help them seize their objective. The military has its own set of do's and don'ts for planning. The following list of do's for novelists will help you maintain your initiative and momentum and keep you and your calendar on the same side as you manage your most valuable asset—time.

Do set your own deadline, if one isn't imposed on you by an outside source. If you're writing your first or second novel, give yourself plenty of time. For those with full time careers—and this includes mothers and fathers at home with children—a twelve- to eighteen-month time frame is not excessive. Too often, a writing project with no targeted completion date will remain unfinished, just as a journey with no destination will never end.

If you do have a deadline determined by an editor or contract, your situation is a bit different. In this case, time management and disciplining yourself to follow your time plan (see below) are even more critical, because you have less flexibility in your battle plan.

Do make a battle plan. How much time do you need? Every individual situation is different, but you can begin your battle plan by allocating each of your writing times/days to one of the following.

- mental preparation
- planning
- invention
- development
- drafting
- revising
- editing
- proofreading

Experienced authors find that twelve months is a good estimate for the total time it will take to complete a novel; you can adjust from this starting point to enable yourself to meet your other obligations. You can allocate your time by using the process below.

1. *Establish your deadline.* When do you want it done? (Or, when have you been told to have it done?)

2. *Cross out time allocated for work, family, vacations, religious observance, exercise, and other obligations.* We'll discuss the phases of your battle plan for writing your novel in greater detail later. For now, take the remaining time and allocate:

- one-third to mental preparation, planning, invention, and development
- one-third to producing a quality draft
- one-third to revision, editing, and proofreading

3. *Mark your calendar with these key dates.* Since you're doing long-range planning, getting more specific at this point is probably counterproductive—there are just too many unknown factors. However, when you begin each new phase of your battle plan, you'll want to follow the guidelines below to set specific weekly and daily goals.

Do set daily goals. Once you begin each phase, plan to accomplish a little each day and you'll keep the momentum going. Writing daily is like earning compound interest—seemingly small amounts add up surprisingly quickly, and nothing motivates writing more than having written. This principle of writing daily has a corollary: Don't set aside whole days for writing. In our busy worlds, these whole days seldom materialize. Even if they did, your powers of concentration would only hold out for a few hours. Instead, work a little each day.

Do plan on vacations, breaks, business trips, and the like. You probably won't write much—if at all—during these breaks, and that's fine. Retreats and time-outs will give your imagination a chance to recharge, and you'll be even more motivated when you again get the opportunity to work on your writing project.

Do give yourself some breathing room—build a "fudge factor" into your time plan. Ask any military planner—the best campaign plan in the world often lives only long enough to come in contact with the enemy or an unexpected event. For novelists, life is full of unplanned events. You can't control those events, but you can build flexibility into your writing plan.

It's imperative that you make your calendar your ally and not your enemy. It's also important to know what your end goal is. To find out more about that, make the time to move on to the next drill.

RELATED DRILLS

Drill 1: Make It Your Mission
Drill 7: Drill Your Way to Success
Drill 49: Know the Unwritten Rules for Quality Drafting
Drill 56: Back Up to Beat Writer's Block

DRILL 5

SEE YOUR TARGET

If you don't care what you're shooting at, anything you hit is okay. But you have a very specific target—your bull's-eye is a completed novel. To hit your target, you need an understanding of what your end product will look like. What you *don't* need is to revisit high school definitions of the elements of fiction or to haul out an academic's tools for analyzing a novel. You need to go back to basics. At the most basic, a novel is a book-length work of fiction. *Book-length* means anything from 55,000 words for some category fiction, such as category romance or men's action (Donald Hamilton's Matt Helm series, for example), to 140,000 or more words for epics (such as Frank Herbert's science-fiction classic *Dune*). Your chosen genre will give you guidelines—sometimes formal, sometimes not—on how long your novel should be.

Fiction means your story is made-up. While actual historical events, current events, places, and figures are fair game for inclusion, your work is imaginary, not documentary. Your novel's job is to tell an entertaining, emotionally compelling story that ultimately causes the reader to have an emotional experience.

At this point, as you're preparing yourself to hit a target that (for now) is in the far distance, you need to be aware of the seven major features of a novel.

- characters
- dialogue
- plot
- setting
- point of view
- style
- theme

A novel has *characters*—imaginary (or imaginary versions of) people. The *protagonist* (hero) and *antagonist* (also known as the *opponent* and sometimes as the *villain*) are normally called *major characters*. You may also have *minor characters*, who are like bit players or extras and have only small roles. (We'll discuss all the kinds of characters in greater detail later.) Characters can be round (complex and fully developed, often prone to change) or flat (one-dimensional, usually of minor importance). Minor characters include those who appear frequently but have only marginal influence on the story, and those who appear only once or a few times with little impact.

Depending on your story, you also might choose to include *foils*—characters who contrast with a major character (such as Laertes and Fortinbras in Shakespeare's *Hamlet*)—or *sidekicks*—steadfastly loyal characters who almost constantly accompany the protagonist but who are less talented and less experienced (and less of everything else). You might also include *minions*, minor characters who work for the story's antagonist. Minions can be anything from flying monkeys to wise-guy enforcers doing the padrone's bidding, but they're always aligned against the protagonist.

Characters communicate through *dialogue*. The term *external dialogue* refers to spoken exchanges between characters, while *internal dialogue* refers, appropriately enough, to a character's inner thoughts.

Your novel has a beginning, a middle, and an end. In the beginning, you introduce your characters or cast, set the genre, and establish some event or crisis that sets the plot in motion.

The *plot* is a series of interrelated, cause-and-effect occurrences that build upon each other as the characters progress through the story. This progress doesn't come easily; your protagonist faces an often ruthless antagonist and must overcome tough opposition. These obstacles yield continuous, intense, and dramatic *conflict*. This conflict becomes more intense and the protagonist's challenges become more difficult as the novel progresses. There may also be *subplots*, secondary plots that can contrast with or complement the main plot.

The ending portion of a novel contains your work's *climax*, the point in which all of the conflicts come to a head and the dramatic tension is at its highest. The conflicts and all the action in the novel are concluded in a *resolution*, and if there are any loose ends to tie up, that gets done in a final *denouement*.

A novel takes place in one or more *settings*—physical locations (earthly, otherworldly, or both) in a specific time period.

A novel's narrative voice comes from its *point of view*, the perspective from which the story is told. *First-person* point of view is signaled by use of the pronoun *I. Third-person* point of view is possible when the narrator does not take part in the story. The third-person narrator can be *omniscient*—seeing, knowing, and telling all, including the interior thoughts of all the characters; *limited*—knowing and relating the actions, thoughts, and feelings of a few select characters; or *objective*—observing the action, but unable to get inside the minds of the characters.

Every novel has a style. *Style* refers to the language conventions used to construct the story. A fiction writer can manipulate diction, sentence structure, phrasing, dialogue, description, narration and other aspects of language to create a unique style. The communicative effect of style is often referred to as a story's or author's *voice* and can be anything from serious to sassy, cynical to fresh, depressing to hopeful.

Finally, novels have themes. *Theme* is the meaning or concept the readers are left with after reading, the big idea behind the novel. Themes can run from *the price for freedom is always high* to a moral such as *good always triumphs over evil.*

While knowing the parts of a novel isn't the same as knowing how to build a novel, you need to have a basic familiarity with what your target looks like in order to reach it. In the end, each of these features will be a part of the work you produce. But as any soldier knows, describing a target and hitting it are two different matters. Now that you know what you're shooting at, you can learn how to better aim and fire.

RELATED DRILLS

Drill 14: Go Beyond *What If?*
Drill 21: Forge Your Setting
Drill 26: Choose Your Cast
Drill 42: Take Three Steps to Story Line
Drill 45: Put Your Book on an Index Card
Drill 94: Conduct the Final Assault: Rewriting

DRILL 6

TOSS OUT YOUR CIVILIAN CLOTHES

Just as a new trainee must put away her civilian clothes so that she can become a productive member of her military unit, so too must you put away your old methods of looking at the novel. Remember high school or college literature classes? Remember how you dissected a novel, plumbing the depths of each character, outlining the main events of the plot, analyzing the symbolism embedded in descriptions? Good. Now forget all that—or at least lock it away in a footlocker under your cot. You're no longer going to look at the novel from the outside; you're going to build one from the inside. Your job is not to analyze but to construct.

Analyzing a novel's plot, denouement, theme, setting, symbolism, and characters only contributes an understanding and appreciation of an existing work. Gaining understanding and appreciation is fine, but those categories of analysis are close to useless when you try to develop your own work. Even knowing that protagonists, turning points, and narrative summary are necessary components of a novel will do you little good. None of the definitions of these components tell you how to design or build those components, how many of them to put in, where to put them, or how specifically to make them work for you and your novel. And knowing what the parts of a novel are certainly does nothing to help you start your novel.

What does get you off to a strong start are a few key "left-right-left" first steps: (1) choosing a genre, (2) creating characters, and (3) developing a story line. The *story line* tells what happens as the character struggles to obtain his objectives in the face of active opposition in a certain locale or setting. Whether you're writing a category romance, a steampunk horror tale, or a mainstream literary novel, stepping off with these three goals gets you marching in the right direction by compelling you to define what is truly the heart and soul of any novel—the story.

Once you set your character in motion on a route across the terrain of your chosen genre, your story and your writing will build its own momentum. As your character moves forward in his story, those components your eighth-grade literature teacher pointed out to you will naturally emerge as by-products of your protagonist's journey.

Put your old analytical tools aside. You'll get new tools to carry out this new approach to writing your novel, and you'll see some of your familiar tools—such as that box full of microprocessors on your desk—in a new way. Yes, even your computer gets a boot camp treatment. Just read on to see how.

RELATED DRILLS

Drill 3: No Sniveling Allowed
Drill 14: Go Beyond *What If?*
Drill 15: Find Your Path
Drill 43: Turn on Your Turning Points
Drill 94: Conduct the Final Assault: Rewriting

DRILL 7

DRILL YOUR WAY TO SUCCESS

In boot camp, Army drill sergeants make new recruits repeat specific skill-training tasks over and over again, until both the action and the idea behind the action are burned into memory—and into physical "muscle memory." These repetitive exercises are called drills (hence the name *drill sergeant*) and cover everything, such as how to fire a weapon, march, throw a grenade, bandage a wound, salute, or render a report. Drills are critical to a soldier's success and survival, because in the super-high intensity of combat, there's no time to figure out what to do and how to do it.

You don't have bullets cracking overhead, but novelist's boot camp drills are critical to your success in building your novel. These drills cover the full spectrum of tasks in the writing process—from developing an idea to checking for spelling errors. There are drills that teach principles and concepts, drills that provide different ways to describe a character, drills that list specific grammar errors to root out during proofreading, and a full line of others.

At the same time, drills allow you to focus your creative energy. By showing you one task at a time exactly what to do and how to do it, a drill lets you concentrate on doing that one task well. And drills actually give you more freedom to exercise your personal creativity. From intensifying the action in a scene to understanding the motivations of a strong female character, a drill will help you accomplish the task and put your own, individualized stamp on the result. With drills, one size does fit all.

Drills can help relieve anxiety. Don't know what to write next? Execute a drill! Drills also help you make progress when you don't feel like writing, and they actually help you get into that oft-talked-about flow state, where you are in what athletes call *the zone* and your writing seems to come automatically and naturally.

You can learn and master these drills by repeating them again and again, each time evaluating your results and taking action to improve. Unlike the recruit, who can never go back and undo sloppy salutes or missed targets on the rifle range, you *can* go back—you can revisit your first attempt at building a main character, again follow the instructions in the drill, and build a more exciting, more compelling, and more emotionally connecting character than you did before.

And while you may not have shells exploding nearby and enemy forces shooting at you, you're still under pressure. If you're at all like most of today's authors, you have at least 1,001 other distractions: people and commitments lined up with claims on your precious writing time, a job (or two), a family, a hobby, a need to eat and sleep, a significant other, and bills to pay. Drills allow you to make the best use of small chunks of time. You'll get the most out of yourself and your imagination and creativity in the few minutes you do have. And as drills teach you critical skills, they also help to instill the mental discipline you need to complete a book-length project and to provide you with a new way of seeing your writing tasks.

As you practice and execute these drills, you'll also learn a new way of reading. For that drill, read on.

RELATED DRILLS

Drill 3: No Sniveling Allowed
Drill 6: Toss Out Your Civilian Clothes
Drill 49: Know the Unwritten Rules for Quality Drafting

DRILL 8

FORGET ABOUT READING FOR ENJOYMENT

They say you can take the man out of the military, but you can't take the military out of the man. The same is true for you in novelist's boot camp. You'll never be the same again.

Disciplining your creativity means you no longer passively wait for creativity to find you. Instead, you kick your creativity in the butt and get it into action by setting writing goals (making a battle plan) and working in a disciplined manner (executing drills) to achieve them. But to succeed, you must also discipline your reading. Before boot camp, you passively let another novelist have his way with your emotions as you read his book. No longer. From now on, you'll read like the novelist you are—with a mission. When it comes to reading other works of fiction, your mission is to learn from what other novelists have done so that you can leverage that knowledge to get better at what *you* do. To accomplish that mission, first do a few push-ups. Then follow the five guidelines below.

Assess structure. When you read a novel, look at its overall structure. Some of the drills in this book teach you how to boil down your story to essentials and how to construct a master story summary (see drills 45 and 46). Once you've read these drills, try practicing them on a few novels that you've read and really enjoyed. You'll find it both entertaining and educational to understand how other authors construct their stories. If you're reading a work that's new to you, see if you can anticipate what kinds of events and challenges will come next.

Zero in on technique. Dialogue. Description. Narration. Action sequences. Setting, large- and small-scale. Characters. Use of technical or historical detail. Management of time. Note how your favorite authors use these techniques, or evaluate a new author whose book you've just opened. Where do the techniques work well? Where do they miss the mark? (Yes, even published novelists—even award-winning novelists—can create less than perfect writing.) Your new focus on technique doesn't mean you should slavishly imitate what you find. On the contrary, another author's methods will—and should—change to become your own as you write your own work. Even if you were to try to imitate a specific author, the result would not compare favorably to the original. If you try too hard to sound like Hemingway, you won't end up sounding like Hemingway—you'll end up sounding like you're trying to sound like Hemingway. You want to become conscious of technique in the fiction of others so that you become more conscious of technique in fiction of your own.

Target the differences. What makes your favorite author's works unique? What makes them stand out from other novels? What made you choose that particular author over others? Depending on what authority you consult, there are only 12, 25, or 112 different plot lines in existence. (Never mind the number—just accept that there are no truly new plots.) How does the author you're reading make the same old story something new and interesting? What are new and captivating ways of portraying old character types? Most importantly, what ideas does this author give you for differentiating your own story?

Capture your learning. Write down what you learn—and not in the books' margins! Marginal notes are a waste of time (and a disfigurement of good books). Do fifty push-ups for even thinking about writing in the margins. Instead, obtain a notebook (or index cards, a journal, or other way of recording the information) you can carry with you—just as you carry a novel to read. When you have accumulated a series of notes, take a few minutes to look over them. What trends do you see? What ideas do your notes give you?

This type of analysis is not the same kind you learned in high school or college English or literature classes. Instead, this is a new, active, focused way of reading, and it requires the same kind of planning and discipline that your writing mission does. The benefits of this type of active reading range from maintaining your motivation to broadening your perspective, and they make reading a crucial part of your battle plan.

Starting today, when you read other novels you'll actively listen for information you can use. However, there are some people in the publishing world you should not listen to. Ever. To learn who those people are, turn the page.

RELATED DRILLS

Drill 3: No Sniveling Allowed
Drill 4: Control Your Calendar
Drill 16: Know the Terrain
Drill 25: Use the Poor Man's Spy Satellite
Drill 45: Put Your Book on an Index Card
Drill 46: Build Your Master Story Summary

DRILL 9

DODGE THE LAND MINES

Land mines. Ambushes. Punji stake pits. Concealed snipers. Camouflaged barbed wire. Booby traps. All these dangers await the unwary or untrained soldier.

You won't pay with your life when you run into the dangers present in a novelist's world, but you can pay with your money, your ego, and your most precious commodity, your time. The novelist's world is filled with a legion of very bad characters, and we're not talking about the ones on your pages. These characters are very real, and their number-one priority is to deliberately and unfeelingly separate you, the new novelist, from your money. They are very good and very experienced at what they do. They have emptied the pockets of very smart, street-savvy, and sagacious writers. They know your strength is also your weakness; they know you have a dream, and they stand ready to exploit it.

If the above scares you, good. A dose of fear helps keep recruits alive and will help keep you from losing your cash to a hustler. Below is list of some of the dangerous criminals—as in committers of fraud—you're most likely to encounter as a novelist.

The crooked vanity publisher. Self-publishing has significant drawbacks but is a legitimate alternative for many novelists. That said, crooked vanity presses and subsidy publishers regularly rob novelists of their savings and their time. A 2005 case in Chicago is typical of this scam, although there are many variations on the theme: A so-called publishing company charged an elderly novelist more than twenty thousand dollars to produce one hundred trade-size copies of his two-hundred-page novel. Although editing and content-development services were billed, none were provided. Ink-smeared pages riddled with errors fell out of the few poorly constructed copies that were delivered. The company owners vanished, of course.

The crooked agent/editing agency team. This scam made headlines in the late 1990s but is still around: You submit your completed manuscript to a literary agent. That agent responds very positively, but says your novel needs work, then recommends a specific editing agency or book doctor. You send your novel and your money to the editing agency or book doctor, who takes your money but gives you little in return. At the same time, the agency is kicking money back to the agent. Months and months pass, and finally you get your "improved" manuscript back and send it off to the agent again. But now—surprise—the market has changed. Your work is no longer saleable, and the agent declines to represent your novel. There are several variations on this scam.

The crooked book doctor. Legitimate professional freelance editors and book doctors do exist. Many well-known published authors have discreetly used the services of book doctors at one time or another. However, a wide variety of less-than-competent (and less-than-honest) book doctors will promise you that publishers will love your book and that literary agents will beat a path to your e-mail inbox if you will just pay the fee for their services.

How do you protect yourself against these crooks—and others? Three methods:

- Be extra wary of those who promise publication for money.
- Keep informed. Become a member of the online writing community, read professional writers' magazines and blogs, and attend conferences.

- Before you spend, ask. Ask a lot of questions of those who would take your money, then check up on them with members of the writing community. And, before you sign that check or hand out your credit card number, ask yourself if all your questions have been answered satisfactorily. If not, put your money away until they are.

Criminals are counting on you being new to the world of publishing, counting on you not having heard of their scams, and counting on you not knowing where to find information about how they fleece their victims. Make them wrong.

Watching out for yourself is something you must do. Something else you must do: Write not what someone else tells you to write, but what you need to write. To find out what that is, go on to the next drill.

RELATED DRILLS

Drill 1: Make It Your Mission
Drill 12: Make Peace With the Publishing Industry
Drill 13: Be More Successful
Drill 16: Know the Terrain

DRILL 10

WRITE WHAT YOU MUST

It's said that military service can build leadership. As a novelist, you need a different kind of leadership, and you need to provide that leadership for yourself. Don't let the market lead you.

You may think that the best way to ensure that your book sells is to analyze what others are buying, and then write your novel accordingly. Yet, two undeniable facts prove this logic fatally flawed. First, the very nature of the writing and publishing process normally defeats attempts to time your writing to match the book market. Second, the nature of the writing process calls on you, the novelist, to write not what others tell you to write but what you are compelled to write.

Leveraging trends in fiction is difficult because there are exceptionally long time lags—several months at least—between coming up with an idea, delivering a finished manuscript to an editor or agent, and seeing the book on a store shelf.

If you had nothing else to do in your life—no day job; no family; no trips to the grocery store, doctor, gym, or movie theater—you might be able to work on your project for ten or twelve hours per day for three or four months and end up with a respectable manuscript. If your work happened to move without any obstacles or delays through the submission process, a literary agent or acquisition editor might be able to review and accept your manuscript in another ninety days. If the publisher then made your manuscript top priority, and you responded to your editor's directions for changes, corrections, and other rewrites with near superhuman speed, your work would be ready to go to press in another sixty days or so. If the publisher then renegotiated its contract with the printing company, completely revamped its schedule of releases, and radically changed its sales force's priorities to convince wholesale and retail booksellers to purchase a book outside their normal buying cycles, your work might hit bookstore shelves

in just under an additional six months. Total elapsed time from concept to store shelf—in a theoretical best-of-all-possible-worlds scenario—would be about eighteen to nineteen months.

Predicting what will be hot in the fiction market eighteen months out is exceptionally difficult. Clearly, even in the dream world described above, you would be making a sucker's bet if you wrote your novel based on anticipated market trends. Now attempt to predict the future in the real world, where a more realistic time frame for writing, selling, and publishing your work is thirty-six months. Knowing and writing just what will be hot three years from now is almost impossible. Some novelists will try, though. They'll also send money in response to e-mails from Nigeria and invest in air conditioners for resort condos on Mars.

The nature of the writing process is such that you must write what you need to write instead of what you think the market might demand in the future. Most novelists take about twelve months—give or take—to grow a novel from idea to proofread manuscript. That's a year. A year of planning, drafting, and rewriting at night, on weekends, early in the morning, over lunch hours, and in the small blocks of time carved from daily life. A year of waking up at 02:00 with an insight on how to execute a certain scene. A year of subvocalizing dialogue in the car while running errands. A year of devoting emotional, mental, and physical energy to making daily progress. Your work is always with you, and very quickly, you and your novel establish an intimate relationship. You will live in close physical, mental, and emotional quarters with your project, through good days and bad, for twelve months—or longer.

Would you like that relationship to be an arranged marriage—your writing "mate" chosen by some anonymous market force—or a relationship with a partner you want and you choose? Will your constant companion and the object of your efforts and affection be something you love, something you want, something you feel compelled to achieve—or something directed by unseen, ever-changing, unpredictable outside forces?

The first person you must please in your writing career is yourself. You will live, intimately, with your project for a year or more. Your novel will be your partner and constant companion. Choose well and wisely what you write. Write what you love. Write what you want. Write what you must.

Then write in the right place—which you can find in the next drill.

RELATED DRILLS

Drill 1: Make It Your Mission
Drill 12: Make Peace With the Publishing Industry
Drill 13: Be More Successful
Drill 16: Know the Terrain

DRILL 11

WRITE IN THE RIGHT PLACE

When soldiers come under fire, they appreciate the protection of a well-dug fighting position or reinforced bunker. When you're slugging it out with a difficult sentence, scene, or chapter, you'll appreciate a well-arranged workspace.

Entire books, many medical studies, and even some laws have been written on the subject of workplace ergonomics. For you, the workspace in question is the physical area you use to move through the phases of your writing project, and you'll need to go beyond ergonomics to make your space the healthiest and most productive. To do so, choose and arrange your space using these four simple guidelines.

1. **Fit the space to the job and time.** There's really only one way to find out whether your workspace is truly comfortable, and that's by trial and error. It won't take long—a chair that encourages you to lean forward will give you a sore neck in short order. Pay attention. If you start to feel pain, tightness, or weariness, change something.

2. **Use good posture.** Your mother was right—good posture goes a long way toward keeping you comfortable, focused, and energized. As you get more involved in your writing, you might find that you tend to slouch or move forward to get physically closer to your work. Consciously fight these tendencies; otherwise you'll find yourself tiring faster, and your muscles will tighten and ache.

3. **Make room to work.** If you're making a time line to organize your story, give yourself the proper space to spread out several sheets of paper or to lay out index cards so you can see how one event or scene leads to another. If you're drafting on a computer, make sure you have the space to display your character cards, scene lists, and other notes.

Set yourself up for success by setting up your workspace to support the tasks you'll be undertaking.

4. **Work where you are.** You don't need a laptop computer, huge oak desk, and hours of uninterrupted solitude to be a writer. Write your scene in longhand during your lunch break, your daily commute, or your kids' soccer practice, then type it up when you get a longer chunk of time later in the day. Your longhand version will, of course, be rough—but when you type that version, you can refer to other notes to improve the dialogue, description, and action. Stuck commuting in a car? Consider dictating to an inexpensive cassette tape recorder—but only when you're not actively driving.

You're going to spend hours and hours (which will add up to days and days, then months and months) writing your novel. Make the best use of the places and spaces you work in, and make sure those places are comfortable, healthy, and productive.

It may seem unusual for battle plan to call for a comfortable and healthy workplace, but this isn't your usual boot camp. It's also unusual for a battle plan to tell you to make peace, but that's exactly what you'll find in the next drill.

RELATED DRILLS

Drill 5: See Your Target
Drill 6: Toss Out Your Civilian Clothes

DRILL 12

MAKE PEACE WITH THE PUBLISHING INDUSTRY

People work better when they understand what's going on around them, and soldiers are no exception. While an individual front-line soldier doesn't need to understand the intricacies of international politics or the grand strategy of a war in order to fulfill his individual mission, he does need to know enough about the big picture to understand how he contributes. The same is true for you within the context of the publishing industry.

Although the mission in front of you is to execute a series of drills to produce a book-length work of fiction, there are several key concepts you need to come to terms with—or make peace with—within the publishing industry. Once you do, you'll be able to work more effectively, and you'll have a greater sense of how you and your work fit in.

Publishing is a bottom-line business. Book publishers and booksellers are in business, and like all businesses, they need to make a profit to survive. There must be a clear line of sight between your novel and an increase in the publisher's bottom line. What this means to you as a novelist is that if your work doesn't fit an editor's understanding of the company's market (strategy, direction, lineup, etc.), then it's highly unlikely you will be offered publication—regardless of how well you've written your novel. Like editors, agents evaluate submissions based on whether they believe a book will make them money. If an agent doesn't think he is the right person to sell your book, he won't offer to represent it.

Publishing takes a long time. You'll likely spend many months—perhaps even a year or two—writing your novel. It may take many more months for you to market and sell your work. Then your novel will wait its turn (the publisher has a business plan for what will get published when) to reach bookstore shelves. Then the process repeats itself as you write your next work. There are really no overnight successes—writing careers form over years, sometimes decades.

It's a big book world out there. Consolidation and market forces in the large, commercial houses can limit traditional publishing opportunities, but there has been an explosion of alternative markets—the Internet, e-books, small and independent presses targeting niche markets, and self-publishing—that can offer you other ways to see your work in print. Just because one door closes doesn't mean your work will never see publication.

It's tough—very, very tough—to get rich. Six- and seven-figure advances, big royalty checks, and a main character merchandised into an action figure—these are the stuff of headlines and many novelists' dreams. Yet these commercial successes make headlines only because they are the exception, not the rule. Some people win the lottery, and there are those in the publishing industry who would tell you that your chances of receiving one of those mega-million-dollar advances are about the same as hitting those lottery numbers just right. However, there are novelists who have

built—over a period of years—nice second incomes from their work. Bottom line: If you have a day job, keep it.

Getting published is harder than it looks. Successfully completing a book-length work of fiction is a challenge understood only by those who have started at page one and disciplined themselves through to *The End*. Going from completed manuscript to published novel is equally as challenging, whether you sell your work to a major commercial publisher or decide to self-publish. Expect hard work, setbacks, disappointments, frustration, missed opportunities, rejection, and a few bruises to your ego.

It's smart to let it go. Many novelists harbor resentment and frustration at these realities. You don't need resentment and frustration—you need a positive attitude and creativity. Let others waste their time and emotional energy—use yours in a productive manner to produce a well-written book. Having trouble letting go? Do push-ups to take your mind off it. Or maybe do something really crazy, like work on your book.

Understand the big picture. Accept the industry's realities and cope with them, then go back to work on that creative project—your novel. Some days will feel like a series of triumphs. Some days, it will seem like you're stuck running and rerunning the obstacle course. But you *can* be successful every day.

How? Start by turning the page to the next drill.

RELATED DRILLS

Drill 1: Make It Your Mission
Drill 10: Write What You Must
Drill 13: Be More Successful

DRILL 13

BE MORE SUCCESSFUL

Boot camp teaches trainees to take pride in small successes, from getting a good shine on a pair of boots to scoring a bit higher on the rifle range to shaving a few seconds off a timed two-mile run. Learning to take pride in personal accomplishments is a skill that can help see you through a process—and a profession—that too often can be filled with negativity.

As a novelist, you will invest a lot of yourself—and many, many hours of your life—in your writing project. At the end—and along the way—you'd like to feel that you've accomplished something. In other words, you'd like to feel successful. First, however, it's important to understand that there are many different kinds of success. Do you know what kind you want?

Commercial success is perceived differently by different writers but can be considered anything from selling one book at a book-signing to making a best-seller list. Becoming a best-seller is the success most authors dream of: the six-figure contract and the big-bucks movie-rights deal. Because of a thousand factors, almost all of which are outside an author's control, commercial success is extremely difficult to attain.

Critical success is also subjective and ranges from the positive e-mail from a fan to a positive review from a tough, learned, knowledgeable book critic to awards from contests and competitions. This kind of success won't always pay the bills but it still feels good.

Personal success is the most achievable and lasting type of success. It's also the most difficult to define because it is, after all, personal. For some, it means overcoming a fear of failure and actually writing, instead of talking about writing. For others, it means completing that first full draft after dozens of false starts. Still others achieve personal success by writing through the sandstorm of minutiae that daily life brings or by taking just one more step on the long journey of pursuing a personal vision.

Writers who leverage the concept of personal success find themselves with daily opportunities to achieve. Setting daily goals and working hard to meet those goals create the potential for positive reinforcement every day, and this positive reinforcement provides the energy to go on to pursue the next day's goals. Which sounds more appealing: to struggle for two or three years, chasing potential rewards that are outside your control; or to see—and feel—yourself progressing steadily day by day, moving from one achievement to the next?

An approach that plans and celebrates daily personal writing successes does not have to be Pollyannaish—indeed, it should not be. Your own life experience will tell you that on any journey there are setbacks, speed bumps, detours, rough roads, dead ends, and some wandering around, lost. Situations and circumstances change, and so too will your plans as you adjust them to new situations, realities, and priorities. Yet, even these changes offer new opportunities to be successful in meeting the challenges they present.

Negativity and self-doubt will work hard to snuff out the candlelight of joy that burns inside your mind. The long and arduous process of writing a novel is filled with opportunities for rejection, disappointment, criticism, and even despair. Yet, this same process is also a treasure trove of opportunities. The novelist who sees and seizes these opportunities is already successful.

Planning to be successful every day is your last step in mentally preparing yourself for the challenge and joy of writing a novel. You *will* be successful in your project, and the way you'll begin that success is by turning the page, starting the next phase of your battle plan, and inventing your novel.

RELATED DRILLS

Drill 1: Make It Your Mission
Drill 3: No Sniveling Allowed
Drill 12: Make Peace With the Publishing Industry
Drill 16: Know the Terrain

BATTLE PLAN BRAVO

INVENTION

MISSION II: INVENT YOUR COMPREHENSIVE CONCEPT 040

Drill 14: Go Beyond *What If?* 041

Drill 15: Find Your Path 044

Drill 16: Know the Terrain 047

Drill 17: Put a Face on Your Idea 049

Drill 18: Find Your Character in Events, Places, and Concepts 052

Drill 19: Find Your Character in Opposites 055

Drill 20: Invent a Better Story Idea 057

Drill 21: Forge Your Setting 059

Drill 22: Forget About Reality … More or Less 061

Drill 23: Research Your Plan of Attack 063

Drill 24: Don't Fool Around Searching for Too Many Facts 065

Drill 25: Use the Poor Man's Spy Satellite 068

MISSION II

INVENT YOUR COMPREHENSIVE CONCEPT

Boot camp not only changes the way trainees think, it also changes the way they do things. Military drill sergeants tell trainees to forget what they learned back on the block and to start over with the basics—and they do. Trainees even relearn how to walk: On the command *Forward—march!* the trainee always takes his first step with his left foot.

Here in novelist's boot camp, it isn't important how you march. However, your first few steps as a novelist are critical. Those first steps are in the invention phase of your battle plan. In the following left-right-left drills, you'll choose your genre, learn why character comes first, select a main character, build a story line, get an idea about where your story takes place, and understand what you need to research and when to do so. The results of these drills will be rough; what you invent now, you'll later develop. In other words, you'll invent a comprehensive concept for your novel that will be the foundation for all that follows. This is much like what military planners term the *concept of the operation*, an overall concept developed before any mission that expresses in broad terms who will do what, when, where, and why.

Just as life in the military is radically different from civilian life, the drills in this phase of your battle plan are likely much different from the writing practices that you've encountered before. You are no longer a writing civilian, so putting just any foot forward will not do. And while (and perhaps because) these drills are so different, they have an undeniable strength: They get you, your imagination, and your creativity marching in step and moving in the same direction. In other words, these techniques work.

So it's time to put invention in motion. Forward—march! Left! Right! Left!

DRILL 14

GO BEYOND *WHAT IF?*

At the heart of every military operation is a concept aptly called the concept of the operation. It's the idea behind the mission. The novelist's boot camp version of the concept of the operation—the central idea behind your novel—is its comprehensive concept.

One common civilian technique for developing an idea for a novel is fairly straightforward: Start with a bit of information that piques your interest, then ask *What if?* But the answers to the *What if?* questions you asked in the civilian world of writing just aren't strong enough to base a novel on. Instead, you need something stronger—you need to move from *What if?* to a comprehensive concept.

A comprehensive concept is a foundation builder. It is a short statement that combines the following four essential elements to form a strong base for your complex novel: (1) genre, (2) main character, (3) opposition, and (4) macro setting.

You can arrange these elements (which will be the focus of upcoming drills), in any order. Here are some example comprehensive concept statements formulated from popular novels.

> In a mystery [genre] set in modern Los Angeles [macro setting], a female bomb squad technician [main character] pursues a mad bomber [opposition] who killed her partner.
>
> —*Demolition Angel* by Robert Crais

> A by-the-book Army officer and a break-the-rules Green Beret [main characters] battle a new Nazi Fourth Reich [opposition] in a techno-thriller [genre] set a newly united Germany [macro setting].
>
> —*Kriegspiel* by Todd A. Stone

Now, to go from *What if?* to comprehensive concept, you need to leverage the *what* in *What if?* That is, begin with your scrap of information—idea, person,

place, thing, tidbit of news, slice of history, scientific observation, or whatever else that sticks and inspires you—then ask specific *What if?* questions designed to formulate each of the four elements of your comprehensive concept.

For example, start with this fictional news item: *Private plan crashes. No pilot found.* Now, instead of asking yourself random *What if?* questions and allowing your train of thought to pick its own destination, focus and direct your *What if?* questions to determine genre, initial main character, opposition, and macro setting. You can address these four elements in any order.

- **Genre:** What role could this fact play in a horror story? What role could this fact play in a spy novel?
- **Opposition:** In a horror story, what kind of monster might be involved? What could that monster do to make planes crash and pilots vanish?
- **Main Character:** What if the protagonist was the missing pilot? What could be his reason for disappearing? What role could his disappearance play in his discovery and pursuit of the monster? What would the main character do to track and kill this kind of monster?
- **Macro Setting:** What kind of setting might be interesting for this story?

Arrange your answers to form a comprehensive concept statement. As long as you focus your questions on genre, main character, opposition, and macro setting, your novel concept will be strong enough that you can confidently move forward. Directed *What if?* questions can not only help generate interesting and unique genre-appropriate characters, settings, and plot lines—and make use of the interesting scrap of information that inspired you—they can also help you go beyond the comprehensive concept and create subplots, backstory, supporting characters, etc.

People. Places. Events. Things. Some combination thereof. A tidbit of news, history, or science. Any and sometimes all of these somehow stick in your imagination. You *feel* there's a novel somewhere in the unique history of an island paradise (*Hawaii*), in the caves near Hannibal, Missouri (*The Adventures of Tom Sawyer*), in a paralyzed crime scene inspector (*The Bone Collector*), in dinosaur DNA preserved in mosquitoes (*Jurassic Park*). In the civilian world of writing, you'd ask *What if?* about an inspiring tidbit of information and hope to get an idea you could turn into a novel. But as many a soldier knows, hope is not a plan. When you leverage the *what* in *What if?* in the context of genre, character, opposition, and setting, you can build interesting essential elements for your novel's comprehensive concept.

Of course, you'll need to further develop this concept, starting with genre. To do so, don't simply ask *What if I turned the page?* Do it!

RELATED DRILLS

Drill 2: Adopt a Principled Approach
Drill 5: See Your Target
Drill 15: Find Your Path
Drill 17: Put a Face on Your Idea
Drill 20: Invent a Better Story Idea
Drill 42: Take Three Steps to Story Line
Drill 45: Put Your Book on an Index Card

DRILL 15

FIND YOUR PATH

Every action undertaken in the military, from marching to cooking to shooting, takes place within the context of preparing for or participating in armed conflict. This context informs the behavior and expectations of every recruit.

When you're writing your novel, everything from the behavior of your characters to the climax of the plot—even the expectations of your readers—will be informed by the overall context of the novel: its genre. But before you can make a decision about which genre is best for you, you need to know what the major genres are and what to think about when choosing one.

First, understand the difference between *literary* and *commercial* fiction (also known as *genre* or *popular* fiction). One way to think of literary fiction is as, well, literature. While literary fiction aims primarily for the head, genre fiction aims for the gut. Some say literary fiction transcends genre and focuses on style and character, whereas genre fiction focuses on plot. But there are so many exceptions that this generalization is not really useful. Still others see literary fiction as just one more genre, with its own expectations and conventions.

Understanding this difference is important because it allows you to point your draft and slant your prose toward one type of fiction or the other. In other words, if you choose to write a more literary work, you'll have more—but not exclusive—emphasis on style and character and less on plot and genre conventions. The reverse will be true if you choose to work on a piece of genre fiction.

Now let's look at the five main genres. Because so much has been written about exactly what constitutes each genre, you'll get a through-the-binoculars look here. Keep in mind that each of these genres encompasses many (perhaps dozens) of subgenres.

- **Romance.** Stories that center around a one-on-one love relationship are considered romances. There are a dozen or more different types of romances, but they all share one thing: a happy ending. So many readers are in love with the romance that romances account for about half of all fiction sales in the United States today.

- **Mystery.** Stories in the mystery genre are centered around a crime—usually a murder—and feature a detective (in or out of uniform), a criminal to be brought to justice, and an investigation.
- **Westerns.** Westerns are novels set in the American West during the 1800s. You'll find lots of nomadic characters (read: cowboys) in Westerns, and the frontier and landscape normally figure very prominently in the story.
- **Science Fiction.** Stories set in deep space, in faraway galaxies, in the future on Earth—wherever science and technology play a major role, you'll find science fiction.
- **Horror.** Run for your lives, this genre is alive! If it drinks blood, eats brains, or slowly disintegrates the flesh off of your bones, you'll find it in a horror novel; horror novels keep readers up all night, either transfixed by the story or nervously listening for things going bump in the night.

Now that you're familiar with the major genres, it's time to start thinking about which one you want to try. There are many ways to select a genre, but if you keep in mind the three options outlined below, you're more likely to be both successful and satisfied with your choice. Note that each genre has pluses and minuses—there's no one best genre. In the end, the choice is personal.

1. Choose a genre that lets you write what you know. This choice gives you the advantage of relying on knowledge you already have, so you don't find yourself overwhelmed with research or out of your depth as you write. Many authors have successfully leveraged their career experience into their novels. Attorneys John Grisham and Barry Eisler have used their legal knowledge to write courtroom dramas. Denise Swanson—a school psychologist—has a school psychologist as her main character in her charming Scumble River mystery series. David Drake's award-winning military science fiction grew out of his experiences in a combat unit in Vietnam.

2. Choose a genre that lets you write what you love. This choice lets you follow your passion. When you choose to write in a genre that you simply can't get enough of, research becomes a reward instead of a chore.

3. Choose a genre that you believe will make you commercially successful. A certain logic dictates that you should look at the markets, study the trends, and then write the kind of book that has the greatest likelihood of commercial success. This very businesslike approach is espoused by many novelists with multiple-book contracts who earn handsome advances and royalties. It has worked for them. It may work for you. That said, long experience, common sense, industry experts, most seasoned novelists, and (most importantly) your boot camp drill sergeant recommend you write what you feel compelled to write, not what some ever-changing market tells you to write.

These three options are not necessarily mutually exclusive; if all three lead you to the same genre choice, you are a lucky writer! Choosing a genre is one of your most important decisions, and one you must make early in the process of writing. Whichever path you choose, you will likely spend a year or more following it, so don't choose quickly—assess the terrain by reading the next drill, then choose wisely.

RELATED DRILLS

Drill 10: Write What You Must
Drill 16: Know the Terrain
Drill 20: Invent a Better Story Idea
Drill 22: Forget About Reality ... More or Less
Drill 45: Put Your Book on an Index Card
Drill 52: Win the First Battle
Drill 92: Circle Back for the Miscellaneous Pass

DRILL 16

KNOW THE TERRAIN

To plan a successful battle, military planners must understand the lay of the land and the effects of weather. If you want to be successful with your choice of genre, you need to understand the terrain and environment of that genre. Military strategists get to know and understand the terrain and climate by conducting a reconnaissance, and you can do the same. However, you can't just wander around soaking in the scenery—you need a reconnaissance *plan*.

In an earlier drill, you learned a new way of reading. Now it's time to learn how to apply that new approach so that it best informs your work. To succeed in your chosen genre, read as much as you can of other books in the same genre. Prioritize your reading efforts so that you don't spend countless hours wandering around in books and stories that, although interesting and entertaining, are not the best use of your time. When time and monetary resources are limited, the guidelines below can help you set priorities and get the most out of your investment of effort and money.

1. **Read the books that seem closest to what you want to write.** Authors of these books are not only your peers, they're your competitors. You can see how they tackled problems you're likely to have.

2. **Read the recognized masters.** Every genre has acknowledged masters. Find and read the award-winning works within your genre. Often, their authors have spent decades writing successfully within that genre.

3. **Read those on the cutting edge.** Even if you're not writing mysteries, do a bit of detective work. Search independent and specialty bookstores and online publishers and booksellers. Check blogs and online discussion groups. You're looking for new novels and new voices from small and independent presses. These works often point the way to trends that will be the mainstream in one, three, or five years.

4. **Read the bestsellers.** Although reading best-sellers certainly helps you understand the market for your genre, best-seller status is so loosely defined and so transitory that these books should rank a bit lower on your priority list.

5. **Read about the genre.** Read fan magazines, reviews, blogs, whatever you can get your hands on. You'll find story analysis, information on new and cutting-edge authors, interviews with the masters, reviews, and perhaps a hint or two. Also check out industry publications like *Publishers Weekly* and *Publishers Lunch*.

Read outside of your genre as well. Both related and unrelated genres can give you fresh insights and perspectives, and may lead you to decide to become a pioneer and mix genre types. Books and articles on the craft of writing can arm you with new techniques to improve how you write.

Military planners know that in order to succeed, they must thoroughly understand the nuances of climate and terrain and know what to expect before the first soldier is deployed. They know that failure to do so results in missions that fail and troops that suffer. You must know what to expect—and what is expected of you—in your chosen genre. Make a plan that supports your writing goal and prioritize your efforts.

Once you've found your way through your genre, you'll want to find your characters. Start looking for them in the next drill.

RELATED DRILLS

Drill 15: Find Your Path
Drill 22: Forget About Reality ... More or Less
Drill 52: Win the First Battle
Drill 92: Circle Back for the Miscellaneous Pass

DRILL 17

PUT A FACE ON YOUR IDEA

Every military unit needs a leader—a person to drive the organization to achieve its mission. A key step in inventing your novel's comprehensive concept is to put a face on your idea: Find a character to play the lead role in your story.

You may want to center your novel around a specific theme or even around a certain place—say, a remote planet in a spiral galaxy two million light years away. Perhaps you're fascinated with a historical event, such as the World War II D-Day invasion of Normandy on June 6, 1944. Maybe your book answers a *What if?* question, such as *What if there were a race of beings who could change genders at will?* Suppose you're burning to write about a moral or ethical issue, such as the price one must pay for personal or political freedom, or man's daily inhumanity to his fellow man. You could even decide you're going to write a novel that's hip, funny, sexy, witty, smart, sassy, and full of cute shoes a la Candace Bushnell's *Sex and the City*.

All completely satisfactory, as long as your themes, issues, places, ideas, and events are a part of a *character's* story.

Creating a main character is a key step in developing your comprehensive concept—in fact, it can be considered the most important step. Like George Orwell's animals in his masterpiece *Animal Farm*, plot, genre, and character are all equals, but character is more equal than the others. Your main character (also known as your protagonist, lead, hero, or heroine) is not just a part of your story. She and her actions in pursuit of her objectives *are* your story.

Later drills will teach you *how* to find and develop your characters, but it's important you understand now *why* character is so critical to your novel. The why has to do with the nature of fiction itself.

The purpose of your fiction is to create an emotional experience in your reader. As a writer of fiction, you want your readers to laugh and to cry, to become angry, to feel fear, to experience the gamut of human emotions.

Your novel stirs these feelings through its emotional connection with your reader. While some readers can feel emotionally connected to things or ideas, as a general rule, the strongest emotional connection is between one person and another person. It is your main character who puts a face on your idea—your character makes your idea *human*.

You establish a connection with your reader not by writing about great ideas, great events, deep concepts, fantastic worlds, or paranormal events—you do so by telling the story of a character driven by a great idea, a character pursuing her objectives against the backdrop of great events, a character whose deeds put deep concepts into action, a character who must face opposition and her own feelings in a fantastic world—a character who establishes and maintains an emotional connection with the reader, even though she routinely morphs into a werewolf.

Many authors have succeeded at inspiring strong emotional connections with their characters. One of the most successful is James Jones in his classic war novel *The Thin Red Line*. The novel recounts the events of two specific days during one battle on one island in World War II; so although it can be classified as a war novel, it really isn't about the war. Instead, it's about the many characters that Jones gives us, the Marines in "C-for-Charlie" Company. These are characters we come to love, pity, despise, fear for, mourn—characters that we emotionally connect with. So *The Thin Red Line* is not about war—it is about men (people, characters) at war.

You've heard people speak about plot-driven versus character-driven novels. The distinction is more than a little artificial, which is all well and good for some booksellers, reviewers, academics, marketers, and backyard barbecue book critics—but not very useful for you as a novelist. Every novel is plot-driven—things happen. Every novel is character-driven—characters make things happen or react to things happening. Some genres call for more action than others, but they still have characters at their centers.

Set your novel in a specific, significant (if only to you) geographic location, center your story around a pivotal historic event, or base it on a strong value judgment. However you start, move out on your march toward a finished novel by choosing your genre and then making the connection with characters.

Now take another step to the next drill.

RELATED DRILLS

Drill 14: Go Beyond *What If?*
Drill 18: Find Your Character in Events, Places, and Concepts
Drill 26: Choose Your Cast
Drill 53: Tell Each Character's Story

DRILL 18

FIND YOUR CHARACTER IN EVENTS, PLACES, AND CONCEPTS

New recruits come in all shapes and sizes and from every part of the country—sometimes from around the globe. Experienced drill sergeants know that someone in each ragged bunch will be a standout—you never know where you'll find a hero.

Whether you're inspired by an event, place, profession, or theme, a critical step in inventing your novel's comprehensive concept is to put a face on it in the form of a main character or protagonist. One way to find that main character—and his opponent—is by generating a list of characters associated with the event, place, profession, or concept around which you're building your story.

Let's say an event inspires you—the December 7, 1941, attack on Pearl Harbor. A list of people associated with that event might include:

- American soldiers, sailors, Army Air Corps pilots, and Marines
- Japanese bomber pilots and sailors
- nurses and doctors
- civilians living on the island (everyone from bankers to petty thieves)
- Japanese Americans (a subset of the civilians listed above)
- government officials from the United States and the Empire of Japan

You can probably think of many more. In fact, you should. Your list will give you a rich palette to choose from. Don't be hasty—consider several options for your main character and how each choice might drive your story in a new direction and provide unique insights. For instance, John Gardner, in his powerful work *Grendel*, retold the *Beowulf* myth from the point of view of the monster.

If a place inspires you, rather than an event, the process of creating characters follows the same process. If a medieval castle is your main setting, then you can identify characters that might normally be associated with such a place.

- the king and queen (or lord or lady)
- their children
- the jester
- serfs
- courtiers, male and female
- advisors
- knights and men at arms
- skilled tradesmen (armorers, blacksmiths, tailors)
- stonemasons
- beggars, thieves, robbers
- tavern wenches, seamstresses, courtesans
- merchants, townspeople

Again, make your list as long as possible to give yourself a full cast of characters from which to choose.

The process of creating a main character when a concept or theme is your inspiration for a work of fiction has two steps. First, narrow and focus your theme or idea until you can make a declarative value judgment. Second, list the key words in the judgment and generate a list of characters you associate with those words. Let's say you're inspired to write a novel about greed. Greed is a big idea—how can you narrow it? What can you say more specifically about greed? For example, you may find that the more focused idea of the *cost* of greed appeals to you—and that's a good start. So what about the cost of greed? After some thinking and refining, you find that the value judgment you want to make is: *The cost of greed far outweighs any wealth a greedy person might accumulate*. That's a much more sharply focused and much more interesting idea than just greed.

Once you have your value judgment, the next step is to find and list the key words in that statement. In *the cost of greed far outweighs any wealth a greedy person might accumulate*, certain words stand out.

- cost
- greed, greedy
- outweighs
- wealth
- accumulate

With this list, you can proceed to the next step. Determine the kind of person who would be associated with or care deeply about the concept each word embodies. For example, you might associate the word *cost* with accountants or expenditure-sensitive businesspeople. *Wealth* might yield bankers, the very rich, oil tycoons, or perhaps owners of giant software companies. The verb *outweigh* might suggest a character or a certain physical description. *Greed* and *greedy* might lead you to list miserly kings, penny-pinching recluses, and scrooges of any era.

If you already have characters—protagonist, opponent, or both—in mind, then this listing method works well to generate secondary characters.

Once you've generated a rough list, retype it, label it *Cast List*, and save it. You'll need it later as you refine and develop the final list of characters who will appear in your novel. Or you might find that you want to add to your list by focusing on the opposite—to learn more, turn to the next drill.

RELATED DRILLS

Drill 22: Forget About Reality … More or Less
Drill 26: Choose Your Cast
Drill 75: Use Micro Setting for Maximum Impact

DRILL 19

FIND YOUR CHARACTER IN OPPOSITES

In ground combat, scouts often travel ahead to seek out the opposing force. Once the scouts find the enemy, the commander can develop a plan based on the number, location, and disposition of the opposing forces.

You can find interesting characters for your novel not by scouting out the opposition but by seeking out opposites. The process of developing characters by seeking out opposites has the advantage of building two critical elements into your novel—conflict and plot development. Opposites can be built around places, events, and concepts. For a closer look at this process, let's go back to the value judgment crafted earlier: *The cost of greed far outweighs any wealth a greedy person might accumulate.* Here's a list of possible associated characters.

- an investment banker
- a real-estate magnate
- a scrooge
- an oil tycoon
- a modern royal similar to King Midas
- an international financier

Now let's expand on that list by generating a list of opposites.

Character	Opposite
an investment banker	a day laborer living paycheck to paycheck
a real-estate magnate	a homeless person
a scrooge	a philanthropist
an oil tycoon	a gas station attendant
a modern royal similar to King Midas	a modern peasant
an international financier	a preacher in a small town in an underdeveloped nation

You can generate even more lists by asking questions beyond *What is the opposite of . . . ?* For example, start with your value judgment and ask questions such as: *Who would care the least? Who would believe the opposite was true? Who has the most to lose if this is true? Whose life would change radically if he came to believe that judgment?*

Don't limit yourself to physical opposites; consider moral, social, economic, political, gender, and other opposites as well. You can find a powerful example of opposites in W.E.B. Griffin's popular Brotherhood of War series. In each book, Griffin alternates between protagonists: one rich from an old-money family, one dirt poor who pulled himself up by his bootstraps; one slight and intellectual, one burly and action-oriented.

Once you've generated a rough list, either add this list to your existing cast list (generated in the last drill), or clean up your list, label it *Cast List*, and save it on your computer or put it away where you can readily find it. You'll need it later as you refine and develop your list of characters.

Interesting conflicts emerge when you build your characters from opposites. So interesting that they may well have an impact on your story idea, which we'll develop in the next drill.

RELATED DRILLS

Drill 14: Go Beyond *What If?*
Drill 18: Find Your Character in Events, Places, and Concepts
Drill 21: Forge Your Setting
Drill 26: Choose Your Cast
Drill 36: Define the Opposition

DRILL 20

INVENT A BETTER STORY IDEA

At the heart of even the most complex military operation is a simple idea: A certain unit must seize or defend a certain terrain and defeat a certain enemy. This idea gets refined, developed, and expanded, but it's this simple and yet essential statement of who must do what against whom that puts men and machines into action.

Your story idea is as fundamental to your comprehensive concept and as critical to your novel as a military planner's initial mission and objective is to the success of a battle. Your objective in this drill is to invent your story idea.

In its most basic form, a story idea (like the idea behind a military operation) is *who must do what against whom*: A protagonist takes action to accomplish something in the face of active resistance from an opponent. This simple description is at the heart of the most beloved stories, from the child's tale "Little Red Riding Hood" to the epic Lord of the Rings trilogy. But it's not as simple as it might look. Note that there is a focus on character, a *someone*. This character must take action (*accomplish* something), whether that action is rescuing Grandma or destroying a magical evil ring. There is also a main opponent or antagonist—a wolf, for example—who wants to keep your character from accomplishing what she must accomplish.

Your story idea should be clearly stated in genre-appropriate terms. In a mystery, for example: *A newly promoted detective must hunt down a murderer*. In a thriller: *A graduate student in volcanology must escape an impending cataclysmic eruption*. In a romance: *A recently widowed ranch owner must get the loner cowboy to commit*. A study of your chosen genre will give you a good idea of the appropriate language and characters for your story idea.

It is critical to develop a sound story idea. Everything you do builds upon it. Get it wrong and your novel fails—it's that simple. Statements like *a beautiful but shy princess lives in a castle*, *a lonely cowboy rides the range*, and *a time traveler accidentally lands on a world where the beings randomly change genders* get it wrong. These are not story ideas—none includes an opponent, so there can be no conflict. And none of the above statements shows the characters taking a genre-specific action to accomplish something. This means that there's no objective, no familiar genre action, and no real beginning, middle, or end—in short, no story.

Inventing your story idea gives you an excellent feel for what is going to happen in your novel—of the struggles your main character will face, and what forces and characters will be arranged against her. By developing a strong story idea, you'll be able to keep your novel on track as you grow a full story line in the development phase of your battle plan.

Once you know who must do what against whom, you can go on to build the next part of your comprehensive concept—the *where* they do it. Where to find out more about where? In the next drill, of course.

RELATED DRILLS

Drill 14: Go Beyond *What If?*
Drill 15: Find Your Path
Drill 41: Change the World
Drill 42: Take Three Steps to Story Line
Drill 43: Turn on Your Turning Points
Drill 45: Put Your Book on an Index Card

DRILL 21

FORGE YOUR SETTING

In boot camp—and in the military—everyone must pull her weight as part of a team to get the mission done. When it comes to your novel, your setting needs to take up its rucksack and do its full duty. If the setting of your novel does nothing more than tell where the story takes place, then it's not making the contribution it could be making to your novel and to your reader's experience. To get the most out of your novel's setting, you need to understand three key concepts.

1. Setting does not have to be a perfect forgery. Most forgers want their forgeries to be indistinguishable from the real thing in every detail. But a novelist can create a setting that *feels* real with just a few bits of information. Don't log innumerable hours of research time in a struggle to ensure that the setting of your story is accurate in every detail. Setting is a *tool* you use to accomplish the goals of your story. Your setting can never be completely real; it's at least several times removed from the real place and time. Moreover, your purpose is not to write an encyclopedic historical catalog; your purpose is to write entertaining, emotionally stimulating fiction. (Many novelists have made a name for themselves—especially in the historical fiction genre—by successfully reproducing for the reader the details of everyday life in the more distant past. But even these authors choose these details carefully for their value in creating an emotional connection with the reader and furthering the story.)

This doesn't mean you can play fast and loose with reality—you can't have the sun rise in the west and expect the reader not to notice—but it does mean you can and must shape and mold reality to fit your genre and story.

2. Setting has certain specific functions. The primary function of setting is to contribute to and intensify your reader's emotional connection with your novel. You don't use setting simply to tell how things were in twelfth-century London, because that's not what your book is about and that's not what your reader expects. If you want to write a book about life in twelfth-century London, write a history book. Your reader expects a novel, not a series of detailed verbal snapshots.

Setting can also establish mood or tone (use a setting like the Great Depression Dust Bowl to magnify a sense of despair and loss), lend tension or suspense (set your story on a rumbling volcano or in Chicago just hours before the Great Fire), increase conflict (use war as a background event), or mark the genre (set your science fiction novel on a planet ruled by intelligent apes).

3. Setting operates on two levels. The first level is the large-scale or macro level, and it's this level you need to be concerned about as you invent your concept. This is the level that answers the question *What's the setting for your story?* Macro setting consists of a time frame and a general geographic location: London, about 1832; a modern, affluent Midwestern suburb; a remote nuclear weapons depot in the near future; a space station on the other side of the galaxy. A novel can have many settings, but macro settings apply to large portions of the book or to the entire novel. You can use macro setting to help accomplish the functions listed in item two, especially to help set the genre of your story.

The other level of setting is the small-scale or micro level. This is the level of setting for a specific scene, which we'll discuss in a later drill.

Nobody loafs in boot camp. Make your setting contribute all it can to your novel by understanding the three critical concepts of setting. Once you do, you can adjust your setting to increase the emotional impact of your novel. Don't worry about how real it is. In fact, don't worry too much about reality at all. Instead, read the next drill.

RELATED DRILLS

Drill 14: Go Beyond *What If?*
Drill 15: Find Your Path
Drill 18: Find Your Character in Events, Places, and Concepts
Drill 75: Use Micro Setting for Maximum Impact

DRILL 22

FORGET ABOUT REALITY ... MORE OR LESS

Sometimes new recruits are surprised and disappointed that the reality of boot camp is different from what they've seen on television or in the movies. To succeed in boot camp, recruits have to forget fictionalized notions of military training and stay focused on the reality. However, when it comes to writing fiction, the reverse is true; to succeed, you often have to forget about reality.

There's an old saying among editors that reality is a poor excuse for bad fiction. Reality is reality and fiction is fiction and *never*—except perhaps during political campaigns and IRS income tax audits—do the two meet. Certainly reality can and should influence your novel, and certainly your novel must establish and maintain credibility, but when it comes right down to it, your novel is not reality.

Clearly, reality and fiction are two different things, but for the author who wants to write a better book, four distinctions are critically important.

1. The purpose of your novel is to entertain the reader and to give that reader an emotional experience. Setting aside discussions of higher powers, reality does not have a purpose. Fiction does. Reality happens, meandering along in a series of events and moments in between. Even if your belief system says that reality does have a purpose, that purpose is not necessarily a good plot for a novel.

2. There's much about reality that's just plain boring. In a novel, however, you must make sure there aren't any boring parts. Even modern armed combat—which is fast-paced and adrenaline-pumping, and life-or-death dangerous—has been characterized as long periods of boredom punctuated by moments of intense fear. Your job in building a better book is not to recount the tedious hours but to build intense excitement into every scene and on every page.

3. Reality is full of people; fiction is full of characters. Most people live their lives in unremarkable ways. In your novel, however, the characters are unique, memorable, and deeply motivated to achieve their goals. They feel more intensely, have flaws that run deeper, have desires that burn much hotter, and have enemies much more cunning and vicious than any in real life. They pursue their goals with single-mindedness, and they're beset by more troubles than most people would experience in a dozen lifetimes.

4. Your novel must do something that reality isn't required to do—your fiction must make sense. In the real world, people often act irrationally. They do things for the silliest of reasons or sometimes for no reason at all. When they do act, they may choose a course that has little chance of success—just because. They inconveniently forget things, miss the obvious that's in front of them, and mysteriously choose to ignore signs of danger or indicators of a problem.

Not so in your novel—your reader won't stand for it! Characters must think and act competently and rationally. If they decide to commit a murder, run for governor, or shape-shift into a princess to rescue an imprisoned prince, they do so because something in their past or in their persona, something that the reader is aware of, clearly motivates them to do so.

After you've tossed out boring reality and created several hundred pages of intense emotion and an experience more riveting than real life, your novel may seem and feel very real to your reader, and that's exactly what you want.

It's for this unreal experience that the reader picks up your book. But just because you're not writing about reality, don't shrug off researching central elements of your story. Turn the page and find how to blend facts with your fiction.

RELATED DRILLS

Drill 14: Go Beyond *What If?*
Drill 20: Invent a Better Story Idea
Drill 24: Don't Fool Around Searching for Too Many Facts
Drill 25: Use the Poor Man's Spy Satellite
Drill 41: Change the World
Drill 75: Use Micro Setting for Maximum Impact

DRILL 23

RESEARCH YOUR PLAN OF ATTACK

Successful military operations require continuous gathering of intelligence. Soldiers have to gather intel on the enemy and the terrain, and factor that information into their battle plan. Likewise, writing a novel requires continuous research. Whether your decide to write in a genre you know, in a genre you love, or in a genre you think will bring you commercial success, you must conduct research during *each* phase of your battle plan: before, during, and after you write your book.

In the civilian world of novel writing, there's an intense debate over whether to research before you begin writing, while you're writing, or after you're deep into your work. All sides of this debate are right (and all are wrong), which is why, in novelist's boot camp, you research at all stages of writing. Here's why.

1. The truth changes. Whether about the physics that govern the universe or the social structure of pre-biblical Egypt, new discoveries are made each

day that change our view of what really is or what really happened. Your ongoing research may lead you to new or better information. You may use that information or you may not, but you can't make a smart choice if you don't know the information is there.

2. The smarter you get, the less you need. Once you get past the initial temptation to dump *all* your research into your work, you'll find that continuous research lets you find more relevant and interesting information and subtly work it into your novel where it will have the best effect. The challenge is overcoming that initial temptation to include it all. Continuous research also gives you a depth of knowledge that will make it easier for you to be more selective about the data you do include.

3. New information can take you and your story in new directions. Although your battle plan leads you to develop a detailed strategy for writing your novel, you should expect to adjust the direction of your work as you draft, revise, and edit. You don't know what new directions you may take, but continuous research means you'll be prepared—and the new information you uncover may well serve as a catalyst for new direction as well.

Just as you read continuously in your genre and about the craft of writing, you need to continuously research before, during, and after you write. Of course, you also need to carefully manage the time you spend researching: You have a writing mission—not a research mission—to accomplish! Find the facts you need. How do you know which facts you need? See the next drill.

RELATED DRILLS

Drill 22: Forget About Reality ... More or Less
Drill 24: Don't Fool Around Searching for Too Many Facts
Drill 25: Use the Poor Man's Spy Satellite
Drill 92: Circle Back for the Miscellaneous Pass

DRILL 24

DON'T FOOL AROUND SEARCHING FOR TOO MANY FACTS

Good soldiers know how to make every shot count. As a novelist, your ammunition is time and energy. Expend them wisely. As you research (before, during, and after you write your novel), you must be smart about your approach because what you don't know—about finding out about what you don't know—*can* hurt you.

For most novelists, research is essential. We're novelists—not detectives, Army Special Forces leaders, Scottish Highland princesses, crypt explorers, or space station commanders. Yet we need to understand their worlds well enough to build believable book-length environments for readers.

But research is also the enemy. Every moment you spend researching is a moment you're not drafting, not rewriting, not editing. You probably have an overcrowded schedule and too many competing demands on your time, energy, and creativity; you need to carefully allocate those three precious resources to make the greatest progress toward your goal. Novelists all too often depend on information gained from research to make their novel seem more real or authentic, and in so doing, they weigh down a good story with excess material.

How do you know how much research is enough? Each project is different, but you can have greater confidence that you're making the best use of time and information by following the guidelines below.

1. Understand the difference between research to learn more about a subject and research to find information to use in your novel. The key difference between these two is that the second—research to find information to use in your novel—has a definitive set of parameters: You are trying to find specific information to support a project—a project that has a schedule and a deadline.

2. Change your thinking about reality. Don't try to use the information gained from research to make a novel "real." By definition, your novel isn't real; it's a made-up story. Too often, history is boring. You don't want to bore the reader, you want to get him emotionally engaged and keep him that way. What you want to do is find—and use—information that will help your story to *feel* real. Fiction—like a forged signature, counterfeit bill, or copied painting—can never *be* real, it can only give the impression of being real. Your research has to contribute to that illusion, and a little goes a long way.

3. Construct a scene list as your guide to what kind of information you need. Your scene list (developed in a later drill) should contain the who, what, when, where, and why for each scene in your novel. Let's say a scene in your historical mystery takes place in an antebellum mansion. You'd need to research the sights, sounds, and smells of the time and place, then decide what bits of information would best contribute to your scene. You may also need research to familiarize yourself with what steps your protagonist might take to solve a problem. This information can help lend an air of authenticity to your story line. Make a list of what you need—it'll be a valuable guide and keep you on track.

4. Make a plan. Allocate blocks of time to (1) figuring out what kinds of information you need, (2) brainstorming and identifying sources, and (3) actually reading or researching to find the information. Mark your calendar with your research plan and with what information you want to have obtained by what dates. Keep track of your progress to keep yourself motivated and focused.

5. Keep good notes. Since there will likely be a time gap between finding information and actually writing it into your draft or revision, you'll need to rely on something other than your memory to keep track of knowledge gained. Additionally, when you're drafting a scene, you want your brainpower focused on the task at hand; when you're drafting a scene, draft a scene—don't try to draft a scene *and* recall research. Keeping good notes also keeps you focused. Once you've written down the information you need on a specific subject for a specific scene, you can go on to the next topic rather than dawdle over unrelated information.

Fiction writing requires that you do some research to evoke places and times and to solidify your own knowledge. Too little realism in a story alienates the reader. But too much research dissipates your precious time and energy, and too much realism weighs down the novel's progress. To find out where to look for interesting facts and figures that can add just the right touch of realism to your work, double-time it to the next drill.

RELATED DRILLS

Drill 22: Forget About Reality ... More or Less
Drill 23: Research Your Plan of Attack
Drill 25: Use the Poor Man's Spy Satellite
Drill 92: Circle Back for the Miscellaneous Pass

MISSION II

DRILL 25

USE THE POOR MAN'S SPY SATELLITE

Today, military commanders can use orbiting spy satellites to zoom in on remote areas. These high-tech digital imagery and remote-sensing tools can distinguish objects from a few inches to a few miles in length. It doesn't matter if a military commander has never been to that location—in just a few minutes a spy satellite can give him all the details he needs.

You probably don't have access to satellite imagery, but you do have digital tools that can make your research on a specific geographic area easier and give you results faster when you can't get to the library—or to San Francisco, Venezuela, Cincinnati, or Kazakhstan.

To be most effective in your research, follow the procedures below.

1. Determine what information you need. Three kinds of information best contribute to your novel.

- *An overall understanding of the area.* You should understand the place where you've set your story—its economy, government, issues, and so on—especially if it's a foreign country. This kind of research helps you more accurately paint your novel's backdrop and can translate into details that your characters see and relate. General information on the economy of an area can tell you what kinds of minor characters might be present and what kinds won't be. For example, if your novel is set at the foot of Russia's Ural mountains, your protagonist can expect to encounter coal miners, not sheep herders.

- *More detailed information on the specific city or town where your story takes place.* Familiarize yourself with local landmarks, events, maps, etc. If your protagonist needs to meet a man by a statue in Trafalgar Square in London and you get the wrong statue, your stumble might derail a knowledgeable reader.

• *Climate data.* Will your protagonist need a jacket? If your story is set in Oxford, Mississippi, in July, anyone dressed in an outfit other than shorts and a T-shirt is going to be soaked in perspiration in short order.

2. Use the most expedient methods to gather information. Several types of Web sites can serve as your own spy satellites when you need to know specific demographics and get a better feel for a distant locale. They can also give you the critical details you need to ensure your readers believe your novel is set in Amarillo, Fargo, or Tel Aviv.

You don't need to be a spy to get this information, but spies have done much work for you. The CIA World Factbook contains detailed country profiles and maps and is available at www.cia.gov/cia/publications/factbook/. These profiles will give you the overall understanding of where your novel is set.

You can get more specific information about cities and towns in the United States from chamber of commerce sites, city guides, and tourist information sites. Such sites can provide you not only with statistics, but also with seasonal event information and the locations of theaters, shops, civic centers, parking, public transportation, and more. Many include maps, but if they don't, you can plug addresses from one site into an Internet mapping site.

Often, cities and towns have Web cams—cameras hooked up to the Internet. Shots from Web cams can be invaluable in giving you a feel for the area as well as specifics about how a city, town, or campus actually looks. Additionally, many chamber of commerce and tourism sites offer virtual tours of landmarks or major attractions, again allowing you to see a place you can't actually visit.

Local news and national weather Web sites can provide specific climate data. National sites often contain historical data so you can check for the biggest storm in forty years, floods, and other natural disasters. Many of these sites also contain monthly or seasonal overviews. Of course, in most locales, it's hot in summer and cool in winter, but in Alice Springs, Australia, the temperature on an early July day will reach only

64°F—no coat necessary, but a light jacket will keep the northwest winds from chilling your main characters.

However, one word of caution—double-check. Many Web sites are just plain wrong, and it's difficult to spot bad info, especially if you're in a hurry. Trust, but verify by finding a corroborating source.

3. Record and save the information. Bookmark your favorite Web sites so you can find your way back easily. It's also a good idea to print out pages with pertinent information and keep them together. Cut and paste smaller bits of information and save them in a file labeled *Setting Notes*. Don't spend a lot of time on this—your notes file is for your use only, so just make sure you can read and use the information.

Establishing and maintaining a sense of realism helps keep the reader emotionally connected. Use your virtual spy satellite to gather intelligence throughout the execution of your battle plan. For now, put down the mouse, pick up this book, and move on to the next phase: development.

RELATED DRILLS

Drill 18: Find Your Character in Events, Places, and Concepts
Drill 21: Forge Your Setting
Drill 22: Forget About Reality ... More or Less
Drill 23: Research Your Plan of Attack
Drill 88: Make a Description and Narration Pass

BATTLE PLAN CHARLIE

DEVELOPMENT

MISSION III: ENLIST YOUR NEW RECRUITS 073

Drill 26: Choose Your Cast 074

Drill 27: Make Your Main Character Unlike You 077

Drill 28: Understand the Alpha Male Character's Motivations . . 080

Drill 29: Understand the Alpha Female Character's Motivations . . 083

Drill 30: Make Your Protagonist Act Like a Dog 086

Drill 31: Distinctly Mark Your Characters 089

Drill 32: Discharge the Wimps 093

Drill 33: Give Your Protagonist a Pointed Personality 095

Drill 34: Open a Window to Your Character 098

Drill 35: Tell Your Characters' Backstories 102

Drill 36: Define the Opposition 105

Drill 37: Put a Face on Evil 107

Drill 38: Define, Objectify, and Personify the Objective 109

Drill 39: Use a Character Matrix 112

Drill 40: Up-Gun Your Character Cards 115

MISSION IV: DEVISE YOUR OPERATIONS ORDER .. 118
Drill 41: Change the World 119
Drill 42: Take Three Steps to Story Line....................121
Drill 43: Turn on Your Turning Points 125
Drill 44: Develop Your Exit Strategy 127
Drill 45: Put Your Book on an Index Card 130
Drill 46: Build Your Master Story Summary 133
Drill 47: Plan Your Characters' Development 135
Drill 48: Sound Off for Equipment Check 138

MISSION III
ENLIST YOUR NEW RECRUITS

You've left your civilian thinking behind, and you've created a detailed comprehensive concept. Now you're ready to build on this solid foundation. In short, you're finally ready to enter the development phase of your battle plan.

The development phase expands and refines the plans and concepts you prepared in the previous phases, and gives you the tools you need to effectively and efficiently execute the next demanding step in your battle plan—writing a quality first draft. Your development phase has two steps.

1. Character Development. Here you'll get your troops in formation. Soldiers are the heart of the army; characters are the heart of your story. Some will be courageous, likeable, and competent; others will be manipulative, greedy, and evil. Your development work here will permeate through every word of the draft that is to come.

2. Story Line Development. Operations orders are the blueprints for execution of military concepts—they set a mission into motion. This part of the development process is all about creating a detailed story line and setting the stage for the upcoming action. You'll build your full story line, prepare a list of your novel's scenes, and write scene summaries. This isn't just a paper drill—you'll be using these tools to make daily progress as you write your draft in the next battle plan phase.

Don't believe me? Do push-ups until you do. Choose your novel's cast well. Train, or rather, *develop* them intensely. Don't let up until they're strong, until they're larger than life, until their personalities push themselves into your readers' memories. At the end of this phase of development, your troops will be ready, and so will you.

DRILL 26

CHOOSE YOUR CAST

Once military planners receive a mission, they carefully determine how many and what kind of troops they'll need—they pick the right members for the team. Too few and there's a chance of failure; too many means support, command, and control problems, and a waste of resources. Choose team members with the wrong skills for the specific mission—send a jungle expert into Antarctica—and the entire mission is in jeopardy.

Hollywood does the same kind of choosing for movies—directors choose just the right actors in just the right number for a certain type of film. As a novelist, you face the challenge of picking the right number and right kind of characters for your novel's cast. Your story and genre will give you some guidelines: Family sagas need families, ensemble stories need ensembles, mysteries need witnesses, and thrillers and horror stories need victims. An action-adventure survival novel will likely need fewer major characters, as will a contemporary romance or a work of psychological suspense. Read broadly in the genre you wish to write in, and you'll get a good feel for the conventional cast size.

As a rule of thumb, plan for the following six kinds of characters.

1. A protagonist. This character is essential. Hollywood writes its screenplays for a lead actor (or actors, in the case of split mains found in the likes of *Butch Cassidy and the Sundance Kid* or in the case of ensembles as in *Ocean's Eleven*). This character is the focus of the novel; your book is the story of his pursuit of his objective.

2. An antagonist, main opponent, or villain. This character is also essential. Your main opponent, like the brilliant serial bomber who faces off against LAPD bomb expert Carol Starkey in Robert Crais's *Demolition Angel*, works actively and passionately to defeat your protagonist. He is skilled, tough, and driven—just like your main character. Note that your novel's main opponent doesn't have to be evil to the core; he may be a rival, competitor, or alternate candidate.

3. A window character for your main character. Give your protagonist someone to talk to—perhaps like Sampson, the partner of James Patterson's detective, Alex Cross. A window character for your lead provides multiple possibilities to make your novel richer and offers opportunities to give the reader glimpses into your protagonist's true nature.

4. A window character for your main opponent or villain. Just as you did for your protagonist, give your opponent someone to talk to. A window character for your antagonist or villain can provide more conflict for the protagonist.

5. Other opposition to your main character. Also known as *other opponents*, and sometimes called *minions* if they work for the main opponent, these characters are also out to defeat your protagonist. They have their own motivations—which may or may not be the same as those of the main opponent—but share the objective of stopping your main character.

6. A character who personalizes and personifies the main character's objective. This character helps your reader establish an emotional connection to your protagonist's objective and gives tangible form to your protagonist's desire to achieve that objective. This character requires some care to keep her from turning into a flat, caricature-like trophy. For example, in Daniel Silva's *The Kill Artist*, art restorer and Israeli intelligence operative Gabriel Allon must rescue model-turned-spy Jacqueline Delacroix from a ruthless Palestinian terrorist, Tariq al-Houraini. Delacroix is also Jewish. If Allon does not stop Tariq, both Israel and Jacqueline will perish. Given the personal history Silva constructs for Delacroix (her parents were Jewish resistance fighters in WWII), her imprisonment by Tariq, her religion, and the close, intense personal relationship Silva constructs between her and Allon, it's clear that Delacroix both personalizes and personifies Allon's objectives. To ensure that Delacroix is more than an empty prize, Silva goes the extra mile in developing the character, telling crucial parts of the story from her point of view, and giving her an active role.

This list may shrink or expand, depending on the genre you're writing in. Your reading in your genre will give you a good idea of how to determine your cast size, which you want to keep as small as possible. One benefit of limiting your cast size is that it helps discipline your creativity. Too often, beginning writers introduce a new character just to provide readers with some quick information. This crutch can inflate your cast size and distract from your protagonist. Although you may need to create more characters to support the kind of story you're writing, keep the focus on your main character by having other characters talk to or about him, get into conflicts with him, deal with changes he has caused, and work to defeat him. It is, after all, his story.

One of the keys to success in both military operations and creative tasks is to choose the right number and the right kind of people to accomplish the mission. Limit your cast size and include the essential players, and when it comes to the main player—your protagonist—take steps to ensure he has all the right qualities for the job. How? A good way to start is with the next drill.

RELATED DRILLS

Drill 2: Adopt a Principled Approach
Drill 5: See Your Target
Drill 18: Find Your Character in Events, Places, and Concepts
Drill 19: Find Your Character in Opposites
Drill 53: Tell Each Character's Story
Drill 85: Make a Character Pass

DRILL 27

MAKE YOUR MAIN CHARACTER UNLIKE YOU

Early in boot camp, everyone wants to be a hero. But being the hero isn't your job—your job is to be the author.

It's natural for you, as the author, to want to make yourself the main character—to give the protagonist your own strengths, weaknesses, knowledge, values, and personality. This pull to place yourself at the center of your novel is especially strong when you write your fiction in the first person (*I*), when you're leveraging your expertise in a specific subject, or when the protagonist has a profession that is the same as or similar to yours.

Yet that's a temptation that novelists need to actively avoid. You need to take definitive steps to ensure you're as removed from the story as you can be.

Why? Although you're surely competent, attractive, intelligent, fascinating, and [insert a string of other of ego-enhancing adjectives here], you're also a real person. Great novels aren't about real people. Rather, they're about characters who are simply and intensely *more*—more competent, attractive, intelligent, fascinating—than any real human being.

Additionally, when you, as the author, sneak in to your protagonist's skin, there's a chance that your character will ultimately be torn in two very different directions. For example, what happens if your natural reaction to an event is different from that required of the character? At what point do you let the character develop into her own person? At best, that specific scene will be awkward; at worst, you'll need to backtrack to redevelop and redefine the character, which also means doing a rewrite to show that character's personality—or rather, *yours*—playing out naturally in the story.

There are five key techniques for ensuring your protagonist is allowed to be her own person.

1. Give your protagonist at least one physical attribute you don't have. Physical differences can be a good start to giving your main character a separate identity. Make your main character short if you're tall, blonde if you're brunette, or fair-skinned if you have an olive complexion. Physical ability is another way of differentiating between yourself and your character. Are you a klutz? Give your protagonist graceful coordination. Play a pretty good game of tennis? Your main character can shoot pretty good hoops. Can't dance? Your protagonist loves to tango.

2. Give your protagonist at least one personality trait you don't have. Go beyond superficial physical differences and make your protagonist different on the inside, too. Your main character should have different likes and dislikes and personality traits. Hate snakes? Perhaps your main character keeps a pet boa. Like cats? Your protagonist is a dog person. Enjoy good old meat-and-potatoes, down-home cooking? Your main character prefers free-range chicken breasts and organic salad. Do you have the patience of the saints combined? Your protagonist doesn't, and she has a temper to boot.

3. Enlarge a personal attribute. We all believe ourselves to be somewhat brave, at least a little insightful, just, fairly smart, and a bit creative. Differentiate yourself from your main character by enlarging these traits, exaggerating them until they are salient and driving features of your protagonist's personality.

4. Put yourself someplace else. Giving yourself a bit part in your larger story is one way to satisfy the need to participate in the story you're creating. Consider casting yourself in a noncritical, secondary character role. That way, you can concentrate your creative energies on developing and refining your major characters, but you still get to play.

5. Develop detailed biographies for your major characters. An exceptionally effective technique for developing and differentiating characters is to write their backstories. Develop and write out a two- to five-page personal history and description for each of your major characters: their personalities, likes, dislikes, fears, hopes, and dreams. Go back to their grandparents to see what seminal influences affected their lives. Develop major events in their lives that made them who they are. As you do so, make sure their histories aren't replays of your own.

You can't escape yourself in your writing. Your work is a product of *your* imagination and *your* personality, so *your* values, hopes, and fears will all manifest themselves in many subtle ways you may not notice until the manuscript is finished. However, to build a book with characters that your readers will love, hate, fear, laugh at, and (above all) remember, take yourself out of your character's clothes and off of your novel's center stage. Instead, give someone else the lead. Where to find that character? Try the next drill.

RELATED DRILLS

Drill 2: Adopt a Principled Approach
Drill 28: Understand the Alpha Male Character's Motivations
Drill 29: Understand the Alpha Female Character's Motivations
Drill 31: Distinctly Mark Your Characters
Drill 32: Discharge the Wimps
Drill 33: Give Your Protagonist a Pointed Personality

DRILL 28

UNDERSTAND THE ALPHA MALE CHARACTER'S MOTIVATIONS

In the military, tough drill sergeants who bellow out orders give boot camp trainees all the motivation they need. As an author, you too will need to provide your characters with motivation, explaining to the reader why they do what they do. One of the most challenging characters to motivate is the alpha male character. Regardless of genre, as you develop the personality for a strong male character, you need to understand what makes him tick.

While your leading man will certainly be likeable, competent, courageous, and virtuous, there are key motivations or needs that make him an alpha male. These don't change with story or genre, and they come into play regardless of other characteristics you give him, such as his sense of justice or his flaw of excessive pride. Let's take a closer look at the six core needs and motivations of an alpha male character.

1. He needs to feel and appear competent. He wants to know what he's doing, and he wants others to believe he does, too. That's why he doesn't ask for directions, ignores installation instructions, and lifts the hood of a broken-down automobile when he has no clue what's going on inside. This trait also makes it difficult for him to admit a mistake.

2. He is goal-oriented and results-driven. Whether or not he hits the target, makes the numbers, or accomplishes the mission, your alpha male never loses his focus. To him, it's more about competence than hard work, more about winning or losing than playing the game. If he has to do an end run around established procedures or defy authority to get a job done, he'll do it.

3. He believes strength is the ability to take it in silence. He hates whining. He can take it—whatever *it* is—like a man, without showing or verbalizing the fear, pain, fatigue, or sadness the *it* brings. He believes that a real man exhibits grace under pressure.

4. He values loyalty to a comrade or team, but also places a high value on independence, individualism, and self-reliance. His word is his bond to buddies and teammates, but at the same time, his earliest heroes were men who stood above the crowd. This trait can make him show loyalty to a friend who has done wrong or refuse assistance even when it's clear he needs it.

5. He values logic over intuition, reason over emotion, and action over discussion. Although he does trust his gut feelings and will play a hunch, he is more comfortable with a logical, well-mapped road toward a definable goal. And he always prefers action to talk.

6. He has a strong sex drive. Attribute it to testosterone, to the instinct to preserve the species, or to genetics; the animal drive to mate is strong in alpha males. He notices physical attractiveness, feels powerful sexual urges, and responds—if only internally—to sexual stimulus, intended or not.

Your alpha character need not be your main character—just make sure he doesn't steal the show. Whether your strong male character has a large or small part in your novel, these traits should be a big part of his emotional and psychological makeup, and they should exhibit themselves in his words and actions. These traits can be strengths or weaknesses—depending on the situation of your novel—and they can lead to both internal and external conflict, but they will always make the alpha male more believable and more interesting.

These traits and motivations are, however, only a start. If you use these traits and only these traits, your hero becomes a stereotype. Your job as novelist is to use them as a point of departure to build a unique, interesting male character.

To find out how to build an interesting alpha female, read on to the next drill.

RELATED DRILLS

Drill 15: Find Your Path
Drill 29: Understand the Alpha Female Character's Motivations
Drill 31: Distinctly Mark Your Characters
Drill 32: Discharge the Wimps
Drill 33: Give Your Protagonist a Pointed Personality

DRILL 29

UNDERSTAND THE ALPHA FEMALE CHARACTER'S MOTIVATIONS

In today's military you find strong leaders and resolute warriors of both genders. In fiction, you'll also find tough men and women alike.

Just as there are alpha male characters—strong, masculine characters who make your readers say *there goes a real man*—so too are there strong female characters—alpha females. An alpha woman can be anything from a soldier (like Major Valerie Mcintyre in my novel *The Best Defense*) to a tomb raider (like Lara Croft), private investigator (like Sara Paretsky's V.I. Warshawski), or plantation owner's daughter (like Scarlett O'Hara in *Gone With the Wind*). What matters is not their profession but their motivations and their character.

What makes strong female characters tick? Like their male counterparts, strong female characters are likeable, competent, courageous, and virtuous. But they're also different. The following motivations and traits are applicable across genre and exist regardless of other specific characteristics that you give your alpha female.

1. She has an unstoppable iron will that drives her to take action. At the core of an alpha female character is a freight train of a will that translates her values into action. While weaker women only talk about wanting to solve a problem or attain a goal, the strong female character makes things happen. Her drive may manifest itself in words, but the strong female character will get physical if she has to. In a confrontation, she won't hesitate to use force.

2. She truly understands right and wrong. In any given situation, the strong female character intuitively knows what is honest and dishonest, what is good and evil, and what is the right and wrong thing to do. This understanding comes not from an external set of rules and regulations but from deep inside. Dishonesty in herself or others is distasteful, and her deep understanding of right and wrong can lead to conflict when her intuitive sense of morality conflicts with the real world's manipulations, dogma, iron regulations, or shades of gray.

3. She is connected to her feelings, her family, and the people and places around her. The strong female character is aware of her own feelings and the feelings of those around her. Although she doesn't allow her emotions or the emotions of others to rule her, those feelings do figure into her calculations. This connection sometimes happens even when she doesn't want it to; she may find it difficult to cut out of her life the family member who is nothing but trouble or the friend who is too needy too often.

4. She sees clearly and deeply. The strong female character is quick to grasp the true nature of another person or situation. Although she can be deceived by appearances, she is usually able to determine the essential qualities of a certain person or of a set of circumstances. While she may temporarily convince herself, for example, to trust a specific individual, there will be a small voice inside her that constantly, quietly nags her if the person in question is not someone she can turn her back on. This can make many social situations uncomfortable for her—she'll be ill at ease when surrounded by friendly smiling sharks.

5. She's solid under pressure. She doesn't break down or freeze up when disaster strikes. When the chips are way down, or when failure or even certain death is seconds or inches away, she digs deeply into herself and finds the emotional and physical resilience not just to endure but to thrive and succeed.

6. She has a sex drive. The strong female character feels the attraction to potential loves and lovers. She accepts, embraces, and enjoys her sexuality. While the potential consequences of acting on her passion or desire may keep her urges in check, she is not afraid to feel those urges or to acknowledge when sexual chemistry or the potential for sexual chemistry exists. Her drive may stem from her primal instinct to preserve the species or from genetics; but whatever its origin, the alpha female notices physical attractiveness and feels strong sexual urges. She will also respond—if only internally—to sensual or erotic stimulations, just as her alpha-male counterpart does.

From queens to starship captains to housewives, alpha females bring their own brand of strength to the challenges and obstacles of stories in all genres. These are women of thought, feeling, and—most importantly—action. These are not the panicky women in high heels who fall helplessly in front of a villain or monster, frozen in terror until the hero fights it off. Instead—because of her indomitable will, her connection with others, her sense of right and wrong, her grace under pressure, and other essential qualities—the alpha female takes action to rescue herself and others from the oncoming evil.

You should take action, as well—turn to the next drill.

RELATED DRILLS

Drill 15: Find Your Path
Drill 28: Understand the Alpha Male Character's Motivations
Drill 31: Distinctly Mark Your Characters
Drill 32: Discharge the Wimps
Drill 33: Give Your Protagonist a Pointed Personality

DRILL 30

MAKE YOUR PROTAGONIST ACT LIKE A DOG

There are units that merely look good, and there are those you *know* are good because when you see them in action, they're kicking tail and taking names. They not only talk the talk, they walk the walk of winners. Your main characters should do this, too—walk the walk and act like the strong characters they are.

Suppose you had to write a story in which your protagonist couldn't talk. Not one word of intelligible dialogue, save for a few unintelligible guttural sounds. How would you let your reader know that your protagonist is a person of indomitable will and bold actions? Without the novelist's critical tool of dialogue, how could you communicate your hero's motivations or the powerful personality traits that drive your heroine?

You'd make the character act like a dog, that's how.

Your protagonist has to express her strength in the small things she does as well as in the large things. From how she holds her head to how she enters a room, her actions must communicate that she is a dignified, resolved character. These actions are often as important as dialogue. Much of human communication is nonverbal, so your words must paint a picture that allows the reader to visualize your protagonist's power, just as dialogue allows the reader to hear it in the words she says and that others say to or about her.

Your dog can't talk, but you know exactly what he is thinking or feeling, what his needs or wants are, and whether he's feeling brave or fearful, determined or apathetic, passionate or angry. Your dog shows you, with his actions large and small, what he's feeling.

What do heroes and heroines do to show readers that they are heroes and heroines? They don't have tails to wag, so they demonstrate who they are in other ways.

- **They will look 'em in the eye.** Whether they are a staring down a deadly opponent prior to mortal combat, comforting a dying buddy, or sharing a soulful glance during a moment of passion, strong characters look directly into those windows to the soul.

- **They will stand up and stand tall.** They don't sit much. Instead, they stand—ready to act. And when they stand, they do so without slouching. Think military bearing and carriage.

- **They will stand still.** They value grace under pressure, so there won't be any nail-biting, awkward fidgeting, hair-twisting, or pencil-chewing. The notable exception is when a male character must deal with his or another's feelings—then count on him to endlessly tie and retie his shoelaces or exhibit some other repetitive behavior.

- **They will get physical.** Strong characters are men and women of action—physical action. Although a male protagonist (especially an alpha male) usually has a code of behavior that mandates he not be brutal against women (no hitting girls), he has no problem hitting, moving, shoving, pushing, or tossing obstacles aside. This can mean solving a dispute with his fists or heaving boulders out of the way. And while physical action might not be a female character's first choice, she's not afraid of it and will fight hand to hand to get what she needs.

- **They will have big body language.** These characters are big and bold, even in the way they do the smallest things. He'll push back from a meeting table to distance himself or make a point. She'll lean forward across that same table to dominate space or drive her point home. If he relaxes, his arms stretch behind his head and his feet go up. He'll pull, gently but firmly, his date onto the dance floor—and then he *will* lead, even if he can't keep time.

So now you have a strong protagonist who walks, talks, and thinks like a *real* man or woman. And now it's up to you, the alpha author, to make sure that each of your characters—the alpha and the beta—is distinct in his or her own right. So, to learn how to keep stereotypes or caricatures out of your work, turn to the next drill.

RELATED DRILLS

Drill 27: Make Your Main Character Unlike You
Drill 28: Understand the Alpha Male Character's Motivations
Drill 29: Understand the Alpha Female Character's Motivations
Drill 31: Distinctly Mark Your Characters
Drill 33: Give Your Protagonist a Pointed Personality

DRILL 31

DISTINCTLY MARK YOUR CHARACTERS

In the military, you always know who's who because of the rank indicators and badges on their uniforms. These badges distinctly mark military men and women.

You can give your characters their own distinctive badges or markers so readers can easily and quickly understand who they are. Writers have only a few seconds to provide readers with an emotional understanding of their characters' personalities. If this understanding is postponed for too long, it becomes difficult for readers to emotionally connect with the characters. Smart writers expedite this process by leveraging stereotypical markers to give their readers starting points for placing, defining, and understanding a character.

These markers go beyond descriptions of sex, race, age, hair length and style, height, weight, and eye color to provide detailed information and insight. Take a look at the following distinctive markers and think about what will work for your characters.

- **Clothing.** Fashion does indeed make a statement, and clothes do make the man—or woman, as the case may be. Agatha Christie's dignified detective, Hercule Poirot, wore his obsession with detail in his perfectly fitted suits. Use a tailored pinstripe suit to make the reader infer a connection with business and wealth. Associate your character with a rebellious biker crowd with a well-worn leather motorcycle jacket. Put your character in a baggy corduroy jacket with leather elbow patches and he becomes a college professor. Dress your heroine in an extra-short mini skirt, stiletto heels, and a low-cut blouse, and she becomes a working girl. Gang colors have strong connotations, as do bib overalls, Hawaiian shirts, saris, and string ties.

- **Speech patterns.** Give your character a Southern drawl, a Kentucky twang, or a New England nasal tone, or have him speak in ethnic slang—

these can all help place your character in terms of geography and class. So too can technical or industry jargon. Want to signal that your heroine served in the military? When asked what time an event occurred, have her respond with *thirteen hundred hours* instead of *one o'clock*.

- **Food and drink.** Does your character's background lead him to sip James Bond's signature vodka martinis or to belt down boilermakers? Is his regular sustenance fast food, or does he eat only haute cuisine at the finest French restaurants? Does he have charm-school table manners, or is the boardinghouse reach his defining mannerism?

- **Transportation.** Provide your character with two Porsches, a Jag, and a Bentley, and he likely has a different background than the driver of a lumbering minivan, a low-slung two-seater sports car, or a hulking SUV. If your character is a veteran big-city dweller, it's possible he's never owned a car; instead he gets about by train, subway, and taxicab, and is at ease (or on alert) in each of these. Take your character out of the driver's seat and put him on horseback, on two wheels, on a tractor, or simply have him walk everywhere he goes, and you have strong indicators of his background and personality. Characters who won't fly and those who fly their own planes, sail their own boats, or race automobiles all have different characteristics and behaviors.

- **Physical markings.** Scars, wounds, tattoos, and body piercings send very strong signals, and in many levels of American society, most of those signals are negative. Incorporate disabilities with care and make them relevant to the story: Captain Cletus Grahame's knee injury figures prominently in Gordon R. Dickson's classic science-fiction series, the Childe Cycle (also called the Dorsai series). Put physical markings on your character with thought—they can never be changed. Cosmetic surgery gives clues to your character's wealth, and repeated cosmetic surgery can say something about your character's vanity or self-image.

- **Smells.** Have your characters reek of who they are: a perfume that costs five hundred dollars per ounce; Dad's aftershave; oil, axle grease, and gaso-

line; horses and saddle leather; mortar dust and sweat; gunpowder; hospital antiseptic; formaldehyde and death.

While many of these markers can clue in a reader to a character's basic type, mannerisms, details, and context often provide deeper insight into what's unique about that character, allowing you to address how your specific character is different from others of his type, and what that character is like inside.

- **Mannerisms.** Like Jeffrey Deaver's Amelia Sachs in *The Coffin Dancer*, your nervous character can constantly bite his nails, or perhaps he has already bitten them to the quick. He can pull at his ear, rub his forehead, bite his lip, chomp on an unlit cigar, tap his foot, or have some other signature mannerism—perhaps chewing on straw—that signals his uniqueness. Be sure, though, to associate this mannerism with something significant in the character's personality and personal history—no lip-biting for its own sake.

- **Telling details.** Your character may wear a suit, but does that suit fit? Is it frayed at the sleeves and collar? Are buttons missing? Clean and pressed or faded and stained? Detectives Hercule Poirot and Spenser both dress immaculately. Accessories—such as hats, pocket watches, pipes, pens, and keepsakes—can also provide insight. Sherlock Holmes had his pipe. Again, these must be connected with that character's personality and not included simply for novelty's sake.

- **Context.** To make a strong statement about your hero's character, have him wear an unusual article of clothing or speak or act in a way that is out of context. For example, a cowboy hat and cowboy boots worn with a business suit send a clear message about a character's background and self-image. Jeans and a black T-shirt at a formal dinner do the same, as do a black power dress and pearls at an informal lunch.

How many and what kind of markers are enough, and how many are too many? That depends on the kind of character. The more important and complex the character, the more detailed the development needs to be; the less important the character, the fewer and simpler the markers. Thus a street vendor or villain's minion who makes only brief appearances may get markers that let the reader type him and move on, while your protagonist and his main opposition will have many markers that reveal themselves over many pages.

Character markers are not the end of character development; they are only the beginning. They offer rich mines of potential story lines, conflicts, and personalities, giving you an opportunity to go beyond caricature and stereotype—to turn character types into real characters.

Some characters are marked from the start as weak. To see what to do with them, move on to the next drill.

RELATED DRILLS

Drill 27: Make Your Main Character Unlike You
Drill 33: Give Your Protagonist a Pointed Personality
Drill 47: Plan Your Characters' Development

DRILL 32

DISCHARGE THE WIMPS

Neither drill sergeants in boot camp nor today's readers will tolerate a passive character. Those drill sergeants will kick ass, and readers will quickly dismiss—or loathe—a character that suffers in passive, silent self-sacrifice.

In all genres—not just in action-adventure novels or thrillers—it is critically important that your characters be persons of action. And while all of your characters must be active, it's most critical for your protagonist to be active. Your story is about a main character who has an objective and who pursues it in the face of opposition. The events in the story come about when that character makes a decision or discovers new information, then acts on that decision or information and deals with the consequences. In other words, your main character goes after the goal with 100 percent of her being. Her actions are in pursuit of her goal, her decisions are in pursuit of her goal, and her dialogue is in pursuit of her goal.

The task of building an interesting, sympathetic main character, therefore, includes actively seeking out and eliminating traits and signs of passiveness. Your protagonist is not God and does not control events. She does, however, face challenges that are seemingly impossible to overcome, and she does have a goal that appears well beyond her abilities to achieve. She may seem woefully outmatched by her opponent. Her friends and allies may turn their backs on her. She may try and fail, try again and fail, and try yet a third time only to fail again. But what she cannot do is quit and stand meekly in place. Readers will simply not tolerate it if she does.

While natural and man-made disasters can throw your main character's world into chaos, she cannot retreat to her bedroom to blandly accept her oncoming demise. Your main character must act in the face of disaster—whether it be an erupting volcano or a sinking cruise liner—to save herself and what she holds dear.

Physical limitations can also challenge your main character. Physical or mental disabilities, such as blindness and depression, can pose great obstacles to her achievement of her goal. Yet to maintain reader interest and move your story, your protagonist must overcome these disabilities to make progress toward her goal, as does Jeffrey Deaver's quadriplegic forensic expert, Lincoln Rhyme. Your main character may be a victim of violence or an accident, or she may have suffered some other kind of devastating loss. Yet, as terrible and immobilizing as these are, your main character must rise to continue the pursuit of her objective.

Part of your protagonist's challenge is to overcome the negativity of others. She can count on being told many times and in many ways that she can't succeed. Her response, of course, is that she can and will. She can counter negativity with words, or, more powerfully, with actions. She may have self-doubt, but she will effectively overcome that negativity in herself and turn off the whining voice inside her that continually bemoans the difficulty of the journey and the impossibility of the goal.

Your protagonist doesn't necessarily have to stoically "take it like a man," but she won't lament her condition endlessly and pitifully either.

Your task as a novelist, then, is to be much like that drill sergeant. No, don't go kick someone's ass. Instead, actively eliminate the passive in your characters. One way to do that is to add some enticing personality points to your characters. What are personality points? Glad you took the initiative and asked. Now see the next drill.

RELATED DRILLS

Drill 17: Put a Face on Your Idea
Drill 26: Choose Your Cast
Drill 28: Understand the Alpha Male Character's Motivations
Drill 29: Understand the Alpha Female Character's Motivations
Drill 31: Distinctly Mark Your Characters
Drill 33: Give Your Protagonist a Pointed Personality
Drill 85: Make a Character Pass

DRILL 33

GIVE YOUR PROTAGONIST A POINTED PERSONALITY

All military recruits start out as civilians; then they sharpen their skills and personalities and become members of the armed forces. The same is true for characters in fiction—when they come to novelist's boot camp, they may start round, but that's only a start. The civilian way is to create round characters. The boot camp way is to create *pointed* characters.

Think of a fictional hero or heroine. Do you see a *round* hero? Courageous? Yes. Lonely? Yes. Competent? Yes. Cynical? Maybe. But *round*? No.

Your characters start out expressing a number of different character traits, including the kind of contradictory characteristics often seen in real people. This is a good definition for a rounded character. It's also only a beginning.

During the invention phase of your battle plan, you chose a main character. You likely had some initial ideas about what kind of person he was. Now you want to begin to develop—enlarge, refine, grow, or improve upon—that character. Your first step is to give your protagonist (or any major character) a pointed personality.

You create a pointed character through the deliberate insertion of positive and negative striking points into that character's personality. Your protagonist obviously needs to have the most well-developed personality, so he should get the most personality points. In your antagonist, the proportion of positive and negative points is reversed. (How could it not be? If the antagonist is such a good person, how could he stand in the way of your protagonist?) The more important the character and the more prominent the role, the more personality points the character should have.

Building your character's pointed personality involves the following three steps.

1. Assign the character's positive personality points. These personality points are, of course, the positive elements of a character, such as optimism, courage, insightfulness, virtue, competence, a strong sense of justice, charm, and determination. These points are present in everything your protagonist says and does. If your character is determined, the sharp point of determination is going to poke through his dialogue, thoughts, feelings, and actions. Behavior is no more than personality manifested. For example, Tom Clancy's CIA analyst Jack Ryan is determined to bring a terrorist to justice in *Patriot Games*. That determination comes through in Ryan's behavior—in how he talks and acts—and drives him from Pentagon mission control room to one-on-one confrontation.

Just as you limited the size of your cast, limit the number of positive personality points you assign your character. Consider assigning your main character three to five positive personality points—any fewer and your character becomes too simple and dull, any more and you're likely to have difficulty juggling all the points.

2. Assign the character's negative personality points. Negative personality points include aggressiveness, excessive ambition, self-centeredness, loneliness, and cynicism. Giving your protagonist a negative personality point makes that character appear more human to the reader, builds conflict (and, by extension, reader interest), allows for emotional growth, and throws interesting emotional wrinkles into what might otherwise be simplistic scenes. Like any good fictional homicide detective, Ian Rankin's Inspector Rebus struggles with cynicism, loneliness, and despair. Part of the great interest in Rankin's novels arises from watching Rebus battle these points to a draw.

In a protagonist, limit the number of negative points to one to three because—antiheroes notwithstanding—readers generally like their protagonists to be good people (even Lawrence Block's lonely hit-man protagonist, Keller, is a nice guy).

3. Cross-check, refine and reassign, and intensify. This step has three parts. First, cross-check your character's positive and negative personality points against other characters. Second, reassign personality points, if necessary, and refine them so you have a mix that is interesting and builds conflict. For example, if your hero is logical, his window character or opponent might be emotional. In general, you want different kinds of people with different kinds of personalities in your novel, so when they come together, things heat up. (The *opposites attract* premise is common in many romance novels.) The third and final step is to intensify. To make your protagonist's personality points resonate with the reader, you'll want to make them pronounced. Does your character have a temper? Intensify it and send your character into violent rages. Are two characters brave? Make one recklessly fearless to get some conflict.

In later drills, you'll learn how to drive these points home to your reader without stacking up adjectives and adverbs so high they smother your writing, as in *Lonely and cynical, Bill gazed out the window as he remembered the brilliant detail missing from his brave performance in court that morning.* For now, put points on your main characters' personalities. Make sure they have weaknesses as well as strengths, then refine their personality points to build interest and conflict.

The civilian idea of rounded characters is a great start, but it's just that—a start. Give your protagonist a pointed personality. And give him a window character as well—you can find one in the next drill.

RELATED DRILLS

Drill 17: Put a Face on Your Idea
Drill 26: Choose Your Cast
Drill 31: Distinctly Mark Your Characters
Drill 32: Discharge the Wimps
Drill 48: Sound Off for Equipment Check
Drill 85: Make a Character Pass

DRILL 34

OPEN A WINDOW TO YOUR CHARACTER

Navy SEALs always dive in tandem. Army Rangers always move in buddy teams. Marines dig their combat fighting positions for two. In the military, no one goes into no-man's-land alone.

Don't send your protagonist out alone either. As you develop your characters, remember that your protagonist needs a partner—but make that partner pull her weight. Instead of giving your character a subordinate sidekick, give your reader real insight into your main character by using a window character.

A window character is a character who spends a significant amount of time with your protagonist and serves as a confidante. Often window characters are major characters. The key function of a window character is to provide a window to your protagonist's true nature. The relationships between partnered cops, pilots and co-pilots, and military officers and their senior enlisted soldiers are just a few examples of this dynamic. A sidekick, minion, or foil may transcend her role and be a window character, as may a close friend or trusted employee, such as a chauffeur or butler. Sometimes even seeming opponents—think Rick and Louis in *Casablanca*—can serve as mutual window characters.

The development phase of your battle plan is the best place for establishing the relationship between your main character and her window character. To get the most from that relationship, build your protagonist's window character and their relationship in five steps.

1. Choose a window character who shares the protagonist's experiences. Suppose you're writing a sea adventure set in the late 1800s and your main character is the ship's captain. His wife is *not* a good choice for a window character. Why? She's not there most of the time—she's in port. Your window character should see what your protagonist

sees, hear what he hears, feel the same fear. To provide the clearest window, your window character must always be able to see your protagonist, so that if your protagonist says she did one thing, her window character can point out that she actually did another.

DRILL 34

2. Base the window character relationship on friendship and/or partnership, not on romance. You don't want either character trying to win the other over, which would temper their responses. Give one or both of them love interests, or otherwise minimize the potential for their romantic involvement by giving them significantly different tastes or ages, or by making them relatives. This allows both characters to share their issues and feelings without romance at stake.

There are many powerful exceptions to this principle, including Nelson DeMille's Paul Brenner and Cynthia Sunhill in *The General's Daughter*. However, having a character serve as both a romantic interest and a window character requires some very difficult juggling.

3. Build in conflict with conflicting personality points. You want your reader to *see* your main character through her interaction with the window character. One effective method for achieving this is to assign conflicting personality points to them. The two don't have to be different in every respect—if your heroine is intelligent, educated, and articulate (like Patricia Cornwell's Kay Scarpetta), she probably wouldn't routinely associate with a fool. However, she might well have a window character similar to Scarpetta's—the street-smart and terse detective Pete Marino, who is also Scarpetta's foil. This built-in conflict is not only interesting, it means that when your main character says something your window character doesn't agree with, the window character will be predisposed to challenge it.

4. Give them different flavors of the same objectives. In a police procedural, like the novels in Ed McBain's 87th Precinct series, one cop (the protagonist) might want to solve the case to see justice done. A second cop (his partner and window character) might want to solve the case to get a promotion. Although they both want to solve the case, their different motivations create opportunities for the reader to see deeper into the protagonist's nature.

5. Keep the main character in the foreground. Sometimes window characters try to steal the show, and it's up to you to put them in their place early in your battle plan. Otherwise, you'll find you have serious rewriting to do. Keep your focus on your protagonist by ensuring that she is the one making the key decisions, taking the key actions, making the key discoveries, and leading the way through key events. For example, if you notice that your window character is the one to discover a new and critical piece of information and your main character only decides what to do about it, it's time to make a change. Instead, have your main character discover the information, have your window character react to it, then have your main character take action.

Remember that what is true for your protagonist and his window character should also hold true for your antagonist (villain) and her window character, if she has one. Could every character in your novel have a window character? Anything is possible, but remember that your story is first and foremost about your protagonist. Your window character functions as a way for your reader to see inside your protagonist's true nature and therefore helps you build the emotional connection between your reader and your protagonist. Given the demands of most genres, it's very unlikely you'll want to take the time and pages away from your protagonist's story to window all the other characters in your novel. For whatever reason, your protagonist honestly reveals her true character when interacting with her window character, so make sure you put serious thought into the development of their relationship. Just how did your protagonist and her window character come to have this close relationship? You'd know that if you'd written their backstory.

Which you'll do in the next drill.

RELATED DRILLS

Drill 18: Find Your Character in Events, Places, and Concepts
Drill 19: Find Your Character in Opposites
Drill 26: Choose Your Cast
Drill 31: Distinctly Mark Your Characters
Drill 32: Discharge the Wimps
Drill 35: Tell Your Characters' Backstories

DRILL 35

TELL YOUR CHARACTERS' BACKSTORIES

Military units keep unit histories because they know that what came before is important to what happens now and in the future. Your characters' histories are important to *your* battle plan as well.

In order to more effectively begin your characters' story on page one, you must start writing well before that. Your characters have histories that have shaped their traits, values, and personality points. To fully understand those characters and to allow them to consistently and credibly act from those values and personality points, you need to understand how the characters came to be who they are. The best way to understand a character's biography is to write it out in the following three parts.

1. The character snapshot. This is a one-paragraph summary, written in the present tense, of who the character is now. The snapshot contains a character description that includes the character's personality points, age, profession, longings, and a brief physical description.

2. A day in the life of the character. This 250- to 500-word sketch outlines the events in a character's typical day and describes where he lives and works. For example, when does he get up? What does he wear to bed? What does he have for breakfast? You can write this in the present or past tense, but the key is to list specific details, and each detail should be a reflection of some part of the character's personality.

Sometimes you may find that you want your character to have a particular habit. For example, he may obsessively brush his teeth with a special toothbrush after meeting new people. If so, be sure to test this against your snapshot description of the character, and then modify either his description or the habit. Be careful not to give your character distinctive marking habits solely for the sake of being distinctive—make each habit or foible stem from the character's personality and history.

3. The character's personal history. Divide this section into two parts: the character's individual history and his family history. Write both in the past tense, because the events took place in the past.

In the first section, take the character backwards from his current age to birth, noting significant, life-shaping events and the character's approximate age at each event. You don't need to consult old calendars unless a date is critical to your story, but you do need to have the flow of events straight. There are significant events at certain ages in all our lives—entering school or puberty, going on a first date, graduating (or not graduating). These events should have individual and cumulative effects on your character and his personality.

In the second section, include biographies of his parents and grandparents. This section should also contain short character snapshots and sketches for each family member. What kind of people with what kinds of goals, values, and relationships would produce your character? What kind of people would produce those kinds of people? How did they influence your character? What did his parents and grandparents say and do that contributed to your character becoming the kind of person he is?

When you're finished, you'll likely have two to five typed pages of character biography. This biography provides you with a set of intimate details you can use or expand upon in your story. Don't worry about how good the writing is—this work is for your eyes and no one else's. You now also have a full understanding of how and why this individual will act the way he does in the crisis he's about to encounter. While your character biography may never find its way into your novel, you can be sure that your understanding of the character will—and that your character and novel will be better for it.

Perhaps your character backstories will even reveal a previously unnoticed opponent with whom your protagonist is destined to spar. If so, you'll want to give this character the special attention the opposition warrants. What special attention? The attention that begins in the next drill, of course.

RELATED DRILLS

Drill 26: Choose Your Cast
Drill 31: Distinctly Mark Your Characters
Drill 32: Discharge the Wimps
Drill 47: Plan Your Characters' Development
Drill 85: Make a Character Pass

DRILL 36

DEFINE THE OPPOSITION

In any military mission briefing, one critical question always comes up: *What's the nature of the threat?* In your novel, the threat consists of the opposition—those who stand in the way of your protagonist achieving her goals. You want your opposition to be powerful; weak opposition means little challenge for your main character and little excitement for your reader. At a minimum, you want your opposition to create apprehension in the mind of your main character and in the mind of your reader; you want them both to believe that the opposition is likely to win. To clearly define the opposition and to make your opponent worthy, follow the five steps below.

1. **Make it all or nothing.** Defeating the protagonist is the main opposition's top priority in life. If your protagonist wins (achieves her objective), your main opponent loses something of great value (in a mystery novel, she goes to jail for murder; in a fantasy, her evil reign is terminated), and there's no negotiation.

2. **Make the bad guys the ones to bet on.** Your main opposition is competent, perhaps even an expert. The opposition must be such a viable threat and so capable of winning that the deck is stacked well against your main character.

3. **Ensure there's no sitting and waiting.** The opposition is active. Like the protagonist, the opposition will take action in pursuit of an objective.

4. **Make the threat really big.** The opposition needs to be larger than life. For example, in J.A. Konrath's first Jack Daniels mystery, *Whiskey Sour*, no ordinary serial murderer would do. Instead, there's a grotesquely violent, brilliant sadist known only as the Gingerbread Man.

5. **Give it a face.** Putting a face on your opposition is the topic of a separate drill, so it's enough to say here that you want your reader to have a

degree of empathy with your opponent. To do that, you'll need to give that opponent—whether he's a mass murderer or an erupting mountain—at least one human, personal, positive quality.

How much opposition is enough? Simply put, more is more. More opposition means more conflict and a greater possibility your protagonist just might fail—which means your reader will keep turning pages to find out if he does. The opposition can include people, the elements, supernatural beings, animals, robots, diseases, forces of nature (such as volcanoes, earthquakes, and meteor showers), or any combination of the above. Choose what works best for your story.

You might think that all your characters—or at least your major ones—should receive a full definition. So what makes the opposition so special? The motivating factor for spending extra time and creative energy on your opposition is that opposition characters have a great influence on conflict, and it is conflict that drives a story. It's during conflict that your hero's character fully emerges. The richer and more developed the opposition, the richer and more complex the conflict, thus the greater opportunity for your protagonist's heroic nature to emerge.

Military planners take care to define the threat to ensure mission success. You can help ensure the success of your story by defining your opposition. Once you do, you can give your story a different and interesting twist by humanizing that opposition. To put a face on evil, turn the page.

RELATED DRILLS

Drill 18: Find Your Character in Events, Places, and Concepts
Drill 19: Find Your Character in Opposites
Drill 26: Choose Your Cast
Drill 31: Distinctly Mark Your Characters
Drill 33: Give Your Protagonist a Pointed Personality
Drill 37: Put a Face on Evil
Drill 47: Plan Your Characters' Development

DRILL 37

PUT A FACE ON EVIL

Military planners know that it's not enough just to identify a threat; they also need to know what kind of person leads the opposing force. To know that person, they work hard to put a face on the enemy.

To maximize your reader's emotional experience of your story, you must put a face on your protagonist's enemy. When this is done well, your reader feels something for the opposition as well as for your protagonist. You want your reader to feel intense, conflicting, and complicated emotions about those forces of opposition. You can evoke those feelings, maximize your antagonist's effect, and enrich the other characters in your novel by humanizing the opposition with the five steps below.

1. Know your opponent's history. Major opponents should get the benefit of a full character biography (although you may include only the most dramatic details in your novel), so you know what motivates them to act and speak the way they do. It's likely your antagonist will have a history of the behaviors he's going to exhibit in the novel. For example, your mystery may contain a homicidal psychopath; most homicidal psychopaths don't go instantly from zero to mass murderer. Instead, they build up their crimes over time.

2. Give your opponent a positive personality point. Adding just one positive personality point to an otherwise evil opponent greatly enriches the character and lets your reader empathize with him. That small bit of empathy leads to emotional conflict in the reader, piquing his interest in how you will resolve it.

3. Make your opponent believe he is right. Your opponent must believe in his heart that what he is doing is the right thing—even if it isn't. For example, in my first novel, *Kriegspiel*, the opponent, German army general Karl Blacksturm, is a patriot who loves his country and believes with all his soul that, for his country to survive, he must forcibly institute a Nazi Fourth Reich.

4. Show the world as the opponent sees it. Whether it is in the form of a passage written from your opponent's point of view or in the form of another character giving his analysis of the opponent's thinking process (just as Hannibal Lecter does in *The Silence of the Lambs*), let the reader see the world through your opponent's eyes, thoughts, and feelings.

5. Show his face. Many authors forget to provide their antagonists with character markers and physical descriptions. Clearly painting an opponent takes nothing away from your protagonist—in fact, your hero will stand out more when your reader has your clearly drawn opponent to compare him to.

Just how many and which members of the opposition get this five-step treatment depends on how prominent a role each plays in your story. The more often your reader sees the opponent, and the bigger the role the member of the opposition plays, the more clearly you should show that opponent's face.

Putting a human face on your antagonist and endowing him with human feelings lead to a richer and more complex emotional experience for your reader. Add in a personified, humanized objective—as in the next drill—and you'll keep your reader turning pages. Like you should, to the next drill.

RELATED DRILLS

Drill 19: Find Your Character in Opposites
Drill 31: Distinctly Mark Your Characters
Drill 36: Define the Opposition
Drill 39: Use a Character Matrix
Drill 85: Make a Character Pass

DRILL 38

DEFINE, OBJECTIFY, AND PERSONIFY THE OBJECTIVE

The impetus behind every battle plan and mission is the objective. Without an objective, there would be no need for (or point to) a battle plan. Objectives play a similarly important role in fiction; without them, there would be no story.

The objective in your novel is what your protagonist wants—it's what he expends energy and takes risks for. Your protagonist pursues both a story objective (arising from the event or crisis that initiates the action of the novel) and a personal objective (arising from your protagonist's personality points). As you begin to develop these objectives, use the following guidelines to ensure that each objective is indeed worth fighting for.

1. Define the objectives. Major characters have two kinds of objectives: story and personal. The story objective is the thing your protagonist wants—in particular, it's the mission he must accomplish, the murder he must solve, the love he must return to. Remember the comprehensive concept you created during the invention phase of your battle plan (*The protagonist must accomplish X against the opposition*)? *Accomplishing X* is the story objective.

In a mystery, the story objective may be to solve the crime and apprehend the perpetrator. In a romance, it may be to win the hero's heart. In a techno-thriller, your protagonist may have the objective of destroying the enemy base. In a travel adventure novel, the lead may struggle to reach a destination. In a suspense novel, the main character's story objective may be to survive the threat. Your antagonist also has a story goal, usually opposite (or at least in conflict with) that of the protagonist.

Each of your major characters should also have at least one personal objective. Personal objectives are less tangible and can encompass inner longings, like the desire for success, personal growth, love, power, redemption, freedom, justice, or victory. Personal objectives can also be feelings, dreams, ideas, or states of mind or being. Your main character may or may not be aware of these objectives or the degree to which they influence his behavior. He may not articulate his desire for his personal objective, but his desire will permeate his words and actions.

Both story and personal objectives are easier for the reader to understand—and easier for you to work with as you develop, draft, revise, and edit your work—when they are specific and stated in the affirmative. In other words, you should tell what the character wants, not what he doesn't want: *The hero wants to find true love*—that's stated in the affirmative—instead of *The hero doesn't want to be lonely any more.*

2. Objectify the objective. This may sound a bit redundant, but keep in mind that an objective is not necessarily a tangible thing. Assigning tangible representations to a character's objectives makes them more real to your reader. To accomplish this, find an object that can be seen and held and that can literally stand for your protagonist's success. For example, if your work is a romance and the story objective is love and marriage, you might objectify this goal with a wedding ring. If your story is a crime drama and your protagonist must solve a mystery, perhaps the goal is objectified by the victim's missing body. Personal objectives should also be given a tangible representation.

3. Personify the objective. Personifying the objective is like objectifying it, only instead of assigning an object to a goal, you assign a person. Think of any story in which the hero gets the girl, and you have a good example of an objective personified. The girl isn't just *a* girl, she's *the* girl—she's the embodiment of the hero's quest for true love, redemption, and growth.

Both major and minor characters have objectives; all characters have motivations for doing what they do. The extent to which you define, objectify, and personify those objectives for your minor characters should depend on how large a role they play in your novel. As a general rule, if you see a character in two or more scenes that directly affect your protagonist or antagonist, then plan on developing that character's objectives.

Perhaps no story provides a better example of story and personal objectives personified and objectified as Dashiell Hammett's classic hard-boiled detective novel, *The Maltese Falcon*. The conscious objective of the protagonist, Sam Spade, and the antagonists, Joel Cairo and Casper Gutman, is to get the Maltese falcon, which is a tangible item and therefore requires no additional objectification. It is also the thing that will help Spade achieve his personal objective: doing right by his partner by solving his partner's murder. Spade also has another personal goal—getting the girl; and if you wonder whether this personal objective is lust or love, Miss Wonderly (also known as Miss Leblanc and Brigid O'Shaughnessy) personifies both.

Objectives are the terrain that must be seized, the ground that must be defended, the enemy forces that must be destroyed, or the route that must be secured. The more a reader can identify, visualize, and emotionally connect to an objective (story or personal), the more that reader can empathize and connect with your character. The more they empathize and connect, the more they care, and the more they're interested and emotionally invested in your story.

How do you keep track of all those characters, objectives, personality points, and other details, while ensuring they are as tightly integrated and interrelated as the characters in Hammett's story?

You proceed to the next drill, that's how.

RELATED DRILLS

Drill 14: Go Beyond *What If?*
Drill 36: Define the Opposition
Drill 37: Put a Face on Evil
Drill 39: Use a Character Matrix
Drill 42: Take Three Steps to Story Line
Drill 86: Make an Objective Pass

DRILL 39

USE A CHARACTER MATRIX

Military operations plans can get complicated quickly—different units with different missions play different roles at different times. Artillery, infantry, airpower, tanks, combat engineers, Special Forces, and support units must all be coordinated. Military planners and operations officers use an execution matrix as a tool to keep things straight. This organization tool also helps ensure that all efforts are integrated toward executing the overall battle plan.

With different characters who have different backgrounds, different objectives, and different relationships, your novel can get just as complicated just as quickly. By using a character matrix, a novelist's version of the military execution matrix, you can help keep your characters' personalities and objectives straight; keep their individual stories interwoven and integrated; and expedite your drafting, revising, and editing.

The character matrix lists the following for each of your novel's main characters: (1) name and role; (2) objectives—story and personal; (3) major personality points; (4) window character; (5) opposition; (6) other opponents.

In matrix format, the list looks like this.

Name/Role	Objectives	Personality Points	Window Character	Opposition	Other Opponents

To get the most from your character matrix, follow these three steps.

1. Fill in the matrix completely. Using the character information you've developed in this phase of your battle plan and starting with your protagonist, begin filling out the character matrix. Once you've finished with the protagonist, go on to the opposition (the antagonist or villain), noting that your villain's main opponent will be your protagonist. Then fill in the rest of your cast in order of importance. Below is an example of what the character matrix might have looked like for some of the main characters in the classic novel *The Adventures of Huckleberry Finn.*

Name/Role	Objectives	Personality Points	Window Character	Opposition	Other Opponents
Huck Finn, protagonist	escape Pap; free Jim; Cairo, Illinois	street-smart; likeable; liar, but strong sense of right and wrong; courageous; competent; resourceful; loyal	Jim	Pap, slaveholders, Widow Douglas	Grangefords, con men, the Mississippi River, Tom Sawyer
Pap, antagonist	Huck's money	alcoholic, violent, liar, manipulative, greedy	none (Huck)	Huck, Widow Douglas	Preacher
Jim, window character	freedom; Cairo, Illinois	competent, naive, submissive, wise, courageous, loyal		slaveholders	con men, Tom Sawyer, Widow Douglas, the Mississippi River

If you can't fill in the matrix, or if one aspect of a character feels light or weak, go back to your character list now so you won't have to rewrite your draft later. Note that some characters won't have window characters; that's fine, as long as your protagonist and (depending on the genre and length of your work) your antagonist do.

2. Use the matrix to check for conflict and integration. When you gave each character a pointed personality, you cross-checked those personality points against those of other characters. It's time to double-check your

DRILL 39

work. Using your completed character matrix, see how all your characters' personality points mesh or conflict with others, and then make adjustments to increase variety and potential conflict. Adjust objectives, opponents, and window characters with the same purpose in mind.

3. Use the matrix as a memory aid during drafting, revising, and editing. Print your character matrix and keep it handy during your drafting, revision, and editing phases. You'll have the big picture of your characters' relationships and goals in front of you, so you can concentrate on what a character wants and how that character speaks, acts, thinks, and feels while you're writing a particular scene.

Your character matrix allows you—and often compels you—to fully understand your characters well before you start planning the twists and turns of your story. Just as a military execution matrix helps ensure success in the field, your character matrix will help you more effectively and efficiently reach your end goal—a finished, revised, edited and proofread manuscript.

Another powerful characterization tool is a powered-up—or, in military parlance, up-gunned—version of that old writing aid, character cards. Find the high-caliber version of these in the next drill.

RELATED DRILLS

Drill 26: Choose Your Cast
Drill 31: Distinctly Mark Your Characters
Drill 33: Give Your Protagonist a Pointed Personality
Drill 40: Up-Gun Your Character Cards
Drill 85: Make a Character Pass

DRILL 40

UP-GUN YOUR CHARACTER CARDS

Experienced soldiers know that a key factor in mission success is not just having good equipment but knowing how to make the best use of it. The same is true for commonly used novel-writing aids, such as the familiar character card. Civilian character cards traditionally include a character's name and age, her positive and negative personality traits, and any striking physical traits or markers. This information is fine—as far as it goes. But to make your cards boot-camp worthy, you'll want to up-gun them in the following ways.

1. Upgrade the card. Character name, traits, and markers aren't enough. To get the most use from your cards during drafting, revision, and editing, you'll need more information. Add to each card:

- the character's objectives (both story and personal)
- the character's window character
- the character's opponent
- the character's other opposition

Adding these elements to your cards helps bring elements that can conjure conflict (objectives, the opponents) out of your memory and onto the page in front of you.

Additionally, make sure you maximize your knowledge of your character by writing not only that character's traits, but the needs, feelings, and motivations behind those traits. For example, noting that your character wears distinctive, can't-ignore-this hats wherever she goes isn't enough. You need to understand what's behind this trait: Is it a need to be noticed, a resentment of authority, or a desire to be wanted sexually or romantically? Your character cards and character biographies must tell you what kind of person the character is.

2. Give everybody a card. Well, almost everybody. Civilian character cards are most often reserved for the protagonist, her opponent, and some other major characters, such as window characters. But in boot camp, even minor characters deserve to be developed. A good rule of thumb is that if a character appears in more than one scene, give her a card. Why? Your reader may not expect much from a minor character the first time she sees her, but when that reader sees the character a second time, there's an expectation that the character will be something other than a cardboard cutout.

What about the nondescript doorman who appears in, say, three scenes but does nothing but open the door for your heroine? Making a card for this individual can challenge your thinking—why is that character so nondescript (read: boring)? What more could he do besides opening the door? Find out by giving him a card—and a personality. Could he be giving out information, opposing your heroine, or maybe providing an alternate point of view? This is boot camp! Give him a card, get him off his lazy duff, and make the slacker pull his weight in your novel!

3. Play your cards every chance you get. Once you've up-gunned your cards and have a full set that includes all your characters, use the following card calisthenics to aid you during the researching, drafting, revising, and editing phases of the writing process.

- *Play your cards during your ongoing research.* When you find an item that seems to fit with a particular character, write it down on that character's card. You never know what might come in handy when you draft a scene.

- *Play your cards as you plan.* As you develop your outline, scene list, or time line, use your cards to keep track of which characters should be present when and how they might act. If you're in need of inspiration, throw an additional card (character) into the scene and consider how that scene might be richer or the conflict more intense. Take a card out to concentrate on fewer characters.

- *Play your cards as you draft.* As you write each scene, display the relevant character cards and refer to them whenever you find yourself in need of big-picture character details (objectives, traits, personality points, and so on) to inform and shape the dialogue, description, and narration you're drafting.

- *Play your cards as you revise.* Your character cards make excellent yardsticks for measuring how well your characters are thinking, speaking, and acting in line with the personality points you gave them. You can also measure how actively they're pursuing their objectives.

- *Play your cards as you edit.* Use your cards to check critical dates and physical features, and to make sure you've addressed any reminders or notes you've made.

For the everyday work of making scene-by-scene, page-by-page progress, make a set of up-gunned character cards. They will help you in all stages of drafting, including the next stage, developing your story line.

RELATED DRILLS

Drill 17: Put a Face on Your Idea
Drill 26: Choose Your Cast
Drill 31: Distinctly Mark Your Characters
Drill 39: Use a Character Matrix
Drill 53: Tell Each Character's Story

MISSION IV

DEVISE YOUR OPERATIONS ORDER

You've developed the *who*—now you need the *what*. Enter operations orders, the blueprints that set a mission into motion. This part of the development phase of your battle plan is all about the action of your novel, and it builds on the character material you prepared in the previous mission. Here, you'll prepare the equivalent of a military operations order—your story line, an index card book summary, and a master story summary. Like your character matrix and character cards, these documents are more than simple outlining aids; they provide you with a solid foundation, clear direction, and practical, functional tools. They also allow you to effectively and efficiently execute one of the most demanding phases of your battle plan—the drafting phase. They will guide the words and actions of every character, the flow of every scene, and (along with the drills in the drafting phase) the composition of every sentence.

No soldier goes into battle without a mission, a clear operations order, and his equipment—neither should you go unprepared into the combat of drafting. The work in this section isn't just a series of paper drills. After all, the better you construct your tools, the better your first draft will be and the better chance your novel has of grabbing and holding your reader's attention.

DRILL 41

CHANGE THE WORLD

Military planners often talk about *when the balloon goes up*, which is jargon for when some catalytic military or political event occurs and troops must deploy. Such an event changes the world in powerful ways for the troops who ship out.

While you aren't starting a war (unless you're writing a military thriller), you, too, need to launch a balloon and change the world for your characters. In novelist's boot camp, the life-changing event you'll create is called the *causal event*, a change in your characters' world that forces your protagonist out of the status quo and into the action. This puts your lead, other characters, and entire story in motion. That event (also known as the critical event, catalyst, first plot point, or crisis) may be a murder (in a mystery), the arrival of a dark handsome stranger (in a romance), or a family crisis (in a literary novel). Whatever your genre, you want to create a compelling causal event. To do so, follow the three guidelines below.

1. Make it logical. Choose events that could—in your novel's world—logically occur, rather than random events caused by freak accidents of nature. Logical events are more believable than random ones. For example, if you plan to have a monstrous white whale attack and sink a whaling ship, you need to set the stage for this event by weaving into the story an old mariner's tales of an intelligent, vengeful sea monster, as Herman Melville's Captain Ahab does in Moby Dick. A close reading of your genre will give you a feel for how much time you have to set up the causal event, but in any genre, sooner is better. Make sure that when you set up your causal event (sometimes called *establishing the premise* or *world-building*) you integrate information seamlessly into your story—don't just dump pages of information on the reader.

2. Make it personal. Ever notice that the victim or potential victim in many mystery novels is related to the protagonist (in Michael Connelly's *The Poet*)? Or that a main character is often set in motion by a request that touches a protagonist's personality point such as loyalty or justice (Robert B. Parker's *Small Vices*)? These authors have made the causal event compelling to the reader by making it matter personally to the main character. Even techno-thrillers that revolve around global political issues make their struggles personal (in Tom Clancy's *Patriot Games*, Jack Ryan's wife and daughter are attacked by IRA terrorists). Almost everyone understands these kinds of relationships, so when you make your causal event personal, you make it matter emotionally not only to your hero but to your reader as well.

3. Make it irresistible. There must be no escape—there has to be one way, and only one way, out—and that's to respond to the event and resolve the crisis. H.G. Wells's Martian invasion in *War of the Worlds* certainly qualifies as inescapable, but you don't need Martians to create tension. You can use a number of techniques, such as geographically isolating your characters, having your characters make public commitments to solving the problem, or otherwise raising the stakes so they can't escape the struggle (later drills will discuss stakes in detail). Make your event big enough that your heroine may not want to become involved in solving the problem, at first; then make sure she has no choice.

So your characters are living their lives when the balloon goes up and a causal event shatters the status quo. What happens next? You turn the page to the next drill to find out how to build what happens next.

RELATED DRILLS

Drill 2: Adopt a Principled Approach
Drill 5: See Your Target
Drill 18: Find Your Character in Events, Places, and Concepts
Drill 52: Win the First Battle
Drill 85: Make a Character Pass
Drill 90: Make an Action Pass

DRILL 42

TAKE THREE STEPS TO STORY LINE

The mission statement tells military planners what needs to be done. What drives *how* these things get accomplished is the *concept of the operation*, which is a summary of how major units will accomplish major portions of the mission.

Your battle plan needs a concept of the operation—called a *story line*—as well. Like the military concept of the operation, your story line recounts the major actions and events that occur as your protagonist pursues her objectives. To build that story line, you'll need to structure the steps your protagonist will take, as well as those actions that your antagonist (opponent) and other opposition will take to stop her.

Take the following three steps to build your story line.

1. Add one of the four *D*s. To set your initial story idea into motion, put these *D*s behind it.

- *Does.* Your protagonist *does* something that she thinks will bring her closer to her objective. This is the most powerful *D* because it is direct action. Your research, knowledge of the genre, and imagination will tell you what actions your characters will take—what they will *do*—and your knowledge of your characters (their personality points, background, and objectives) will tell you how they will do it. In one of Kathy Reichs's best-selling Temperance Brennan mystery novels, the lead, a forensic anthropologist, travels across the continent and visits everywhere from a deserted farm to religious communes, risks her life, applies her forensic skills, battles reluctant officials, and finally single-handedly confronts a killer. She does these things because her personality points of bravery, intelligence, strong sense of justice, and determination compel her to do so. Note that every action (every *does*) has a consequence—so when you add a *D* such as *does*, you'll find that as a consequence of this action there is a *discovery*, a reaction to *deal with*, a *decision* to make, and so on.

- *Discovers.* Your protagonist *discovers* new information that impacts her quest for her objective. (Note that to drive your story, this *D* must be followed by other *D*s, as in *decides* what to *do* based on the new knowledge.) Again, your research and your genre will determine just what your character discovers. Through her investigation into a victim's background, Dr. Brennan *discovers* new evidence that links Canadian outlaw bikers with a murder in Florida.

- *Decides.* Your protagonist *decides* to try something new to reach her objective. Be wary of thinking that making a decision is an action. (Note that to keep your character in motion after she decides, she must *do* something based on that decision.) Dr. Brennan decides to pursue the case and so *does* something—she flies to Florida.

- *Deals with.* Your antagonist takes action, or an event happens and your protagonist responds to or *deals with* it. Dr. Brennan discovers that her chief witness is actually a suspect, and she deals with this information by *doing* something—changing her plan and actions accordingly. The witness-turned-suspect now has her actions and motives placed under Brennan's scrutiny.

Note that your *D*s can come in any order—your protagonist can begin her journey to attain her objectives by *deciding* something, by *doing* something, by *dealing with* something, or by *discovering* something.

2. Follow with *and so*. When you add a *D*, insert an *and so* behind it. Doing so should lead you to another *D*, either from your protagonist, her opponent, her other opposition, or another character. That D is followed by another *and so*. This sequence helps to build a sense of cause and effect, keeps your characters focused on their objectives, and keeps your story in motion. You can also connect events with terms like *and*, *then*, and *but*.

3. Expand, refine, and cross-check. You'll need to expand and refine your *D*s to get to the level of detail necessary to develop your scenes. For example, Kathy Reichs may have started with something like *Dr. Temperance Brennan investigates a child's death.* Using the four *D*s, the simple statement becomes more specific. For example: What does she *do* to investigate? *She conducts an autopsy, interviews witnesses, and researches the criminal gangs.* Now these actions can be refined by adding *and so.* For example: *And so* what, specifically, does she do when she conducts the autopsy? *She prepares the body, makes a Y-shaped incision.... And so* what does she discover? *She discovers that the victim was dead before the fire was started.* You then cross-check the believability and necessity of each of these actions:

- against your research, for accuracy
- against your protagonist's objectives, to ensure her actions are focused on achieving those objectives
- against the opponent's objectives, to see what actions the opponent might take

Then expand and refine each *D* to ensure that you can insert *and so* to connect one series of actions with another, that the overwhelming majority of your *D*s have your protagonist doing the doing, and that you have a good intuitive fit with your genre.

This three-step process isn't the end. You'll also need to bring the story line to a conclusion (also known as the *resolution*), but we'll resolve that discussion in a later drill.

And so you want to know in what book Dr. Temperance Brennan made these decisions, did what she had to do, dealt with those challenges, and discovered what she discovered?

Deadly Decisions, of course.

And so now you'll turn the page.

RELATED DRILLS

Drill 2: Adopt a Principled Approach
Drill 5: See Your Target
Drill 43: Turn on Your Turning Points
Drill 45: Put Your Book on an Index Card
Drill 49: Know the Unwritten Rules for Quality Drafting
Drill 86: Make an Objective Pass
Drill 90: Make an Action Pass

DRILL 43

TURN ON YOUR TURNING POINTS

There's an old story in the military about the general who was asked what the decisive moments—or turning points—of a certain battle were. His response? "Before, during, and after."

There's wisdom here that novelists can learn from. If you eschew conventional ways of thinking, you can make every point of your novel an intense, conflict-filled, high-stakes turning point. Worded another way, it's time to turn on your turning points. That is, make *every* decision, action, and discovery (which are all points in your novel's plot), interesting, significant, conflict-filled, and intense. How? The five techniques outlined below will serve novelists across all genres.

1. Point in the right direction. Orient every action toward achieving your protagonist's story and personal objectives. If your character is doing something she doesn't care about, why should your reader care?

2. Don't try to make one point more important than another. Make every action important, in its moment, as it takes the character toward her objective. Don't deliberately build in little decisions or actions just to have them lead to bigger ones. You don't want to build boring into your book. Have a little action that seems unimportant? Cut it out or make it matter.

3. Don't just raise the stakes; pile them on. Later drills will go into detail about specific ways to raise the stakes, but keep in mind that your character should have as much to lose as possible at every turning point.

4. Meet genre expectations, but don't be limited by them. Certain genres have expectations that will necessitate the inclusion of specific critical actions. For example, readers of category romances expect to see a large amount of emotional energy around the meet (the heroine and hero's first meeting), the moment of truth (the heroine and hero realize they truly love one another), and the dark moment (when the obstacles to their union appear too great, and they understand that love is not enough). However, if your story calls for decisions or actions that are outside genre standards but that put the attainment of your protagonist's objectives in jeopardy, include them.

5. When in doubt, add opposition. If a decision or action seems too easy for your protagonist, get her opposition involved. Your character shouldn't be able to lace up her combat boots without opposition, which means she should have something to lose if she leaves the laces too loose.

Toss out your civilian ideas about turning points and plot points with the potato peelings from KP. Make every action a turning point. Your novel should be one turning point after another, right up to the story's end.

And that's the point of the next drill.

RELATED DRILLS

Drill 14: Go Beyond *What If?*
Drill 19: Find Your Character in Opposites
Drill 36: Define the Opposition
Drill 42: Take Three Steps to Story Line
Drill 90: Make an Action Pass

DRILL 44

DEVELOP YOUR EXIT STRATEGY

A military operation, like a novel, has a beginning, a middle, and an end. If you listen to news commentators discuss the endings of major military operations, you'll hear them toss around the term *exit strategy*, which is a plan for satisfactorily winding up and closing out an operation.

To bring your novel to a satisfactory conclusion, you need an exit strategy for your story. Map out your ending now in order to give yourself an objective to write toward. The following three techniques will help you build a more integrated, compelling, and memorable ending.

1. Set up a one-on-one confrontation. This key event in your novel's ending takes the conflicting issues, ideas, and characters down to a personal level. To build this decisive, personal confrontation between your protagonist and villain:

- *Exhaust all the other options.* Your protagonist *must* face off against your antagonist.

- *Block all exits.* Later drills will talk more about setting and time pressure, but for now, keep in mind that, in your final confrontation, there should be no time left and no place to run.

- *Take off the kid gloves.* Create both physical and emotional stress for your characters by increasing the amount of action, moving the level of physical contact up a notch or two, and increasing the intensity with which of each character's personality points are expressed.

Depending on your genre, this confrontation may involve words, arrest warrants, or interstellar weapons. In the end, your charge is to bring your characters' struggle to a face-to-face contest of wills, the outcome of which will determine who succeeds and who fails in accomplishing the objective.

2. Satisfy the readers' hearts. Your ending must *feel* right to the reader. An emotionally satisfying ending does not necessarily mean a happy one, but it does mean two things: First, your ending must be genre-appropriate. Does your heroine always have to win? Romances require happy endings. In crime thrillers, sometimes a villain gets away—so she can be pursued in a sequel. Sometimes an otherwise happy ending is marred by an intimation of trouble to come: In *The Maltese Falcon*, Sam Spade does solve his partner's death, but a woman—his partner's widow—reappears in Spade's office with a problem. Her reappearance is a signal to readers that Spade's world remains a dark place and that his troubles are not over—all is just as readers feel it should be.

Second, your ending must clarify and confirm the reader's feelings about the characters. If you built in tension and conflict by giving a character opposing personality points, your ending must put that character in one camp or another. There's no need to nominate a protagonist for sainthood—tarnished heroes are just fine, as long as the reader feels that they're still heroes. At the end of the film *Casablanca*, we want to feel good about both Rick and Louis. The movie's famous ending lines give us good cause to do so.

3. Satisfy the readers' minds. Your novel's logic—its cause and effect—must work. Your protagonist's world changed with a causal event. Throughout your novel, your protagonist responds to that change. How does that work out? As you choose your cast, develop your story line, and raise the stakes, you introduce a variety of characters and complications. Your ending must address these characters and complications, and bring them to a resolution. Sometimes called the *denouement*, this portion of your ending is your chance to tie up loose ends. Be careful, though. A danger to watch for—and a sure sign of incomplete planning—is the introduction of new information in the ending. Pulling a rabbit out of your authorial hat is a sure way to provide your reader with a disappointing conclusion.

So you have a plan for your novel's beginning, middle, and end. Now it's time to put your book on an index card so you'll reinforce in your own mind—in clear and certain terms—what your book is about.

How? Turn the page to the next drill.

RELATED DRILLS

Drill 14: Go Beyond *What If?*
Drill 42: Take Three Steps to Story Line
Drill 46: Build Your Master Story Summary
Drill 86: Make an Objective Pass
Drill 90: Make an Action Pass

DRILL 45

PUT YOUR BOOK ON AN INDEX CARD

At the end of detailed orders briefings, military planners take one minute to review the most critical elements of the operations plan—the mission and the concept of the operation. This one-minute summary brings all the planners and operators back to the central ideas of what must be done, who will do it, and how it will be accomplished. To keep your energies focused, you'll want to summarize your story as well—in a book on an index card (or BIC).

The BIC summary helps you to establish a clear outline of your novel's plot and critical actions, the major characters, emotional issues to be resolved, and the climax your work should build toward. It also helps you prepare your pitch for your query letters or in-person meetings with editors. The BIC format consists of seven key elements that encapsulate the critical items in your book. We've already discussed most of these elements, so here's a summary of each.

1. **The causal event.** This critical event is the first major turning point in your novel, and it shatters the status quo of your protagonist's world. It's an event she can't ignore and must respond to.

2. **The main character.** This is your protagonist, the character who makes decisions and takes actions to achieve her goal. You may have more than one main character.

3. **Personality points for the main character.** Personality points are sharp positive or negative character traits—in this case, specific to your main character.

4. **The opposition.** This is the antagonist, and as such, your protagonist's main opposing force. The antagonist can be played by a person or group of people, by an animal, or even by Mother Nature.

5. **The four *Ds*.** These include what your protagonist and antagonist *do*, *discover*, *decide*, and *deal with* in order to achieve their objectives. These steps are interrelated—one leads to the next—and you connect them with words such as *and so*, *and then*, and *but*.

6. **An objective.** This is what your main character wants—the goal that she must achieve in order to solve the problem created by the causal event. Your protagonist has both a story objective (related to the causal event) and a personal objective (related to her personality points). The main opponent in your novel also has story and personal objectives.

7. **A final confrontation.** This is the personal, one-on-one, genre-appropriate battle between your main character and your main opponent. The final confrontation resolves the main character's quest for her story objective but does not necessarily resolve her attempts to achieve her personal objective.

Your BIC won't contain numbered items. Instead, it should be written as a short paragraph. To succinctly outline what your book is about, address the BIC elements in chronological order. (Feel free to rearrange the seven BIC elements, as long as your arrangement either directly conveys or clearly implies the necessary information.) A generic, fill-in-the-blank version might look like this.

> When [a causal event] happens, a [main character, with personality points] must [accomplish objective], so [the main character] [does A] in the face of [opposition], and then [the main character] [does B], and then he [discovers C], but [the opposition] [does D], so [the main character] [decides to do E], which makes [the opposition] [do F], which leads to [the final confrontation].

This is what your book is about!

Here's what Robert Crais's crime thriller *Demolition Angel* would look like in BIC form.

When a member of her bomb squad is killed defusing explosives [causal event], a cynical, physically and emotionally scarred female police bomb tech [main character with personality points] must solve the crime to stop the serial bomber from striking again [objective]. So working against both the bomber and official resistance [opposition], she deciphers the clues from bomb fragments [action A], traces the components [action B], and finally confronts the bomber in a one-on-one life-or-death struggle [final confrontation].

Spend some time developing and revising your BIC before you begin your first draft. The investment pays off: The clearer your BIC, the tighter and more focused your final novel will be.

Once you have your BIC in hand, you're ready to create a tool that will guide you through the daily task of creating your first draft. You've developed the *who* and the *what*, now it's time to spell out *how*.

How? Turn the page to the next drill.

RELATED DRILLS

Drill 14: Go Beyond *What If?*
Drill 42: Take Three Steps to Story Line
Drill 44: Develop Your Exit Strategy
Drill 46: Build Your Master Story Summary
Drill 90: Make an Action Pass

MISSION IV

BUILD YOUR MASTER STORY SUMMARY

Your grandfather probably wouldn't recognize much about today's military, just as your seventh-grade English teacher wouldn't recognize the novelist's boot camp master story summary as a book outline. A master story summary expands the story line you summarized in your BIC into a scriptlike tool that you can use every day to determine exactly what you need to write. Your master story summary consists of two parts: (1) a scene list and (2) scene summaries.

1. Your Scene List. Adapted from screenwriting, the scene list is simply a listing of your scenes (location and time) in chronological order. The scenes in your scene list originate from your book on an index card (BIC). The BIC helps you develop your plot by outlining the major events (the *D*s) of your story line.

A simple scene list might look like this one, which is based on my first mystery novel, *Close to Home*.

Bertrands' bedroom—morning
Kraag's ADMS office—afternoon
Kraag's car—afternoon

2. Your Scene Summaries. Create an expanded version of your scene list by including with each item a short summary of the actions and characters in the scene. When you add a scene summary to a scene you've listed, it might look like the ones below.

BERTRANDS' BEDROOM—MORNING
The murderer ambushes Susan Bertrand as she comes out of the shower. He lies in wait for Pastor Thomas Winston (Susan's lover), kills him too, and poses the bodies.

KRAAG'S ADMS OFFICE—AFTERNOON
Kraag receives a call from Mayor Dorland about the murder; blows off an executive meeting with corp. bigwigs to respond.

KRAAG'S CAR—AFTERNOON

Kraag calls Dorland for details. Kraag flashes back to his time in covert operations and how his detective skills failed him then.

Prepare a summary for every scene in your novel, from beginning to end. Scene summaries allow you to do something you don't get to do in your novel—they give you the chance to tell instead of show. In fact, scene summaries are all telling—there's no dialogue, no description (with the possible exception of short notes to yourself), no introspection, and no detail. These come later, when you use the scene summary as a guideline for drafting each scene. To keep your focus, don't do more than summarize the description, mood, dialogue, etc. Because only you will read the scene summary, include any additional notes you want.

A well-developed master story summary helps you keep time and events straight and avoid annoying errors of logic and continuity. It keeps the action and the main character in the foreground and helps ensure your story doesn't stray into digressions that have nothing to do with your main character striving for his objective.

Master story summaries, BICs, story lines, character cards and matrices—these are all powerful tools that, if constructed well, lead you to a higher-quality draft. Once these are complete, you can ensure that your characters' development and growth make sense and progress logically.

Which leads us, logically, to the next drill.

RELATED DRILLS

Drill 14: Go Beyond *What If?*
Drill 38: Define, Objectify, and Personify the Objective
Drill 44: Develop Your Exit Strategy
Drill 90: Make an Action Pass

DRILL 47

PLAN YOUR CHARACTERS' DEVELOPMENT

In boot camp, a trainee follows a defined path from civilian to soldier, mastering skills and drills and growing emotionally. Your main characters must show the same kind of development over time. Your characters must move forward—forward in pursuit of their objectives and forward in their development as individuals. This means that, as your novel progresses, your main character needs to grow and change on an emotional level.

Your character's development is too important to be left to chance. You have only a limited number of pages to make changes in him. To get the maximum effect in the short time you have, take three crucial steps to effectively develop your protagonist.

1. Get a good fix on your protagonist's starting point. In an earlier drill, you gave your protagonist personality points. This is where you start. When you thoroughly understand your character and his salient personality points, you're ready to move forward.

2. Decide where you want your main character's emotional journey to end. Having found the beginning of your protagonist's developmental journey, you next need to identify his emotional destination. At the end of your story and his development, how far will your protagonist have progressed? It's tempting to take your main character all the way—to have him completely rid himself of negative personality points. However, this is a temptation you should avoid. Keep your character believable: Have him make significant progress toward eliminating negative character traits, but don't turn him into a saint (unless, of course, you're writing a story about a saint).

You don't have to go far into Charles Dickens's *A Christmas Carol* to see that Ebenezer Scrooge has several well-defined negative personality points. In fact, the entire story centers on Scrooge's denial that he has these

negative traits, his eventual realization that he indeed does have them and that they have cost him much, and finally his triumph over these traits on Christmas morning.

Did Dickens go too far? Not for the kind of story he was writing, for his market, or for the audience expectations of the day. But even Scrooge has his limits. Although he becomes generous after his epiphany, Scrooge is not generous to a fault. He doesn't sell the business and distribute the profits among the poor or take the homeless into his lodgings. Instead, Scrooge finds the essential good nature he had as a boy, allows it to mature, and, thus, becomes the generous, caring man he was meant to be.

The lesson is clear: Keep the end result of your protagonist's growth larger than life but still believable (based on genre, character, and circumstances).

3. Select markers and checkpoints along the way. Stay the course by using events, decisions, and discoveries as waypoints in your character's emotional journey. How far, how fast? Today's savvy readers expect character development, but they expect it to happen gradually, rather than in a tacked-on epiphany near the end of your book. For the most part, people change in small steps that therapists call *shifts*. That's a good term, especially for novelists facing the question of how much their protagonist should change and when. But here's where your characters again differ from real people: Your protagonist's development is a case of cause and effect. The main character's decisions, major discoveries, and reactions all offer opportunities for you to shift his personality. Significant events affect your lead and cause changes in his thoughts, feelings, and actions.

For an exciting emotional ride, don't be afraid to throw it in reverse now and then. In the epic movie *Casablanca*, Rick, we know, has a character conflict—at heart he's dedicated to higher ideals, but outwardly he sticks his neck out for nobody. The audience can track him as he leans further toward his devotion to a higher cause, but Rick apparently reverses to his cynical self before he puts Elsa on the plane with Robert. This reversal builds tension, which is released at the end of the movie, when Rick returns to his true nature.

With your protagonist's emotional development carefully planned and the rest of your development tools ready, you're about to jump into the drafting phase of your battle plan. But before you jump, read the next drill.

RELATED DRILLS

Drill 19: Find Your Character in Opposites
Drill 42: Take Three Steps to Story Line
Drill 44: Develop Your Exit Strategy
Drill 46: Build Your Master Story Summary
Drill 53: Tell Each Character's Story
Drill 85: Make a Character Pass

DRILL 48

SOUND OFF FOR EQUIPMENT CHECK

You've constructed a suite of tools that will put your creativity and characters in motion. You're probably anxious to put those tools to work and begin your next phase, writing a quality first draft. Essentially, you're poised like a paratrooper, ready to jump from a high-flying military aircraft, standing in the open side door and looking down at the ground rolling beneath you.

The drop zone—the drafting phase of your battle plan—is coming up quickly. You're a little scared and a lot nervous. Surrounding you are your characters, ready to make the jump with you. When a green signal light glows, you'll leap into space and wait for the static line to yank your parachute open. Your characters will follow right behind. But how do you know if you're ready? If *they* are?

Before you send your characters (and yourself) plummeting into space, do like paratroopers do: Sound off for equipment check! (Yell loudly to be heard over the aircraft engine roar.)

Drop zone in thirty seconds! All characters at maximum intensity?

All characters ready! Check the adjectives you use to describe your characters. The more pronounced and intense your characters' personality points, the more interesting those characters will be. To help ensure you've created compelling characters, list the adjectives you use to describe their personalities, and then intensify them. Use a dictionary or thesaurus, or brainstorm to replace weak choices with strong ones. You want only the sharpest characters with the most pointed personalities going out the door with you.

Drop zone in twenty seconds! All verbs at maximum intensity?

All verbs ready! Check the action in your scene summaries. By definition, these summaries need verbs, because verbs are actions. The more intense the verbs , the more interesting the action, and the more interesting the story. For example, if you write that two characters discuss their relationship, that's all they'll do—boringly yack. If you instead write that they fight about their relationship, that's what they'll do—and your reader will remain riveted. Review and intensify the verbs in your scene lists and summaries.

Drop zone in ten seconds! All Ds *at maximum intensity?*

All *D*s ready! Check your BIC and story line—could your character take a more dramatic, more intense, more decisive, more forceful, more dynamic action as she *deals with*, *decides*, *discovers*, or *does* something? Instead of reading about a treasure map at a museum, could your character break in at night and steal the map on display? List alternative *D*s and intensify what your character does.

Drop zone in five seconds! All equipment ready?

All equipment ready! You have only a few seconds left, so get your equipment organized. And not just your computer and a ream of paper. Preparing a quality draft is an intense experience that can last for several months. Are your character bios complete and legible? Character cards ready? Scene list done and scene summaries written for every scene from first to last? BIC ready? Are these documents printed out and put together in one place where you can use them? Backup copies made? Your work area set up for you to work? Get everything ready now. It's too late to do so when you begin writing your first draft, because unless there's a problem, you'll be 100 percent focused on going forward, not back.

Get this done quickly. You're about ready to—

Green light! Go! Go! Go!

You step out the door into nothingness and a 200-mile-per-hour wind tosses you like a rag doll in a hurricane. Three seconds later your chute opens and yanks you up like a puppet on a string. You're descending slowly and there's a strange stillness as you float down. Your equipment is strapped to your side. All around you are forms—people, your characters—gently dropping down with you. It's just you and them and blank page and a battle plan.

Welcome to the drafting phase.

RELATED DRILLS

Drill 14: Go Beyond *What If?*

Drill 28: Understand the Alpha Male Character's Motivations

Drill 29: Understand the Alpha Female Character's Motivations

Drill 42: Take Three Steps to Story Line

Drill 44: Develop Your Exit Strategy

Drill 49: Know the Unwritten Rules for Quality Drafting

Drill 85: Make a Character Pass

Drill 90: Make an Action Pass

BATTLE PLAN DELTA

DRAFTING

MISSION V: CROSS THE LINE OF DEPARTURE ...143
Drill 49: Know the Unwritten Rules for Quality Drafting 145
Drill 50: Occupy Your Main OP 148
Drill 51: Make the Reader See Your New POV 151
Drill 52: Win the First Battle 154
Drill 53: Tell Each Character's Story 157
Drill 54: Hang Your Readers Off a Cliff—Repeatedly 161
Drill 55: Button It, Soldier! 164
Drill 56: Back Up to Beat Writer's Block 166

MISSION VI: COMMIT YOUR RESERVES..........169
Drill 57: Go More Public 170
Drill 58: Make It More Personal 172
Drill 59: Be More Moral 175
Drill 60: Get More Physical 178
Drill 61: Draft Some Victims 181
Drill 62: Wind Up the Clock 184

MISSION VII: SOUND OFF! 187
Drill 63: Learn How to Fake It 188
Drill 64: Dispense With the Pleasantries 190
Drill 65: Make Your Dialogue Multitask 193
Drill 66: Aim for the Gut 196

Drill 67: Talk Like a Man 199
Drill 68: "Keep It Simple," He Said 201
Drill 69: Give Your Dialogue a Good Beat(ing) 204
Drill 70: Know When to Say *Well* 208
Drill 71: Make Your Characters Try, Try Again 211

MISSION VIII: EXECUTE SHOCK AND AWE 214
Drill 72: Find the Devil in the Details 215
Drill 73: Go to Time-and-a-Half 217

MISSION IX: UTILIZE STEALTH TECHNIQUES .. 220
Drill 74: Do More With Description 221
Drill 75: Use Micro Setting for Maximum Impact 224
Drill 76: Know That You Are Not a Camera 226
Drill 77: "Stonewall" Your Description 228
Drill 78: Lob a Hand Grenade 230
Drill 79: Zoom In and Out 232
Drill 80: Leverage the Intimacy of the Senses 235
Drill 81: Eliminate Deadly Modifier Buildup 238
Drill 82: Mix It Up 240
Drill 83: Try a New Technique 243

MISSION V

CROSS THE LINE OF DEPARTURE

Your preparations are over. You've advanced out of the friendly territory of preparing, inventing, and developing your story idea. You've crossed the line of departure into enemy territory. Now it's you, your imagination, and your tools facing off against a blinking cursor or a blank sheet of paper. Like dug-in enemy troops, those blank pages stand between you and your objective—a completed quality draft. And like the infantry that fixes bayonets and closes with entrenched opposition, you're going to have to take those pages down one at a time: word by word, sentence by sentence, page by page, scene by scene.

Welcome to the drafting phase of your novelist's boot camp battle plan.

Your goal in this phase is not just to finish a draft—that's what writers in the civilian world do. Instead, you want to create a *quality* draft. Use your master story summary (your scene list and summaries) as your maps. Write from scene to scene applying boot-camp techniques and using the tools you created, such as your character cards and character matrix.

The drills in this section are powerful tools for your drafting phase, and will help you advance steadily toward your goal. How? When a blank page rises up to halt your progress, consult your scene summary for what you must write, then apply a drill found in this chapter. Don't panic, don't quibble, don't snivel, don't freeze, and don't muse about the 1,001 possibilities—execute a dialogue drill, an action drill, or a stakes-raising drill. Your creativity and the proven techniques in this chapter will yield not just any sentence but a quality sentence. Then another, and another, until your blank-page enemy goes down.

Note that, unlike the drills in previous sections, many of the drills in this phase need not be executed sequentially. Use the drills when you need them—dialogue for when your characters fight with words, action to show what happens, description to make connections with the fictional world you've constructed.

Note too that there's a built-in contradiction in drafting—you're doing the best work you can, only to change it later. Why not do a great first draft and call your novel done? Because neither the writing process nor your brain works that way. Remember the seven principles from drill two in the preparation phase (revisit them if you don't)—you don't want to fight fair. Focus all your energies on creating something—your draft. In the next two phases of your battle plan—revising and editing—you will focus your energies on improving your draft.

Read the drills in this section carefully, take out your pad and pen or turn on your computer, buckle your helmet's chinstrap and make sure you have a full canteen of water, make sure that your bayonet is sharp, and that your tools from the development phase are by your side.

There's a blank page straight ahead.

DRILL 49

KNOW THE UNWRITTEN RULES FOR QUALITY DRAFTING

There are many unwritten rules of combat, such as *Never share a foxhole with someone braver than you are* and *When in doubt, empty the magazine*. There are unwritten rules of drafting as well, and the five below will help you make more and better progress toward those two words that signal your success: *The End*.

1. Write the best draft you can, but turn off your internal editor. There's no excuse for a sloppy draft—don't write a sentence you know is weak, leave a misspelling, allow a member of your cast to act out of character, or use excessive narration when you know you have better choices.

At the same time, don't worry about how a sentence, paragraph, or scene reads. Your internal editor will tell you that a sentence isn't perfect or that the dialogue you just wrote isn't best-seller quality. Of course it's not, but no writing in a draft is perfect—that's why it's called a draft. Get those sentences down and move forward. No one will read this draft but you. It doesn't have to be perfect, it just has to be good. You'll make it great later.

2. Concentrate on what's right in front of you, not on the big picture. You've likely heard that the best novels are organic, that each part is an integral subsection of a larger whole. This is true, and the most effective way to make your novel that way during your drafting phase is to forget about the larger whole altogether. That's what I said, trainee: Forget about writing a novel. Instead, concentrate on doing your absolute best to make your characters' personality points and objectives come out in the scene you're writing right now. This will help you focus your energies each day, and because you worked hard on your BIC, character matrix, scene list, and scene summaries, you've already built an organic structure.

3. Every day, set realistic writing goals. Avoid blocking out large, continuous chunks of time to write, because the odds are that you'll end up wasting a considerable portion of it. If you schedule two hours to write, for example, you'll likely find yourself spending twenty to thirty minutes of that time reading e-mail, paying bills, searching for that one fact you want before you write the scene—anything but adding another sentence to the scene you're on. Our lives are over-committed and too full of multitasking; who gets two or three hours of uninterrupted time to work? That only happens to characters in novels.

Instead, schedule forty-five to fifty minutes for drafting, which is about the amount of time an adult can focus on one task before his attention span and ability to concentrate drop off radically. In that time—as you learned during the preparation phase—assign yourself a specific task or tasks. *Work on book* is not specific enough. *Draft first half of scene where protagonist discovers her best friend is working for antagonist and then she confronts best friend* is just right.

Have only fifteen minutes? Remember this is boot camp, so no sniveling and no excuses. In fifteen minutes you can draft a sentence—maybe two or three. That's one, two, or three more than you'd have if you did nothing. Would you rather spend those fifteen minutes doing push-ups?

4. Resist the urge to warm up by revising what you did the previous day. This common method of getting into the writing mood is one of the biggest time-wasters going and is a truly inefficient way of revising or editing. Yes, everybody does it—but it's a civilian way of working, so *you* shouldn't. If you must warm up, do so by reviewing what is supposed to happen in the scene you're drafting by reviewing your development tools (character cards, scene summary, character matrix, BIC) or by using the techniques found in this phase. And by the way, this warm-up doesn't count towards your forty-five minutes—or even your fifteen.

5. Log your progress. Success breeds success. You already have target dates for the phases of your novel-writing battle plan and for completing the various tasks within specific phases. Use that same calendar to track your progress. For each day, write down the number of pages you write, check off the tasks you complete, and make notes where you get ahead (or behind, heaven forbid). Feel free to draw a smiley face or give yourself a gold star for a good day. The more you see yourself making progress, the more progress you'll make. Didn't have a good day? This is boot camp—do more push-ups.

These unwritten rules will help you make daily progress, and it's daily progress that yields the best results—a quality draft—in the least amount of time. So just as soon as you decide who is telling your story (the narrator or point-of-view character), write that draft one sentence, and one day, at a time.

To find out who should tell your story, turn to the next drill.

RELATED DRILLS

Drill 1: Make It Your Mission
Drill 2: Adopt a Principled Approach
Drill 5: See Your Target
Drill 13: Be More Successful
Drill 45: Put Your Book on an Index Card
Drill 52: Win the First Battle

DRILL 50

OCCUPY YOUR MAIN OP

Before any battle, a military force's commander decides where he's going to position himself to see how the conflict unfolds. He'll likely receive information from multiple sources that have observation of battlefield areas, but before the action begins, he'll choose his main command and observation post (OP).

Your novel will have a main observation post as well, only yours is known as a point of view or POV. To keep it in simple terms (in boot camp we like to KISS—*keep it simple, stupid*), POV is the perspective from which your story is presented. To choose the best viewpoint for your work, you need to know your POV options and take into account some major considerations for making the choice.

- **First-Person POV.** This is the *I* narrator. The *I* can be your protagonist (a tradition in mysteries, including Robert B. Parker's acclaimed Spenser series), a witness to the events (Watson in Sherlock Holmes stories), or a reteller of the story—someone who wasn't there but who is telling the tale of what happened. Yann Martel used this POV in his award-winning novel *Life of Pi*, as did Alice Sebold in *The Lovely Bones*. Other first-person POV novels include Stephen King's *Dolores Claiborne* and Jules Verne's *A Journey to the Center of the Earth.*

- **Second-Person POV.** In second-person POV, the narrator tells the story to another character from that character's point of view: *You ordered a pizza and then ate it all by yourself.* Its main use has been in choose-your-own-adventure novels. You probably won't use this point of view—it's seldom found in fiction. You, therefore, should KISS and not worry about second-person POV.

- **Third-Person POV.** Third-person POV tells the story from the perspective of someone who is not involved in the action of the story: The first- and second-person pronouns *I* and *you* are replaced by the third-person pronouns *he, she, it,* and *they*. There are three main flavors of the third-person point of view: omniscient, objective, and limited. The third-person omniscient (or unlimited) POV provides readers with access to the thoughts, feelings, and actions of every character. This is the only POV not limited in some way. Tom Clancy's *The Hunt for Red October* features this POV.

Third-person objective is considered the fly-on-the-wall POV, allowing readers to see and hear all, but never revealing the inner thoughts and feelings of the characters. This point of view is objective in the same way a newspaper report is objective or in the same way *Dragnet* detective Joe Friday was objective—"Just the facts, ma'am." Your reader interprets what the characters think and feel by what they do. Ernest Hemingway used this POV in his classic short story "Hills Like White Elephants."

The default choice for most fiction is the third-person limited point of view. This POV is similar to first person in that the reader sees the story from a single character's perspective and knows that one character's thoughts and feelings. Toni Morrison's *Beloved* showcases this POV.

Most novels have one main point of view. You'll need to choose, but there are no hard and fast rules for doing so. No one point of view is best, and in the end the choice is personal, but there are several considerations to keep in mind when choosing.

- *Genre points the way.* Look to your genre to determine which POV is most appropriate for the type of novel you're writing. Some genres, like category romance, have very specific guidelines that writers must follow. Hard-boiled detective fiction and literary novels tend toward first person. Third-person omniscience is very popular in Westerns and espionage thrillers. Most of Tom Clancy's techno-thrillers feature a mix of third-person limited and third-person objective POVs. You are, of course, free to push genre conventions—just be conscious that you're making that choice. When you color too far outside the lines, you take the risk of turning off more tradition-bound readers.

- *I has its limits.* First-person POV is often more challenging because it limits what your narrator can know. Your reader may also become bored with the repetitious use of the pronoun. At the same time, *I* can be the most personal, and it carries the potential for a greater emotional connection with the reader.
- *Playing God has benefits and liabilities.* An omniscient narrator gives you the most flexibility to show your story's world from multiple perspectives, and it gives your reader access to the thoughts of all of your characters. However, this third-person POV carries with it the danger of head-hopping. No, this is not a Navy term for going from bathroom to bathroom. Head-hopping occurs when you shift POV too many times too fast, which leads to reader confusion. Try to limit your POV shifts to scene or chapter changes to ensure that your reader doesn't become disoriented.

You should choose a primary POV for your story and tell most of the story from that perspective, but you can incorporate multiple points of view in your work as well. To do so effectively, you'll need to clearly signal the change from one POV to another.

And that sentence signals that it's time to move on to the next drill.

RELATED DRILLS

Drill 5: See Your Target
Drill 33: Give Your Protagonist a Pointed Personality
Drill 47: Plan Your Characters' Development
Drill 51: Make the Reader See Your New POV
Drill 53: Tell Each Character's Story
Drill 92: Circle Back for the Miscellaneous Pass

DRILL 51

MAKE THE READER SEE YOUR NEW POV

Remember the sound of bugles in old civil-war or cavalry-on-the-plains movies? That's the sound of leaders trying to avoid confusion. In battle, whatever can be confused, will be confused. In the heat of battle, leaders rely upon all types of communication—radios, flares, whistles, anything they can use to send signals to their troops. If those signals fail, there is confusion in the ranks, and that can put the mission in jeopardy.

In the heat of writing your novel, you need to avoid confusing your reader. This is especially true when it comes to shifting points of view. Confusion is your biggest enemy when you switch POV. Your reader needs to understand what is happening in the scene (even if your characters don't) and what the narrator's perspective is. If your reader isn't sure who is narrating the scene, the scene will lose its emotional impact. You don't need flags, bugles, flares, or radios to make it work; instead, use the techniques below.

1. Signal the change with words. Deliberately place clear word clues to show who is doing the narration. Use one of these three techniques for signaling a POV shift with words.

- *Cue with a pronoun and a verb.* Begin the sentence that starts the new point of view with the appropriate pronoun followed by a verb. For example:

  He thought ...
  She ran ...
  I didn't understand ...

  Starting the first sentence with a new pronoun is an effective, efficient cue that the narrative is progressing from a different point of view.

- *Cue with character name and verb.* You can also signal a point-of-view change by starting a paragraph or sentence with a name and a verb. There are many variations, but as long as the name of the POV character is close to the verb, the technique is effective.

  Bill stared …
  Sammy, the undertaker's daughter, believed …
  One lawman down, Billy the Kid thought, *three to go*.

- *Cue with an introductory phrase.* This cueing technique combines either a name or pronoun with an introductory phrase or clause. Because your reader understands grammar, she'll understand that your introductory phrase is establishing the point of view. Example phrases or clauses might be:

  From her perspective, …
  As they all knew, …
  As I saw it, …

  Or even the more direct:

  From Bill's point of view, …

2. Signal the change with white space. As a general rule, you should make a change in point of view when you make some other change, such as starting a new chapter or switching ideas. Your reader understands that breaks in type—such as chapter breaks, paragraph breaks, and extra blank lines—signal breaks in thought or topic. You can leverage these visual cues to signal a change in point of view.

- *Use chapter breaks.* Understand that chapter breaks are placed to help you signal to your reader that you've made a change. That change may be a jump in time or location, but it can also be a change in point of view. Chapter breaks are the strongest and clearest uses of white space.

- *Use paragraph breaks.* Like Ms. Grunty told you in grade-school English, a new paragraph means a new idea. Readers understand that the small white space of a paragraph indentation marks a change.

- *Use an extra line of white space.* If you are typing, simply hit the return key twice, leaving an extra line of white space. Again, readers understand that a break in text means a change, and they subconsciously prepare themselves for something new. Because this technique is somewhat artificial and can bring attention to itself, make it your third choice.

Once you know how to showcase your multiple points of view, you'll be able to shift readers into each subtle vector. Now it's time to get that story started and your reader hooked. To find out how, turn to the next drill.

RELATED DRILLS

Drill 5: See Your Target
Drill 33: Give Your Protagonist a Pointed Personality
Drill 47: Plan Your Characters' Development
Drill 50: Occupy Your Main OP
Drill 53: Tell Each Character's Story
Drill 92: Circle Back for the Miscellaneous Pass

DRILL 52

WIN THE FIRST BATTLE

No day at boot camp is more challenging than your first; no parachute jump is more intimidating than your first; no battle is more terrifying than your first; and no page, paragraph, or sentence is more challenging, intimidating, terrifying, or important than your first.

Your first page—indeed your first sentence and your first paragraph—is your first real up-close-and-personal meeting with your reader. If your first sentence, paragraph, and page are compelling, the reader will turn the page and keep going. If they're not—if you lose this first battle and fail to capture your reader's attention—there's a better than even chance that the rest of your novel won't get read. However, if you spend days and days trying to write the ideal first sentence, the perfect first page, there's an even better chance your novel won't get written.

To build an opening hook that will serve as a solid base for your coming revisions and be strong enough to allow you to continue to make progress on your draft, follow the guidelines below.

1. Follow your genre. You've read widely in your genre to find your path. Now take a second look at what works in your genre by reviewing how some of your favorites open. Do they jump right to the causal event? Is the main character present on page one? Which openings feel stronger to you, and what do they do that contributes to that feeling? You don't have to slavishly imitate what you see, but you should understand what the expectations are.

2. Follow your battle plan. Too many beginning novelists want to make up a separate opening—one that doesn't really figure into the action of the novel—and tack it onto the front of their story. Don't. Your opening comes from a scene in the scene list and that scene's summary. The scene comes from the *D*s in your story line and your book on an index card. Use the first

scene in your scene list. Note that if that scene, standing alone, sounds boring, you need to cut the entire scene and start over with one that isn't.

3. Start with the scene's essential conflict. Your reader should see your characters—preferably your main character—in some kind of fight (be it physical or emotional) on page one. If you must, write the mood-setting description, internal dialogue, or backstory summary that leads to the confrontation in your scene. Then cut all those—and your opening will be the scene's essential conflict.

4. Start in the middle of the fight. You want your reader to walk into a scene where things are already happening. This is sometimes referred to as *entering the scene as late as possible.* If your reader is witnessing a murder, a breakup, or a beast ravaging a victim, show that reader—right away—the dead body, the *"It's over,"* or the big shark having a snack.

5. Cut the scene early. Your goal is to build intrigue that will make the reader turn the page. Intrigue comes from unanswered questions: *Who are these people? What are they doing here? Why are they fighting? Who killed the victim? Why are they breaking up?* As an author, your natural instinct is to answer these questions, and your reader's natural instinct is to search for the answers. Avoid giving in to your instincts and, instead, plan on manipulating the reader's desire for answers.

Entire books have been written on constructing an opening hook, including Georgianne Ensign's *Great Beginnings and Endings: Opening and Closing Lines of Great Novels*, which is worth incorporating into your reading plan. The opening page of your first draft won't rank among these outstanding beginnings—and it shouldn't. These are some of the best and are the result of much revising, rewriting, editing, blood, sweat, and probably tears. You are drafting. Your opening scene doesn't have to be perfect, but like all your work in this phase, it should be damn good.

You'll be back to revise your opening several times. For now, get it written and move on to the next scene. You have a story to tell; in fact, multiple stories. So move on to the next drill.

RELATED DRILLS

Drill 2: Adopt a Principled Approach
Drill 45: Put Your Book on an Index Card
Drill 49: Know the Unwritten Rules for Quality Drafting
Drill 94: Conduct the Final Assault: Rewriting

DRILL 53

TELL EACH CHARACTER'S STORY

In military Special Forces units, every individual is trained to perform at exceptionally high levels. As a mission goes on, each one of these elite warriors gives 110 percent to accomplishing the team's objective. This is how small bands of fighters can obtain results that are several orders of magnitude larger than you would expect.

As you write your draft, you can make all your characters—not just your protagonist and antagonist—high-performing elite warriors as well. How? By telling each character's story as if he were the main character. You can increase the depth and breadth of your minor characters—and so add to the richness of your text and improve the connection with your readers—by applying modified "lite" versions of the techniques you used for developing your protagonist.

1. Build a modified BIC. Use a variation of the book-on-an-index-card you used for your protagonist, modifying the format to give a minor character an objective, personality points, and a path to follow.

Let's say your main character is a brilliant but emotionally traumatized former Special Forces profiler who, after a mission gone wrong, retires to a small town to heal her wounded heart, mind, and soul. (If you think this sounds like my first mystery, *Close to Home*, you're right.) The town's appearance-conscious mayor, an old family friend of the profiler, is a minor character in your story, and although he's a likeable character, he's also a hypocrite. When a serial murderer threatens the town's safety and reputation, the mayor asks your protagonist to intervene to "quietly" help his cops find the killer. A modified BIC might read:

> When an appearance-conscious, hypocritical (but likeable) small-town mayor finds his village's safety and reputation threatened by a serial killer,

DRILL 53

he persuades an emotionally traumatized but brilliant former Special Forces profiler to help his cops solve the case.

A good start. But things never go as planned.

But the killings go on unabated, so the mayor teams the profiler with his two lead detectives (who hate each other) to crack the case. Then state and federal politicians get involved, and the mayor interferes with progress as he desperately tries to get the press and investigation under control.

The harder the mayor tries, the faster the situation goes downhill.

In the process, the mayor accidentally reveals that he has had an affair and that corruption is rife in his small kingdom. To stop the rising tide of bad publicity, the mayor takes the profiler off the case and arrests an unlikely and probably innocent suspect. The mayor's philandering and miscarriage of justice are revealed when the profiler corners the real killer.

This minor-character BIC gives you the character's motivation for each and every scene in which he appears.

2. Build an abbreviated character card for each minor character. You don't need to go into the same detail as you do with your protagonist or villain, but you should list most of the same information.

- the character's name
- the character's objectives (both story and personal)
- the character's major personality points
- the character's window character, foil, or sidekick (note that minor characters may not have these)
- the character's opponent or opposition
- the character's age and striking physical traits or markers

3. Build an abbreviated backstory for your minor characters. Use a "lite" version of the backstory format.

- *The character snapshot.* For minor characters, this may be only a sentence or two.
- *A day in the life of the character.* You won't need more than a few lines of description of the minor character's typical day.
- *The character's personal history.* This is a quick list of major events and people in your minor character's life.

4. Let your minor characters shine. As you draft the scenes in which your minor characters are present, have them play their parts (speak, act, and think) as if they were the stars of the story. Write each minor character just as you would a major character—fighting at 100-percent intensity to achieve their goals. This will increase not only the richness of your scenes and story but the level of conflict as well.

5. Mine every character. As you revise and edit your draft, look for places where you can add richness and depth to your minor characters. Remember that the focus of your story is still on your protagonist. However, enriching your minor characters increases your reader's interest in the story and so in its protagonist.

How small a character is too small to warrant the treatments above? Remember the golden rule of two: If a character appears in two or more scenes, enrich that character. Characters who appear only for a scene or two and/or have very little or no dialogue or interplay with the major characters need less of an investment of time, energy, and creativity.

As you develop your minor characters, remember that building reader interest in those characters cuts both ways: While it keeps the reader connected to your story, it also imposes upon you, the author, an obligation to resolve that character. While your readers likely won't care about an almost-anonymous doorman, they will want to know what happens to the mayor. You have a responsibility to finish the story—to not leave your readers hanging. You owe it to your readers to tie up the loose ends.

Minor characters are more interesting—for the reader to read and for you to write—if they act with the same intensity as the protagonist or main character. Strong minor characters help build even stronger emotional connections for your reader. This means you can do things with these minor characters, such as hang them off a cliff, and keep the reader's level of excitement high.

What cliff? Turn to the next drill.

RELATED DRILLS

Drill 2: Adopt a Principled Approach
Drill 5: See Your Target
Drill 26: Choose Your Cast
Drill 31: Distinctly Mark Your Characters
Drill 39: Use a Character Matrix

DRILL 54

HANG YOUR READERS OFF A CLIFF—REPEATEDLY

The military is known for its policy of *hurry up and wait*, which is usually a bad thing. However, in fiction you can use *hurry up and wait* to your advantage. You can increase the tension and quicken the pace of your fiction by incorporating cliffhangers. *Cliffhanger* is a term taken from the movies in which the viewer sees the hero or heroine dangling over the edge of a cliff and is then suddenly taken away to a completely different scene. A cliffhanger keeps the readers' attention focused on what will happen next, and thus keeps them turning the pages. The four essential elements of a nail-biting cliffhanger are: (1) a character in jeopardy, (2) high stakes, (3) an interruption, and (4) a resolution.

1. A character in jeopardy. Let's say your opponent or villain has kidnapped two children, as in James Patterson's *Along Came a Spider*. Readers will be concerned for the children—kidnap victims may or may not be returned alive, even if a ransom is paid. Patterson keeps his protagonist, Alex Cross, in the foreground by focusing in on the detective's actions and describing his reactions to the pressure.

2. High stakes. For a cliffhanger to succeed, the danger to the characters involved must be imminent but uncertain. It also must affect the main characters in some significant way. In James Patterson's novel, Alex Cross is informed during an interview with one child's parents that the child has a potentially fatal medical condition, and that the child will die if not rescued soon. The kidnapped children were already in danger, but now one of the children is in grave, immediate danger.

3. An interruption. Before it is resolved, the action has to be interrupted. Your reader sees the setup. Your reader infers the potential consequences.

Your reader understands the sense of urgency and immediacy. Your reader then anticipates an answer—but you do not give it to him—not immediately, anyway. The reader must go to the next chapter, or even the chapter after that, to find out what happens. Patterson cuts back and forth between several scenes before resolving the cliffhanger.

4. A resolution. Somehow the hero triumphs or the victim is rescued—or not. Cliffhangers don't necessarily have happy endings. In fact, one technique for ensuring that your reader understands just how dangerous your opponent is and how deep his evil goes is to set up a cliffhanger early on in your novel in which the opponent triumphs. In the case of Patterson's novel—

Nope, not giving that away.

So how do you hang your readers off a cliff? There are many techniques, but the following are especially useful.

- *Change the way you think about scenes or chapters.* Civilians tend to think of chapters as a unit of cause and effect—starting with a setup and ending with a payoff. But that's not how it works in novelist's boot camp. Instead, begin your chapters or scenes with the payoff from the previous chapter or scene, and end it with a setup for the next chapter or scene. This can be as simple as cutting and pasting a paragraph or a page, or it may require significant rethinking. You can always leverage the power of the computer to draft one way and revise another (copy, cut, and paste functions have their merits). Even a quick look at Patterson's novel will give you several examples of this technique.

- *Move your scenes around to make the reader wait for the payoff.* Patterson does this, as does Kathy Reichs in *Deadly Decisions*. The reader finds the child in danger, the villain getting the drop on the hero, a forensic discovery about to break open the case—and in the next chapter, the reader gets backstory, the story from the point of view of another character, or the beginning or continuation of a subplot. Patterson and Reichs make the reader wait. You should make your reader wait, too.

- *Edit the sentences at the end of your scene or chapter so they are shorter, simpler, and faster.* This picks up the pace of the reading, and as that pace gets faster and faster, reader anticipation for the payoff grows.

It's not necessary or even advisable to end every chapter or scene with a cliffhanger. Your reader's central nervous system will only tolerate so much suspense. Better to follow the advice of established mystery, thriller, and Western writer Loren D. Estelman and "let the poor devils breathe every now and then."

Chapter- or scene-ending cliffhangers improve tension, increase suspense, and quicken pace. They are useful tools that novelists in any genre can employ to keep readers turning pages.

You can use them, too; you just can't talk about them. Why not? See the next drill.

RELATED DRILLS

Drill 38: Define, Objectify, and Personify the Objective
Drill 42: Take Three Steps to Story Line
Drill 43: Turn on Your Turning Points

DRILL 55

BUTTON IT, SOLDIER!

During World War II, posters and pundits across the United States counseled, "Loose lips sink ships." Don't go blabbing about the war, officials warned; you never know who might be listening, what they might do with the information, or if letting slip even the slightest detail might be detrimental to the war effort.

This wartime advice is applicable to today's novelists. When it comes to talking about that novel you're working on, keep your mouth mostly shut. Give nonwriting friends and acquaintances a sound bite in the form of a modified book on an index card, and unless they're novelists you want specific feedback from, give them nothing more.

There are three reasons why you want to keep your project mostly to yourself.

1. They just don't—and won't—get it. As cocktail party conversations reveal, most people believe they could write a book, are thinking or have thought about writing a book, or know someone who is writing a book. But for most of these folks, being an author is all about the image; an image conjured up either by Hollywood or by high school literature teachers. Very few take the steps you have taken or do the work you've done to make their dreams a reality. Those who don't get it can even include your spouse or significant other, children, friends, neighbors—really, anyone who isn't familiar with and hasn't experienced the writing process.

If you tell them you're writing a book, you'll inevitably hear this next question: *What's it about?* Your best response to that question is a shortened form of your BIC. Give them the genre, main character type, and the main character's objective: *It's a political thriller about a cold-hearted killer turned social worker who must rescue an innocent family mistakenly targeted by terrorists.*

2. You need to safeguard your concept and your time. Many writers worry that someone will steal their idea, though this is a needless worry. There are lots of great ideas for novels running around, and since copyright law protects only the execution of an idea and not the idea itself, you can't copyright an idea. Nonetheless, circumvent this feeling by giving the curious the modified version of your BIC discussed above—that's enough to give them an understanding of the book without giving away your idea. Responding with an abbreviated BIC will also keep you out of time-wasting explanations or lengthy discussions that meander to nowhere.

3. You need to limit what you say in order to do your best work. This might sound counterintuitive. After all, it seems like the more input you get on your novel, the better it will be. But this isn't necessarily true, especially when it comes to input from casual observers and cocktail party critics. When you're writing your novel, you don't need emotional reactions based on personal likes and dislikes. You need insightful advice and recommendations cast in terms you can understand and act on. The broad brushstrokes your friends and acquaintances use won't contribute much to your work and may even be detrimental.

With some very specific exceptions, when it comes to talking about your novel in progress—just don't. This is difficult. Writing book-length fiction is hard work, but it can also be exciting. You may want to open up to everyone you meet. You can, but be smart about it. Most people don't understand the true nature of writing book-length fiction. Protect your ideas, your ego, and your time.

Your friends and acquaintances are neither your critique partners nor your editors. Save the detailed discussions of your work for other writers you're working with and give everyone else just enough for polite conversation. If the subject of writer's block finds its way into one of those conversations, you can tell 'em the truth: You know how to beat it. Find out how in the next drill.

RELATED DRILLS

Drill 5: See Your Target
Drill 20: Invent a Better Story Idea
Drill 45: Put Your Book on an Index Card

DRILL 56

BACK UP TO BEAT WRITER'S BLOCK

You never hear of a recruit failing to turn out of his bunk because of soldier's block. If such a thing ever happened, there would surely be a raging drill sergeant to "help" that trainee find his way to work. You may not have a drill sergeant to help you with writer's block, a condition that can bring a novelist's progress to a dead halt, but you can prevent and cure it.

Writer's block is defined as the inability to write. Most often, novelists talk about writer's block as if it were a disease: *I got a bad case of writer's block, and I couldn't finish the scene*, or *I was blocked for three days, but then it got better.*

But writer's block isn't an illness—it's a symptom. You can (and many do) simply treat the symptom, but your relief will only be temporary. To get real relief, you must address writer's block in a different way: You must identify and alleviate the underlying condition.

1. Take an ounce of prevention. Most often, writer's block comes when you're drafting—when you're trying to create something out of nothing. When writer's block hits, you can't visualize or focus enough to create a scene, much less concentrate on what the characters are saying and doing in it.

In other words, writer's block happens when you're trying to create from scratch an interesting, integrated, powerful scene—plus dynamic dialogue, intriguing description, *and* riveting action. That's a tall order. You're trying to do too many things at once, which leads not just to an inability to do any of them well but to an inability to do anything at all. Writer's block is a clear indication that the writing process is managing you, not the other way around.

Your book on an index card, character biographies, character cards, and master scene summary are all excellent preventative medicines and powerful cures for writer's block. When you complete each of these before you start drafting, you inoculate yourself against writer's block. Once completed, they work together to answer the question *What do I write?* As you're drafting, there's no need to even ask the question. Your tools tell you what happens next—that's what you have to write.

That leaves only the question *How do I write it?* Your notes help answer that question as well. Your scene summary tells you what your characters have to do. Your character cards and character biographies tell you what their goals and personality points are and what critical events in their personal histories might resonate in a given situation. These are all factors that tell you how they will react—and that's how you write it.

2. If prevention fails, look backward to go forward. No system is foolproof, and that's true of the plan outlined in this book as well. Sometimes, regardless of the work you've done planning and prewriting, you may find yourself stalled. If this happens, return to your planning tools.

First, review your scene list. Look for clear, definitive descriptions of what happens next, and measure how strong they are. The stronger these descriptions, the easier it will be for you to proceed. The weaker they are, the more you're likely to flounder.

Sometimes a bout of writer's block will reveal a weakness in these documents. If you find a gap, stop working on your draft. Return to your character cards or character biographies and rework your characters until they are clear and strong. Otherwise, you'll run into the same problem again later.

3. Step over the fear of imperfection. What you write may not be Pulitzer Prize-winning material or even your best work, but it will be committed to the page. Leave it there, and avoid the energy-dissipating trap of trying to edit or revise as you go. Once you have a complete draft, you can bring your creative energies to bear revising and editing that draft.

Although you're focused on getting to *The End*, the process of drafting your novel isn't linear. A case of writer's block can have you backing up to sharpen the tools you prepared in your development phase.

The act of drafting will spur your imagination and creativity. Leverage this effect by making your novel more interesting as you go. How? One way to do so is to raise the stakes, and the way you learn how to raise them is by turning the page to the next mission.

RELATED DRILLS

Drill 33: Give Your Protagonist a Pointed Personality
Drill 37: Put a Face on Evil
Drill 42: Take Three Steps to Story Line
Drill 45: Put Your Book on an Index Card

MISSION VI

COMMIT YOUR RESERVES

There are stakes in boot camp—fail at a task and you can find yourself doing push-ups, *lots* of push-ups. Whether it's push-ups or pride, in boot camp something is always on the line.

Something is on the line in your novel, too. Your characters have story and personal objectives. Of course these are at risk, but the drills in this mission will show you how to heighten the tension and level of conflict in your novel by raising the stakes even higher.

What are stakes? Stakes are what your characters have to win or lose. Raising the stakes—putting more at risk—increases the importance of each choice the characters make, the gains if they choose well, and the losses if they choose poorly.

As you draft, deliberately review each scene and apply the drills in this mission to put more at risk with each decision or discovery your characters make, each action they perform, and each event they deal with. Raising the stakes makes each scene more important, more powerful, and more entertaining for your reader.

Drafting your novel is not simply a matter of passively following the notes in your master story summary. Drafting requires your active engagement and the aggressive use of your creativity. The novelist's boot camp battle plan is engineered so you can bring the full force of your creativity to bear on small writing tasks. Leverage that power and give your characters even more to lose: Raise the stakes.

DRILL 57

GO MORE PUBLIC

A wise old soldier once counseled a new recruit to never allow a journalist to take his picture in uniform, because when it was published, someone—from a concerned citizen to a commanding general—would find something wrong with his appearance.

Your characters may want to follow this advice and stay out of the public eye, but don't you let them. Instead, raise the stakes in your novel by making your protagonist's and antagonist's stakes more public. When you bring a character's problems out of a closed room and open them up for public inspection, you automatically increase the amount that character has to win—or lose. Here are two methods for taking your protagonist's struggle public.

1. Give your protagonist an audience. Doing something difficult is a challenge when no one is looking, but it's an even greater challenge when the whole world's watching. Giving your main character an audience changes the situation of the conflict so that great numbers of people are aware of your protagonist's success or failure. This is a powerful shift—everyone has secrets, and tapping into the reader's own fear of being exposed and potentially embarrassed in front of a group builds empathy.

2. Make it a big deal. You can also alter the nature of your protagonist's fight by giving her weighty objectives affecting public or social policy. Tom Clancy uses environmental terrorism as the backdrop for action and intrigue in *Rainbow Six*. However, you're not limited by genre if you want to weave social issues into your story. Carla Cassidy asks just how far someone can go to eliminate the scourge of drugs in her action-laced romance *Get Blondie*.

There are, however, three cautions if you invoke social issues. First, carefully screen your characters' dialogue for speech-making. Characters should use dialogue as a way to fight for what *they* want, not as a shortcut to the soapbox.

Second, beware of painting an issue as black and white, right and wrong. Few issues have only one side. Even if they do, one-sided issues are by definition flat, and your readers want a richer, more complex story.

Third, keep an eye on your BIC (book on an index card). This will remind you that your story is not about racism, sexism, class wars, or environmentalism; your story is about people whose needs are in conflict.

Now that you've dragged your heroine's struggle into the open for all to see and made it a matter of social consequence, turn around and go to the heart of your character and of the matter.

How? Personally, I'd go to the next drill.

RELATED DRILLS

Drill 18: Find Your Character in Events, Places, and Concepts
Drill 21: Forge Your Setting
Drill 35: Tell Your Characters' Backstories
Drill 36: Define the Opposition
Drill 38: Define, Objectify, and Personify the Objective
Drill 86: Make an Objective Pass

DRILL 58

MAKE IT MORE PERSONAL

If you look into the history of great battles, you'll find that they come down to clashes between personalities. In battle, what's at stake is the fate of the opposing forces—and the personal sense of success or failure of each commander. The fate of man and nations may not be at stake in your novel, but you can make your fiction more entertaining, your characters more compelling, and your readers more invested by making what's at stake more particular and more intimate.

In other words, make it more personal.

Personalizing objectives, as you should remember from drill 38, means imbuing your character's story and personal objectives with personal significance.

You do recall drill 38, don't you?

I see you starting to turn back the pages. I hope you have an extra toothbrush, soldier, because you're going to be scrubbing the shower floor with yours.

In this drill, you'll build on the initial personalization of the causal event as discussed in drill 38. Your personalization here will be focused and directed inward. That is, you should personalize your protagonist's story objectives by tying them to a deep need that is rooted in his personality and his personal history. Whatever your main character wins or loses in your story, the victory or defeat should both come from and deeply effect who he is.

While this may sound like the stuff of relationship-focused romances or slice-of-life literary fiction, raising the stakes by making winning or losing more personal is applicable to all genres—even those with the most violent of subjects and set in the most historically significant of places.

An exceptionally powerful example of manipulating the stakes in this manner can be found in Michael Shaara's classic *The Killer Angels*. This fictionalized retelling of the Battle of Gettysburg foregrounds the deeply per-

sonal stakes for military legends such as Robert E. Lee, James Longstreet, J.E.B. Stuart, John F. Reynolds, Joshua Chamberlain, and others.

We'll focus here on Shaara's treatment of his fictionalized Robert E. Lee, for in this treatment there's a subtle yet powerful example of how a story objective (to win the battle) is made more personal by being tied to a personal objective (to honor a promise made before God).

What is at stake for Lee is not the Confederate cause but something deeper and much more personal. In the dark before the final day at Gettysburg, Lee broods on how far he has come and what he has at stake in the next day's battle. Shaara portrays Lee as a deeply religious man who had served long and well in the U.S. Army before joining the Confederates. At West Point, Lee made an oath before God to protect and defend the United States from enemies foreign and domestic.

The vow broken by Lee's defection to the Confederate army still haunts him; the only way to know that his actions are justified, the only way to somehow wipe out that sin of breaking a vow before God, is to win the coming battle. What is at stake for Shaara's Lee, then, is redemption.

To raise the personal stakes in any situation, tie the character's story objectives to needs in that character's personality—his personal objectives. In most fiction, these needs really boil down to three: the need for growth, the need for redemption, or the need for both. Growth occurs when your character accepts and overcomes his problems. Redemption occurs when your character releases himself (or another character) from blame or when he makes up for some failure. Many people (especially in our Western civilization) believe that although a person can never change the past, he can redeem himself for past transgressions. In fiction, your protagonist may feel the need to redeem himself publicly, privately, or both. We can find both needs in Shaara's novel of the Gettysburg battlefield.

Get more personal about your protagonist's stakes and you'll get more personal with your reader, increasing his interest and emotional commitment to your story. Is it right to raise the stakes and so manipulate your reader's emotions in this way? In boot camp, we're not afraid to address questions of right and wrong—and we do so in the next drill.

RELATED DRILLS

Drill 2: Adopt a Principled Approach
Drill 18: Find Your Character in Events, Places, and Concepts
Drill 41: Change the World
Drill 47: Plan Your Characters' Development
Drill 85: Make a Character Pass
Drill 90: Make an Action Pass

DRILL 59

BE MORE MORAL

It's an old military adage: Seize the high ground. That can be good advice for novelists, too—if the ground your character is after is the moral high ground.

Your main character badly wants something—the story objective—and he will take drastic action to get it. He also has a personal objective—a feeling or idea that he wants to achieve, even though he may not comprehend that he wants it. We've already discussed how to raise the stakes of your story by personalizing and by investing public interest in the objectives of your characters. You can also effectively raise stakes by giving those objectives moral implications or connotations.

Even in this day of relative morality, shades of gray, and tarnished heroes, most people still have at least an intuitive understanding of right and wrong. It's wrong for the strong to bully the weak, wrong to exploit the unsuspecting, to steal, or to hurt innocent bystanders. Most people accept that right doesn't come from might and that killing is wrong. Although religious beliefs and cultures vary, and although many people have a hard time precisely defining evil, most know true evil when they see it.

This same understanding of right and wrong is present in fiction, where we want good to triumph. You can find this sense even in darker fiction—such as hard-boiled detective stories, in which the protagonist operates in a world where the bad guys make the rules and win most of the time. There is a sense that fighting the good fight or lighting a candle against the darkness is the right thing to do, even if the effort is futile.

When you press a reader's intuitive hot buttons by leveraging his sense of right and wrong, you take the stakes up a notch. To do so, frame the moral implications of your protagonist's objectives using the following techniques.

1. Use the generalized notion of right and wrong held by your readers. Your readers will likely represent a wide spectrum of definitions of good and evil. Your job as an author is to affect as many of those readers as possible. Framing the moral implications of your character's objectives within a more generalized interpretation of right and wrong will help you to do this. Keep in mind, however, that some specialized genres or subgenres—like religious fiction, category romance, and young adult fiction—operate within narrow and specific boundaries (for example, no premarital or outside-of-marriage sex allowed).

2. Use your character's sense of morality. Your character will have—and must operate within—his own understanding of right and wrong based on his background and personality. For example, if your main character is an undercover spy, then lying, cheating, and stealing are okay if done in an attempt to preserve justice. After all, that's what he does, and he believes himself to be a patriot for doing so. While there is surely a long list of things that are not okay for your secret agent, one of the things he would likely consider morally reprehensible is abandoning a source to the enemy.

3. Use your own feelings about the nature and definitions of good and evil. Even though you may fully research and develop your characters into distinct, separate individuals, you're still the voice behind the curtain. Your understanding of right and wrong will come through in your writing. It's best, then, to know where you stand, even if it's with both feet firmly planted in midair. When you understand your own sense of morality, you can ensure that the moral agenda in your novel is one that you want, not one that sneaks in.

As you apply all three of these techniques, it's possible that you will find yourself in conflict with them. You'll have to decide for yourself if you're willing to operate within the boundaries of your readers and of your chosen genre. Additionally, the characters and the situations you create for them may shake your own understanding of right and wrong. Sometimes the process of writing fiction can be as cathartic for the writer as it is for the reader. You may well find that your work challenges and changes your beliefs. Don't fight this challenge; embrace it. You'll find yourself a richer writer (and person) for it.

After you've contemplated your beliefs—or the beliefs of your characters—you may decide you need something other than mental exercise. Instead of doing push-ups, get physical another way—turn the page to the next drill.

RELATED DRILLS

Drill 17: Put a Face on Your Idea
Drill 19: Find Your Character in Opposites
Drill 52: Win the First Battle
Drill 85: Make a Character Pass

DRILL 60

GET MORE PHYSICAL

One sure way to get a recruit's attention in training is to use live ammunition. When those real bullets start flying or real explosives go off and there's the danger of real physical harm, trainees pay close attention. You don't need live bullets or real bombs to raise the stakes in your fiction, but you can introduce the threat of physical danger—or the other side of the coin, physical intimacy—to raise the stakes in your story.

A character's life is one of the ultimate stakes—after all, if the protagonist isn't alive (in most genres), she can't worry about achieving her objectives. Although history is full of stories in which people have sacrificed their lives for moral, political, or personal reasons, threats of pain, torture, bodily harm, and death remain powerful motivators for action or inaction. In general, people don't like pain, will avoid risking injury, and won't throw their lives away without a tremendously compelling reason.

However, ramping up the potential for pain (and perhaps loss of life) only works when you've established an emotional connection between your reader and your main character. If your readers don't care about your protagonist, then they won't care if she meets an untimely end, no matter how painful. If you do build that interest and establish that emotional connection, then readers will anticipate the cost of the loss, keep turning pages to find out if it happens, hurt if it does, or be thankful if doesn't.

The less your character can do to save herself from physical harm, the more effective the threat. Maybe a great ocean liner is about to slip beneath the icy North Atlantic waters and, at the last moment, your heroine jumps overboard to save herself.

The stakes go up if your character has been temporarily blinded in an explosion below deck.

They go up even more if she can't swim.

Further still if there's only one lifeboat.

And even more if that one lifeboat is already so full that it's sinking.

Physical harm, not just in the form of loss of life, can also be a threat to another character. Again, you must have established an emotional connection between readers and the potential victim, and the stakes are that much higher if there's an emotional relationship between the victim and the protagonist as well.

While introducing physical harm or the potential for physical harm can raise the stakes in your story, so can introducing physical intimacy. Introducing physical intimacy lends a different perspective to any relationship. In Nelson DeMille's *Up Country*, the relationship between hero Paul Brenner and Susan Weber—who is at times his partner, at times his opposition, and at times his lover—becomes enormously complicated. The implications of their intense physical and emotional attraction to each other enrich Brenner's dogged search for the truth, Susan's willingness to carry out her covert orders, and the collision of the two.

Whether your couple develops, intensifies, and consummates their relationship depends on how you want your story to proceed, but the limits of your genre may have something to say about that as well. What *is* certain is that the potential for (or the results of) physical intimacy can raise the stakes in novel, just as it does in DeMille's.

Introduce the potential for physical harm as your main character pursues her objective, introduce physical intimacy or the potential for it between characters, or introduce both. When you get physical with your characters, you get physical with your readers—in the form of faster heartbeats and the continuous turning of pages.

When you raise stakes by adding physical danger, you'll inevitably need a pool of potential victims. Want to know where and why to find these sacrificial lambs? See the next drill.

RELATED DRILLS

Drill 5: See Your Target
Drill 10: Write What You Must
Drill 18: Find Your Character in Events, Places, and Concepts
Drill 71: Make Your Characters Try, Try Again
Drill 72: Find the Devil in the Details
Drill 73: Go to Time-and-a-Half

DRILL 61

DRAFT SOME VICTIMS

Military commanders always try to avoid civilian casualties and so-called collateral damage. However, as a novelist you should seek them out.

Drafting some potential victims increases your reader's investment in your story by establishing a more complex emotional connection. When you add victims or potential victims, the reader isn't just worried about the protagonist, he's worried about the victims as well. The stakes are no longer hinged to one person's success or failure. Other characters have something to lose, too. Not only do potential victims make a protagonist's objectives more public—others are at risk now, after all—they also add an element of physical danger. Plus, your lead may feel morally obligated to try to save the victims, and, whether he succeeds or fails, the incident is likely to personalize his objectives. He's witnessed the suffering of others, and now he wants justice. Talk about raising the stakes!

Here are three techniques to put all kinds of innocent people at risk—at least in your novel.

1. Identify characters connected to your protagonist. Ideally, all the characters in your work are connected in some way to your protagonist. Your task is to identify those with the strongest connections, because they are the most likely to have something to gain or lose by your protagonist's success or failure. You can then go on to identify characters with weaker connections—characters that care less if your protagonist succeeds or fails.

If you find you have a novel full of minor characters that have no stake in your protagonist's success or failure, consider revising to consolidate or eliminate those characters. Remember that your novel is about your main character's struggle to achieve his goals; scenes or characters unrelated to that struggle belong somewhere else. For those characters who have only a weak connection to your main character's, consider strengthening the connection by tying their fate more closely to your protagonist's. You can use the stake-raising drills in this section to do so.

2. Choose sides. There's no neutrality or sitting on the sidelines here. Decide if the connected characters are supportive of or opposed to your protagonist. Think about what each has to gain or lose if your protagonist achieves his story and personal objectives. If a connected character only has intangibles (such as pride or status) at stake, then identify a tangible item that can represent the loss or gain. (Objectify the stakes just as you would objectify an objective.) In Shaara's *The Killer Angels*, the Confederate battlefield flag serves as a recognizable item the reader can easily associate with the intangible stakes of the battle. As you decide who is for your protagonist and who is against him, remember that more conflict leads to more interesting fiction; the more opponents a main character has, the more he has to overcome. Don't be afraid to stack the deck against your hero.

3. Eliminate the passive, but not the helpless. Anyone can be a victim, but good fictional victims have certain qualities that press down harder on your reader's emotional hot buttons. The ideal victim should make an attempt to save himself, but he should not be able to escape his fate without the successful intervention of your protagonist. The more innocent the potential victim, the better. Finally, while it's certainly acceptable to include multiple victims, your reader has to see those multiple victims as discernable individuals, not as a faceless number.

Remember, too, that you must start what you finish. Today's reader expects an emotionally satisfying resolution to the story. That doesn't necessarily mean a happy ending, but it does mean that the conflicts have to be worked through and characters' stories resolved. For example, if a character opposes your main character by spying on him and reporting his movements to a criminal gang, the conflict between your protagonist and that spy must be resolved by the end of the book. So, too, must the fate of potential victims be resolved.

Will your protagonist have enough time to prevent the innocent civilians from becoming victims? That depends on how much time you give him, and how much time you give him depends on the next drill.

RELATED DRILLS

Drill 3: No Sniveling Allowed
Drill 37: Put a Face on Evil
Drill 42: Take Three Steps to Story Line
Drill 91: Make a Logic Pass

DRILL 62

WIND UP THE CLOCK

One of the first tasks in military planning is to plan the use of available time. You can raise the tension quotient of your fiction by making that precious commodity less available to your characters. Put your characters under increasing time pressure—wind up the clock in your story.

Time is a powerful motivator, and too often the clock is not your friend—just ask any writer who is pounding out copy as her timepiece's digital numbers count up all too quickly toward a deadline. Time is a finite resource—neither you nor your main character can stall it, steal it, borrow it, or recover it once it's lost. Your readers know this, so putting your lead in a time crunch automatically raises the stakes and the tension in your work. If your mystery's heroine has only a day, then the stakes are much higher—there's no time to lose.

In novelist's boot camp, two general rules apply to time. First, in most fiction, time is linear—that is, your story starts on day one and ends after day one (on day nine, for example). Handle anything that is outside this normal flow of time—such as flashbacks, flash-forwards, and scenes or chapters that repeat the same sequence of time from different perspectives—very carefully. These should not be too plentiful.

Second, while you don't have to inform the reader of the passage of every hour, you do need to keep the reader generally oriented on how time is progressing. If you look across genres, you'll see novelists using subtle, almost generic time markers such as:

> The digital numbers counted down the remaining ten seconds.
>
> I checked my watch. I'd wasted two hours in the meeting.
>
> By Tuesday, it was clear there would be no ransom note.
>
> The winter snows came and went, giving way to the spring thaw.

Think of time not as *real* time but as *story* time—the amount of time, broken down into units, that covers your protagonist's pursuit of her objective. How much story time you use depends on the nature of your story and how your genre's readers commonly understand and process time. While some genres—action-adventure, thrillers, and most mysteries—are usually more time-crunch oriented, you can put any heroine in any genre under the (time) gun.

Clearly some stories take longer (in story time) than others. Some stories play out over days so the protagonist can fly back and forth between London to Sacramento. Others may require years for a young main character to come of age. While you should try to use the amount of story time that's most common in your genre, you should also try to use the minimum amount possible—the fewer hours or days, the better. After all, the tighter the time frame, the more pressure there is on your protagonist, the easier it is for your reader to conceptualize the span of the story, and the easier it is for you to keep your reader focused on the central issues.

Family sagas that span generations are no exception. Sagas don't chronicle every minute of every passing year. Sagas open windows on the

story of different generations of a family, and those windows can open for a few minutes, hours, or days, and close as years go by.

If your story takes place in one to two days, consider selecting a specific time span of twelve, eighteen, twenty-four, or forty-eight hours. Why? Not just because a specific time frame puts your characters (and you!) under more pressure, but because these time frames are commonly understood and so make your story's time line—and your story—easier for your reader to conceptualize. Robert Crais's *The Last Detective* makes wonderful use of a shortened time frame, and Greg Iles's crime thriller *24 Hours* (just one in a long line of books with this title) puts the time limit right in the title.

You must intuitively understand the blocks of time in your novel so you can put them to good use. Consider making a time line either before or while you create your scene list. This will help you identify key events, keep your chronology on track, and avoid many errors in logic.

The key to the effective use of time in your novel is to keep the overall length and smaller time units conceptually manageable. Keep the clock ticking by summarizing long stretches of time, planning or revising your novel to fit into a smaller amount of story time, and keeping your outcome and your heroine's success in doubt until the last possible moment.

And now it's time to move on to the next mission of the drafting phase, dialogue.

RELATED DRILLS

Drill 3: No Sniveling Allowed
Drill 37: Put a Face on Evil
Drill 42: Take Three Steps to Story Line
Drill 91: Make a Logic Pass

MISSION VII

SOUND OFF!

Let them hear it loud and proud: name, rank, and serial number!

From General George Patton's fiery speeches to the simple *Follow me!* shout of an infantry leader in battle, great military leaders lead with great words that complement their great deeds. Military leaders know that what they say and how they say it are instrumental in motivating fighting forces and leading them to victory.

This mission is all about writing better dialogue. Your characters' words are just as critical to your work's success as military leaders' words are to success on the battlefield. In fiction, nobody skips the dialogue. Your characters' words become tools or weapons in the struggle to achieve their objectives, and those words must show more than they tell. Review and practice the drills in this mission, and your characters will sound off in ways that can move your readers to sound off as well—about the riveting nature of your writing.

In this mission, you'll change your civilian way of thinking about dialogue and look at this critical, powerful tool in a new way. When should you practice these drills? Learn as you work by executing these drills as you go forward with your draft. Do the best you can with each drill, but don't worry if your results aren't perfect. You'll have several opportunities to improve your first rough attempts.

Ready? Move out and sound off!

MISSION VII

DRILL 63

LEARN HOW TO FAKE IT

Camouflage is a tool soldiers use to deceive and manipulate their enemies. Good camouflage doesn't just hide something—a truck, a tank, or an individual soldier. Instead it convinces the viewer that what is there is real and part of the scenery. In a sense, it alters reality.

In fiction, your dialogue works the same way. It's not a simple transcription of what people say or how they might say it. Just as camouflage is an imitation of real life, dialogue is an imitation of real speech.

Why must it be an imitation? Because real speech is, for the most part, deadly boring. Dialogue—good dialogue, boot-camp dialogue—is not. Listen to real speech at the next party you go to, when you're standing in line at a grocery store, or when you're sitting in a restaurant. The overwhelming majority of real dialogue is dull, drab, empty, and boring, filled with *uh*s, *well*s, *er*s, *like*s, mindless repetition, and long empty spaces.

Put speech like that in your novel and your reader will quickly lose interest. Besides, your reader can get that speech for free at the same places you got it. There's little motivation for your reader to pay—in the form of buying your book—for what he can get for free by eavesdropping in line at the convenience store.

Instead of thinking of dialogue as real speech, think of it as forged speech. Use your characters' objectives, personality points, speech markers, the given situation, and words to create dialogue. Through your tools, you'll create dialogue that is *like* the real speech, only better: a forgery that outshines the real thing. Your forged dialogue should be more intense, more emotional, more confrontational, and more interesting than real speech.

Ultimately, dialogue is a tool that your characters use to try to get what they want. There are many ways to use tools—you can pound, pry, smooth, cover up, slice, manipulate—and your characters can do all these things with the verbal tool known as dialogue.

Dialogue also makes a great weapon. Because your characters have differing objectives and contrasting personality points, conflict will naturally come out in their verbal exchanges; somebody must win, and somebody must lose. Your characters open their mouths because they want to win—to get what they want. How will a character in your story use words to get what he wants? That depends on the character's personality points, the situation, and the character or characters with whom he's fighting. A more manipulative character will use more manipulative language; an honest character's dialogue will be more honest.

Good dialogue begins not with techniques of writing, but with techniques of understanding—understanding how dialogue differs from real speech, understanding your characters and their personalities and goals, and understanding what you want to accomplish in a given scene.

Now you should understand that it's time to move on to the next drill.

RELATED DRILLS

Drill 3: No Sniveling Allowed
Drill 7: Drill Your Way to Success
Drill 33: Give Your Protagonist a Pointed Personality
Drill 49: Know the Unwritten Rules for Quality Drafting
Drill 87: Make a Dialogue Pass

MISSION VII

DRILL 64

DISPENSE WITH THE PLEASANTRIES

Wandering off course can be hazardous to the health of a military vessel in shallow waters or to a soldier patrolling near a minefield. Wandering off course isn't healthy for your dialogue, either.

Dialogue is most effective when it comes from characters' conflicting drives to achieve conflicting objectives. Dialogue manifests these objectives in words in the immediate scene—the here and now. Dialogue is much less effective when it digresses from the immediate conflict.

One such digression is a form of a trip into the past. It's a digression you want to avoid when you're drafting, and one you must hunt down and eliminate during revision. This digression is the *feather duster*. This term comes from a technique that was once common in English mystery stage plays. The purpose of the feather duster scene was to give the audience backstory. On stage, a feather duster scene begins when a maid (or butler, or cleaning lady, or housewife) arrives on stage to dust. The phone rings. The maid puts down her feather duster and answers. The audience listens in on the maid's side of the conversation until all the relevant—and irrelevant—background information is revealed. A feather duster scene is narrative backstory thinly disguised as dialogue. There are no characters with opposing needs and there is no conflict. The audience is simply being told background information.

In another type of unpleasant digression, characters restate information they already know purely to inform the reader.

> "Your brother called earlier," George said.
>
> Laura said, "You mean Bill, who has six kids by three wives?"
>
> "Yes," said George. "The connection was bad because he called from the train he has to take to and from work since quitting his job as an investment banker to become a tollbooth operator."

The sole purpose of this exchange is to give the reader information about Bill and his tribulations. Do George and Laura have needs? Yes. They appear to need to bore the reader to tears with background information masquerading as dialogue. These needs aren't in opposition and there's no conflict; the two characters work together to ensure boredom.

Let's make one point clear right now: Write dialogue to *show* your characters in conflict, using words as tools or weapons to get what they want. If you need to reveal backstory or convey other information to show the reader a character's personality or to set the mood or tone through dialogue, then do so in the course of verbal combat—not through a casual, emotionless exchange.

Do novelists write dialogue for the purpose of conveying information, showing emotion, or setting mood or tone? Yes, they do. They also write run-on sentences, create boring characters, forget to tie up loose ends, write pages of irrelevant description, and put in thirty pages of backstory before the first real crisis. You are never to do so.

But …

Never.

But ...

Never! Now drop and give me twenty.

Stay on target with your dialogue by keeping it in the here and now. And remember that good dialogue is primarily a tool your characters use to get what they want.

Now that you understand the primary function of dialogue, go to the next drill to see what else it can do for you.

RELATED DRILLS

Drill 3: No Sniveling Allowed
Drill 7: Drill Your Way to Success
Drill 28: Understand the Alpha Male Character's Motivations
Drill 29: Understand the Alpha Female Character's Motivations
Drill 33: Give Your Protagonist a Pointed Personality
Drill 87: Make a Dialogue Pass

DRILL 65

MAKE YOUR DIALOGUE MULTITASK

A military unit usually has a primary mission—the number-one thing it is to accomplish. However, it may also have secondary missions as well—things it's expected to accomplish as it fulfills the number-one obligation.

Dialogue works the same way. The primary mission of dialogue is to serve as a tool or weapon to help your characters get what they want. If your dialogue isn't working toward that mission, rework it or cut it altogether. If—and only if—your dialogue is accomplishing its primary mission, you can also assign it secondary missions. What else can dialogue do for you?

1. Dialogue can extend the action. You can extend and intensify a physical confrontation (or action scene) by interspersing lines of dialogue within the blow-by-blow account of the fight (or other action sequence). In doing so, you introduce verbal combat into the scene, extending the suspense and increasing conflict and tension.

2. Dialogue can convey needed information. As characters use words to get what they want, they can use information as a weapon. This information can be a chunk of backstory, information critical to what's happening in the moment, or information that one or more of your characters will use later. Dialogue can be used to sneak in clues crucial to a later scene, without signaling to the reader why the information is important. Take a look for yourself.

> [The homeless man] was unshaven again and the slight look of dementia was still in his eyes.
>
> "Your name is Faraday," Bosch said, as if speaking to a child.
>
> "Yeah, what about it, Lieutenant?"
>
> Bosch smiled. He had been made by a bum. All except for the rank.

"Nothing about it. I just heard that's what it was. I also heard you were a lawyer once."

"I still am. I'm just not practicing."

Michael Connelly doesn't spell out the significance of the information in this exchange between Detective Harry Bosch and a vagrant in *The Concrete Blonde*, but his readers file the information away, knowing that Connelly didn't just happen to write it.

3. Dialogue can break up description. Even a few strategically placed sentences of dialogue can add variety to long passages of description, whether that description is of a person, process, setting, or thing. In *The Concrete Blonde*, Detective Harry Bosch searches a suspect's apartment for more than an hour (and for five pages), cataloging and considering the implications of each item as he rifles through drawers and cabinets. Under time pressure, Bosch throws open a closet door, mistakes a foam ball holding a wig for an ambusher, and throws himself backwards. His weapon drawn, Bosch barks out, "Ray! That you?" These three words break up the pages of description and internal dialogue, providing a small but welcome bit of variety while keeping the tension high.

4. Dialogue can summarize past events or foreshadow future ones. In the interchange below, between Harry Bosch and a timid assistant district attorney, there's no doubt about what's going to happen, no doubt about what Harry Bosch wants, and no doubt about the forcefulness of Bosch's personality.

> "Then, when we get more evidence, if you are still attached to this case, you will file multiple counts under theories of linkage between the deaths. At no time will you worry about the so-called package you will hand off to the trial attorney. The trial attorney will make those decisions. Because we both know that you are really just a clerk, a clerk who files what is brought to him. If you knew enough to even sit in court next to a trial attorney you would not be here. Do you have any questions?"

"No," he said quickly.

"No, what?"

"No, ques—No, Detective Bosch."

Now *that* is an example of dialogue fulfilling its primary mission (to get a character what he wants) and knocking off a secondary mission as well.

Get more out of your dialogue by assigning it both a primary mission—to carry on the conflict as characters use it to get what they want—and secondary missions.

Now your primary mission is to turn the page to the next drill.

RELATED DRILLS

Drill 6: Toss Out Your Civilian Clothes
Drill 33: Give Your Protagonist a Pointed Personality
Drill 47: Plan Your Characters' Development
Drill 87: Make a Dialogue Pass

MISSION VII

DRILL 66

AIM FOR THE GUT

In rifle marksmanship, there's hitting the target and then there's hitting the bull's-eye. Both are hits, but a dead-center shot beats one that clips the outer edge any time.

When your characters ask and answer questions, they can either wield a clunky verbal blunderbuss or pull the trigger on a precision sniper rifle. In both instances, your characters' questions and answers are weapons, but to hit the conflict bull's-eye with your questions *and* with your answers, try the following.

1. Fire off specific questions, not general or rhetorical questions. When you use questions in your dialogue, go straight for the jugular. In a mystery novel, a question such as *Who would commit such a crime?* is too general. It invites an equally general answer, such as *A very evil criminal.* Does your reader know any more than she did before she read the exchange? No. Do twenty push-ups.

Questions have the potential to catalyze verbal conflict, but if a question is weak, the conflict is likely to be weak as well. A more specific and stronger question, such as *What makes you think this is a murder and not a suicide?* or *What makes you think this is the work of a disorganized serial killer?* gets right to the point and right to the details of the story—it hits the bull's-eye.

2. Fire off open-ended questions. A question that can be answered with a yes or no, such as *Did you have sex with that woman?* is closed. Closed questions can easily bring the question-and-answer interchange to a halt. An open-ended question, such as *How could you have had sex with that woman?* can help keep the interchange going by demanding more complex replies.

Closed questions are best used—and have the most power in—the final confrontation of your story. It's then you can deliver the answer to *Do you really love me?* or *Did you commit the crime?* not only with words, but with your story's climactic actions. If you must use a closed question elsewhere, make your reader wait as long as possible for the answer by making the question a cliffhanger as discussed in drill 54.

Which you clearly remember, isn't that right?

That question requires a yes or no answer. If your answer is no, don't hang yourself off a cliff. Just drop and give me fifty-four.

Some other situations—such as courtroom exchanges—may demand closed questions and yes-or-no answers. In such situations, mix it up (drill 82). Intersperse dialogue with description, action, and narration.

3. Fire off high-intensity questions, not gentle ones. *Where are you going?* is a low-intensity question. *Where the hell are you going?* and *Where did you get the stupid idea that you can just go out any time you please?* are high-intensity questions. High-intensity questions up the emotional ante in a scene very quickly.

As you're drafting, you may find that you initially write general, closed, or low-intensity questions but follow them with questions that are closer to the target, almost as if your characters (or you) are warming up for the real fight. While the general rule of drafting is to keep moving forward, don't be afraid to make an immediate improvement by deleting or crossing out questions that miss the mark. Skip the warm-up and get right to the guts of the conflict.

4. Fire back with a reply that doesn't answer the question. When a romance heroine asks "Do you love me?" have her reluctant—or devious—suitor reply "You know I care for you." Responses that simply don't answer the question demand that the conversation go further. Your reader wants an answer as much as your heroine does and will keep reading until she gets one. String them both along (like the dastardly suitor) by not answering.

5. Fire back with a lie. The truth may be stranger than fiction, but as an answer to a question it can be a dead end. A lie as an answer almost always provokes interest, especially if your reader, the character doing the questioning, or both know or suspect that the answer is a lie. Lies can raise interesting questions and lead both your reader and your characters down interesting paths to find that elusive truth (and the motivation behind the lie).

6. Fire back with a high-intensity response. One good *Where the hell are you going?* deserves a *Down to the bar to drink until I get drunk, and you can't do a damn thing about it!* response. If one character ups the emotional ante with a high-intensity question, have the character on the receiving end give back as good as she gets. The result will be a highly combative, highly emotional exchange.

Questions are powerful weapons, but to keep your dialogue on target, understand the difference between a near miss and a dead-center shot.

Now, to get your strong male character's dialogue on target fast, turn to the next drill.

RELATED DRILLS

Drill 31: Distinctly Mark Your Characters
Drill 63: Learn How to Fake It
Drill 64: Dispense With the Pleasantries
Drill 82: Mix It Up
Drill 87: Make a Dialogue Pass

DRILL 67

TALK LIKE A MAN

Military leaders are encouraged to develop what is called a command voice so they sound like leaders. If your male character is going to be the alpha male character, he'll have to sound like one. One of the most difficult challenges for a novelist is writing dialogue for an alpha male character without having that character come off like a brute. The key to meeting this challenge is leveraging stereotypical speech patterns to give your reader starting points for placing, defining, and understanding your strong male characters.

The external dialogue of your strong masculine characters should have several defining characteristics.

1. It should be more logical. Your alpha will be concerned with the hard facts and nothing but the hard facts. Consider this exchange from W.E.B. Griffin's World War II military thriller *Battleground*. Sergeant John Marston Moore has just translated a secret Japanese message that tells him the Japanese will starve American prisoners captured at Bataan—on what history now knows as the Bataan Death March. His superior, Lieutenant Pluto Hon, is a hardened operator and knows that, because the fact that the Americans have broken the Japanese code must be kept secret, the prisoners are doomed.

> Moore thought that over, and horrified, blurted, "Jesus, meaning, 'fuck the prisoners, they're beneath contempt, let them starve'?"
>
> "That's how I read it," Hon said. ...
>
> "My God!"
>
> "Why are you surprised?" Hon asked. "You grew up there. ...
>
> "I still can't accept this," he said. "Jesus Christ, can't we complain to the International Red Cross or somebody? Maybe they'd arrange to let us send food."
>
> "We cannot complain to anybody," Hon said. ...
>
> "We have their goddamned messages," Moore plunged on. "Why the hell not?"
>
> "In about ten seconds, that will occur to you."

DRILL 67

2. It should be more direct and decisive. Alpha males don't make requests or try to build a consensus. Alphas give orders, and they do so with the expectation that others will comply with their directives. Alphas also take orders without flinching, and they carry them out despite all obstacles. Yours should too, without complaint.

3. It should be more clipped and reserved. Silence can be extremely powerful, and your alpha is likely to show his strength and self-control by being taciturn. No matter what he thinks or feels, his sentences will be short, his words direct.

Are these characterizations of strong male speech stereotypical? Yes. Do they apply to real strong male characters? They can't, because *real characters* is a contradiction in terms. The debate about the validity of stereotypes aside, it's safe to say that your reader will pick up on these cues and place your character in the right box.

Remember, though, that your job as a novelist is to take the reader beyond that box. It's up to you to create the other parts, to make him more than a stereotype or caricature.

It's also up to you to keep your dialogue simple in order to keep it moving. Find out how to do that simply by turning the page.

RELATED DRILLS

Drill 6: Toss Out Your Civilian Clothes
Drill 28: Understand the Alpha Male Character's Motivations
Drill 63: Learn How to Fake It
Drill 87: Make a Dialogue Pass

DRILL 68

"KEEP IT SIMPLE," HE SAID

When it comes to both military plans and dialogue tags, simpler is better and less is more.

There are two kinds of dialogue, external and internal. External dialogue involves conversation between two or more characters. Internal dialogue (also known as internal monologue) is a character's thoughts. External dialogue is set off by quotation marks and relies on dialogue tags to identify the speakers. Internal dialogue is not set off by quotation marks; instead, it is italicized and/or identified by an attribution such as he thought.

There are two key techniques to make your external and internal dialogue seem natural and unforced.

1. Keep the attribution simple, and cut it when you can. An attribution is a phrase like *he said* that precedes or follows a line of dialogue and identifies who is speaking. When you are writing external dialogue, use *said* as your default instead of verbs and verb phrases like *chortled*, *spat out*, *hissed*, or *barked*. Make the actual words your character speaks demonstrate that character's state of mind. Give each character dialogue-related personality points and speech markers, and note these on your character cards.

Let's say you are writing dialogue between two characters—Nick and Kyla. Nick is authoritarian, combative, suspicious, and angry with Kyla. Kyla is an attractive southern belle who is also duplicitous, deceptive, and manipulative. Suppose that one night, Kyla comes home very late without calling. One way to write the beginning of this scene might be:

> Kyla walked past Nick without glancing his way.
>
> "Why are you late?" Nick demanded.

In this bit of dialogue, Nick's tone is implied through the use of *demanded*, but there's no emotion in the dialogue itself. Take a look at what happens when Nick's speech reflects his feelings.

> Kyla walked past Nick without glancing his way.
>
> "Stop right there and tell me just why in hell you are so damn late," Nick said.

There's no doubt now that Nick is angry—his words show his emotion. It's also clear Nick doesn't really want to know the answer; he wants to start a fight.

If there are only two characters in a scene or if the circumstances of the scene and the nature of the dialogue make it clear who's talking, you don't need to include an attribution tag with every line.

Attributing internal dialogue is a little bit trickier than attributing spoken dialogue, but the same general rules apply. Keep things simple using the attribution verb *thought* instead of *pondered*, *mused*, or *wondered*.

> Detective Johnson stared at the gun on the floor. *The killer left this here for a reason,* he thought.

Or, simply eliminate the attribution altogether.

2. Find the attribution's adverb and delete it. Adverbs modify verbs, and in the case of dialogue, they modify the verb in the attribution. But using adverbs in attributions *tells* the reader how the character said something instead of *showing* it. Again, make your characters' speech show the characters' emotional states and reveal their traits. In the example below, notice that the adverbs are not only unnecessary, they actually detract from the effect of the dialogue.

> Kyla walked past Nick without glancing his way.
>
> "Stop right there and tell me why in the hell you are so damn late," he said angrily.
>
> "Why, whatever makes you think I've been anyplace special?" she said coyly.

In this case, you don't need the adverb to tell the reader how Nick and Kyla felt when they said what they said—their feelings and personalities are clear from the language they use.

Adverbs also make your reader do double the work. If you use an adverb to tell how your character is speaking (instead of making it clear from the speech itself), your reader must read the characters' speech, then read the adverb, then reread the speech and mentally cast it in the tone the adverb provides. This doubling back interrupts the forward movement of your scene and story.

Keep your dialogue moving and enhance its feeling of authenticity by using *said* and *thought* as attributions. When you can, cut these attributions. And as a general rule, steer clear of more vivid verbs and adverbs in your attributions. When you write strong dialogue, you don't need to beat your reader over the head with colorful verbs and adverbs. However, you do need to give your dialogue a good beat(ing). To learn how, see the next drill.

RELATED DRILLS

Drill 2: Adopt a Principled Approach
Drill 7: Drill Your Way to Success
Drill 64: Dispense With the Pleasantries
Drill 87: Make a Dialogue Pass

DRILL 69

GIVE YOUR DIALOGUE A GOOD BEAT(ING)

Good military commanders know that one way to keep an enemy off balance is to vary the tactics used against him. One attack to seize an objective may come at dawn. The next attack may come in the form of troops descending from helicopters at last light. A third attack may begin with heavy artillery fire, then continue as troops enter under a thick cover of smoke.

Dialogue also benefits from variety. A good way to maintain your reader's interest is to insert a variety of beats into your dialogue. Beats are descriptions of physical action—minor or major—that fall between lines of dialogue. Use the following principles to spice up your dialogue with a variety of beats.

1. Use facial expressions. When a character raises an eyebrow or furrows his brow, this action (beat) interrupts the dialogue and telegraphs a change in the character's emotional state. As an exchange progresses and the emotional intensity rises—as the character's dissatisfaction grows into anger, for instance—a character might set his jaw, bite his lip, or narrow his gaze. His eyes may darken, his face may redden, his nostrils may flare, and so on. These are all conventional and commonly understood signs of anger. You can read a dozen clinical texts on which facial expressions most strongly signal which emotion, or you can watch a few good dramatic films or TV shows with the sound off. It won't take you long to see how the actors use facial expressions to signal emotion.

2. Have 'em talk with their hands. Characters can point, steeple their fingers, make a fist, pound a table, hold their hands up to surrender, cross their arms in front of themselves , throw up their hands in resignation or despair (although this gesture is much overused), or twiddle their thumbs (does anyone actually do that?). In a time when tobacco wasn't politically incorrect, characters took long drags on their cigarettes, puffed on their pipes, and blew smoke rings or chomped on the unlit stubs of their cigars. In the example below from the best-selling novel *Wonder Boys*, notice how author Michael Chabon instills movement and tension into the dialogue by focusing on what college student James Leer is holding.

> "It's a fake," said James Leer, holding out his hand to me, palm upward. Upon it lay a tiny silver pistol, a "ladies' model" with a pearl handle, no bigger than a deck of cards. "Hello, Professor Tripp."
>
> "Hello, James," I said. "I didn't know what you were doing out here."
>
> "It's my mother's," he said. "She won it in a penny arcade in Baltimore, in one of those machines with the claw. When she was in Catholic school. It used to shoot these little paper caps, but you can't find the right kind anymore."
>
> "Why do you carry it around?" I said, reaching for it.
>
> "I don't know." His fingers closed around the little gun and he slipped it back into the pocket of his overcoat. "I found it in a drawer at home and I just started carrying it around. For good luck, I guess."

3. Get 'em moving. Your characters can cross the room or push back from a desk or table to get physical and emotional distance from a heated conversation, intimate moment, or even another character. They can move in closer to become more threatening or more intimate, or to drive a point home. If a character puts a piece of furniture or some other object between himself and another character, that's a clear signal that he's blocking the other character—emotionally, physically, or intellectually, depending upon the nature of your scene. However, coming out from behind a piece of furniture or other object may not be a signal that all is right—it can signal an attack as well as a move to make peace. It's not hard to spot the building hostility in this exchange from Khaled Hosseini's debut novel, *The Kite Runner*.

> "Amir agha and I are friends," Hassan said. He looked flushed.
>
> "Friends?" Assef said, laughing. "You pathetic fool! Someday you'll wake up from your little fantasy and learn just how good of a friend he is. Now, *bas*! Enough of this. Give us that kite."

Hassan stooped and picked up a rock.

Assef flinched. He began to take a step back, stopped. "Last chance, Hazara."

Hassan's answer was to cock the arm that held the rock.

"Whatever you wish." Assef unbuttoned his winter coat, took it off, folded it slowly and deliberately. He placed it against the wall.

4. Don't forget the big stuff. If it's within your character's personality points, don't be afraid to have him take big actions—throw a fit, throw a plate, or throw a punch. And don't be afraid to skip the buildup if a character's personality demands it. For example, if a character has a hair-trigger temper, he may bypass any eyebrow-raising or jaw-setting and go straight to stomping around the room, kicking and breaking the furniture.

Make sure the various actions you choose to use are consistent with your character's traits and personality points. Every action should be a reflection of the character's objectives and emotions, and of the scene at hand. Don't have a character move just for the sake of moving. If your dialogue needs beats to break it up (and almost all dialogue does), insert the actions

that contribute to the scene and that reflect the characters' emotions and pursuit of their goals. When your character pauses in his dialogue to cross the room, have him cross it for a reason and cross it in a way that telegraphs his emotional state.

If your character seldom shows emotions, focus in on small details that show his emotions leaking out—a tightening around the corners of his eyes, a deliberate forcefulness in each step as he walks across the room, a tighter grip on a pen. Some scientists have called these tiny leaks of emotion microexpressions. You can call them microbeats if you like, but they are still strong indicators of emotion.

Beats make it easier for your reader to see and feel the emotion in your dialogue. You also want to make it easier for that reader to get to the emotion in your dialogue's words as well. To do that—well, you'll need the next drill.

RELATED DRILLS

Drill 33: Give Your Protagonist a Pointed Personality
Drill 71: Make Your Characters Try, Try Again
Drill 87: Make a Dialogue Pass
Drill 90: Make an Action Pass

DRILL 70

KNOW WHEN TO SAY *WELL*

Military boot camp trainees may have to run an obstacle course, but you don't want to put any obstacles in front of your reader—and that includes awkward, mind-numbing dialogue. If dialogue wastes time and stops or delays your novel's progress toward resolving the conflict, it must be cut, pared down, or rewritten. Remember, too, that your dialogue is a verbal expression of your willful characters trying to get something critically important to them. Your characters don't want to wait through an unnecessary conversation, and neither do your readers.

To more quickly get to the conflict in your dialogue, cut the niceties, cut the fillers, and cut the echoes.

1. Cut the opening niceties. In real speech, we open most conversations with introductions and small talk. In fiction, these introductions and small talk do nothing but get in the way.

> "Good morning, Sam."
>
> "Morning, Wally."
>
> "How are you?"
>
> "Fine. Nice looking day today, isn't it?"
>
> "Very nice. How's the family?"
>
> "Well, thank you."
>
> Sam and Wally may soon reveal their needs in conflict, but why wait? Cut the niceties and get to it.
>
> "Good morning, Sam."
>
> "It would be, if I didn't have to look at your backstabbing face so early."

There's no waiting and no doubt at all what the conflict is here.

2. Cut the pauses to think. In real speech, we use filler words or sounds to buy time to think about what to say next.

"Ah, what's the status of the Corbin Project," said Al.

"Well," said Linda, "there are serious problems."

"Uh, that's not satisfactory. I told you I wanted that project straightened out by now."

In dialogue, *well*, *ahem*, *ah*, *uh*, *er*, *you see*, *now*, and like words dilute the conflict and get in the way of its progression. If your character needs time because she is under pressure or doesn't want to talk, have that character do something that signals her need to stall or her reluctance to answer.

"What's the status of the Corbin Project?" said Al.

Linda bit her lip and looked down at the floor. An eternity of tense seconds passed.

"There are serious problems."

"Unsatisfactory. I told you I wanted that project straightened out by now."

Now the conflict is more intense, the action moves much faster, and we know Linda is in hot water.

3. Cut the echoes. Real speech is full of echoes. We use them to ensure understanding, to buy time to form a reply, or to continue a conversation.

> Pat said, "I went to see Fred today."
> "You saw Fred, did you?" said Lois.
> "Yes, I saw Fred. We talked about the Jackson case."
> "You discussed the Jackson case? With Fred? Whatever for?"

Rewriting to delete the echoes and to foreground the conflict yields a much more intense passage.

> "I saw Fred today," Pat said. "We talked about the Jackson case."
> "You had no right to do that," said Lois.

Give your readers what they want—characters in conflict fighting with their words—and give it to them fast. Use echoes, fillers, and niceties in your draft if you must to prime your writing, just make sure you take them out before they drag down your reader.

In boot camp, if you had to be told something three times before you got it, you'd be doing push-ups instead of reading this. When it comes to dialogue, however, three is a good number. Understand why by reading the next drill—at least three times.

RELATED DRILLS

Drill 7: Drill Your Way to Success
Drill 33: Give Your Protagonist a Pointed Personality
Drill 67: Talk Like a Man
Drill 87: Make a Dialogue Pass

DRILL 71

MAKE YOUR CHARACTERS TRY, TRY AGAIN

Three on a march may have very negative effects—especially for soldiers facing a sniper, but three tries during dialogue can lead to some interesting scenes.

Now that you understand that dialogue is spoken conflict, it's time to zero in on how to get the conflict started, how to keep it going, and how to end it. At the same time, you want to ensure you have an interesting mix of dialogue, action, and description that entertains the reader as the conflict goes on.

To get and keep the fight going, you'll want to go around a couple of times (or three) and mix up (three) different kinds of writing.

1. Make three tries. Your characters want their objectives so badly they won't take no for an answer. If at first they don't succeed (and they shouldn't, because your story is more interesting if they don't), they should feel compelled to try, try again. As a general rule, have your character try three different times to get what he wants. And, while these three different ways should be consistent with the character's personality, remember that your character has access to all the emotions available to any person. When your character gets stymied, he has the capability to switch methods. In this short telephone exchange from W.E.B. Griffin's *Battleground*, Marine Corps Colonel Rickabee responds definitively to the stalling tactics of his reluctant subordinate, Major George Dailey.

> "I want you to catch a train as soon as you can, Major, and come down here, . . ." [Rickabee said.]
>
> "Sir, would . . . day after tomorrow be all right?"
>
> "I'm talking about this afternoon."
>
> "Sir, that would be difficult. I have a . . .
>
> "Get your ass on a train and get down here this afternoon, Major," Colonel Rickabee said, and then hung up.

Rickabee has to repeat his original request twice—each time getting more specific and more direct—but in the end there's no doubt that Dailey is going to obey. Rickabee cuts off further debate by punctuating this exchange with a beat—he hangs up the phone. Note that Dailey is also trying to get what *he* wants, so he repeats his attempt to wiggle out of complying with Rickabee's order.

Be wary of verbal conflict solely for verbal conflict's sake. Constant fighting over conflicting objectives and emotional needs makes for interesting dialogue. Constant fighting just for conflict's sake makes for a whining aggravation—just ask anyone who has raised a two-year-old or a teenager, or any boot camp instructor who has heard excuses as to why a trainee could not do more push-ups. Make sure that your conflict-conveying dialogue is in line with your character's objectives and that you don't overuse the three-tries technique.

2. Mix three things. Screenwriters have a rule of thumb: There should be no more than three sides (a side being one back-and-forth exchange between two characters) of dialogue before there's some kind of major action or change in the scene. While this is not a hard and fast rule, it is a good guide for you as you draft the verbal conflict in your scenes.

Just as powerful is an option not available to screenwriters—an expansion of the technique of adding beats. This expansion consists of mixing dialogue, action, and description. In novelist's boot camp, we'll call it DAD.

When you write dialogue, you want to give your reader a smorgasbord of stimulation. Intersperse your characters' spoken conflict with action and description that are relevant to the verbal conflict that's taking place. In the scene below—also from Griffin's *Battleground*—a woman reluctantly sees her man yanked off to war for a secret and priority mission.

> The horn on the MP car blew.
>
> "Shit," he said.
>
> He walked out of her bedroom ... and began stuffing his belongings into his seabag.

"Is there anything I can do to help?"

"I can handle it," he said. ...

... He reached inside [his waistband] ... and came out with a Colt .45 and four extra magazines. ...

"I decided I needed that pistol more than one of the classified documents messengers," he said. "So I signed it out before I left the basement. If they come looking for it, send them to Guadalcanal."

My God, he really is going to the war! He is too beautiful to be killed!

She stepped into the room and closed the door after her.

She walked up to him and put her hand on his cheek, then raised her head and kissed him lightly on the mouth.

"You think they'll wait another five minutes, Baby? ... "

This passage combines dialogue, action, description, and interior thought. The possible combinations are endless, but they all serve one purpose—to entertain your reader by enriching the verbal conflict of your dialogue.

Enough talk! Let's get some action going! Start with a powerful, decisive action—turn the page to the next mission.

RELATED DRILLS

Drill 18: Find Your Character in Events, Places, and Concepts
Drill 31: Distinctly Mark Your Characters
Drill 47: Plan Your Characters' Development
Drill 67: Talk Like a Man
Drill 87: Make a Dialogue Pass

MISSION VIII

EXECUTE SHOCK AND AWE

Combat is hours of preparation, some of it tedious. Combat is hours of nervous waiting, followed by a flood of adrenaline. Combat is mere minutes—sometimes only seconds—of violence, deafening roars of exploding munitions, and life-or-death struggles. Combat is immensely powerful moments of organized chaos that sear in memories that last a lifetime. Combat is action with life-and-death consequences, and combat is often difficult for veterans to relate.

The action in your manuscript must be the same, only you don't have the option to remain taciturn. As you write your draft, your action scenes must give your reader the intense feel of being there, the roller coaster ride of conflict in which success or failure hinges on every action. Your action must remove the wait and the tedium and compress the hours, while simultaneously extending the minutes and seconds for many, many pages.

All genres, from romance to literary fiction, have some degree of action in them. Whether your novel is more character-driven than plot-driven or the other way around, you're still writing a story in which characters are set in motion toward their objectives.

This mission's two drills focus on how to write compelling, high-intensity scenes centered on a violent physical confrontation, but the techniques are applicable to any action scene: car crash, fist fight, domestic argument, cliff-scaling, face-to-face altercation, sports contest, and so on.

As you write your draft, take action to make your action feel real. The drills that follow will tell you how.

DRILL 72

FIND THE DEVIL IN THE DETAILS

Ask any soldier who's ever stood inspection and had his dress uniform scrutinized by a fastidious first sergeant—attention to detail is important. For a novelist writing an action scene, attention to detail is important as well. If you pay close attention and use those details well, you can extend the life of those action scenes and raise the level of excitement in your reader.

Good action scenes are great—they get a reader's heart rate up, make his hands tremble as he compulsively turns pages, and make him collapse in exhaustion when the tension passes.

But the problem with action is that it's so active—it just happens too fast. Fights, escapes from burning buildings, car chases, desperate attempts to destroy a monster, air combat, and other high-tension action scenes last only scant seconds in reality. Yet a fast reality makes for poor fiction, while slow scenes make for a bored reader.

You don't want to slow down the action scenes in your novel; you want to stretch out the amount of time your reader spends experiencing those heart-pounding thrill rides. One effective way to do so is to shift focus to the details of (or surrounding) the action and to your character's thoughts, then shift back to the larger action itself. Focusing on descriptive details—sights, sounds, smells, tastes, and thoughts—keeps your reader caught up in the moment's tumult longer and pulls him deeper into the given scene and the story at large.

In this scene from James Patterson's *Pop Goes the Weasel*, detective Alex Cross swims in open water in pursuit of a deranged killer named Shafer.

> I swam harder, trying to gain some sea on Shafer. The boats were still a good way away. He was still going strong, though. No sign of tiring.
>
> I played a mind game of my own. I stopped looking to see where he was. I concentrated only on my own stroke. There was nothing but the stroke; the stroke was the whole universe.

My body was feeling more in sync with the water, and I was buoyed as it got deeper. My stroke was getting stronger and smoother.

I finally looked. He was starting to struggle. Or maybe that was just what I *wanted* to see. Anyway, it gave me a second wind, added strength.

What if I actually caught him out here? Then what? We'd fight to the death? . . .

The closest boat was no more than a hundred, a hundred and fifty yards away.

"*Cramp!*" he called out. "Bad one!" Then Shafer went under.

It's important to note that you have to keep shifting the focus back to the physical confrontation to maintain the action—after all, it is an action scene. That physical confrontation doesn't have to be hand-to-hand combat—it can be a mountaineer's struggle against an avalanche, a firefighter's battle against a blaze, or a stock car racer's high-speed duel with his rival through the last turn. A good action scene will have an almost rhythmic arrangement of more general action and descriptive detail, and could include shifts in point of view and perspective as well.

Stretch your action scenes by weaving description from your five senses into your fast-paced critical moments and you'll not only keep the scene going, you'll sustain your reader's interest and heart rate.

Of course, one way to keep that heart rate up is to just slow down. To find out what that means, turn to the next drill.

RELATED DRILLS

Drill 16: Know the Terrain
Drill 21: Forge Your Setting
Drill 73: Go to Time-and-a-Half
Drill 79: Zoom In and Out
Drill 90: Make an Action Pass

DRILL 73

GO TO TIME-AND-A-HALF

Veterans will tell you that in combat, events sometimes unwind in a kind of slow motion. That's good information for a novelist writing action scenes.

You see, even when you extend the scene by shifting focus to the details of the action, then back to the larger action itself, you may find your action scene ends sooner than you desire. After all, if your main character is in a life-or-death situation, you'd like that ride to last more than a few paragraphs—and so would your reader.

That said, you don't want to slow down the action scenes in your novel—who wants to write (or read) a scene that moves slowly? Instead of slowing down the action, slow down time and come in close. Just as if you had filmed your action scene and were replaying a part of it in slow motion, describe selected parts of your action scenes in slow motion. When you do, you'll naturally focus on the details of what's happening and extend the action.

As an example, let's look at a scene from my own military action-adventure novel *The Best Defense*. In this scene, Victor (a hulking, brutal killer) has critically wounded Valerie's love interest, Mark. As Mark lies helpless nearby, direly in need of medical attention, Victor turns on Val-

erie. Victor is twice her weight and strength, but she must defeat Victor in mortal hand-to-hand combat to save the life of her lover.

In reality, this fight would be over quickly. But you can use the slow-motion technique to extend the action and the experience.

Victor's eyes burned with rage. He towered over her, bigger, stronger, faster.

He lunged for her throat.

Spin, high block. Barely missed. She was off her game.

Punch. Left block. *Punch*. Right block. *Combination punches*. Blocked, blocked, one connected.

The wind went out of her. She backed up.

She flashed in, kicked Victor dead center. He took it and shook it off.

Val backed off.

A half-conscious Mark rolled onto his side and moaned.

"To save yourself, he dies," Victor said.

Val glanced down at Mark.

Victor charged, knocked her arms out of the way, grabbed her throat.

She tugged at his iron grip, punched his face, kneed his groin.

He tightened his hold, brought his face inches from hers.

Almost out of air.

Her hand slid down to her belt, fumbled with the snaps, lost the grip, slipped, found it again.

Victor grinned, squeezed.

"How does it feel," Victor said, "to look into the eyes of your executioner?"

She jerked her switchblade from its belt sheath. Squeezed the handle, pushed the button. She felt the blade shoot out, metal sliding against metal. The knife bucked ever so gently as its blade locked into position.

She brought her arm up, her vision growing dimmer as he ratcheted the life out of her, her thorax and neck bones crunching in his grip.

She rammed the knife into his neck, twisted it left. His blood spurted into her eyes. He held his grip as he fell back, pulling her down with him. She landed on top of him, face to face.

She pushed the blade in harder. His eyes bulged. The vise of his fingers loosened. She sucked in precious air.

Blood frothed out of his mouth. He died staring at her.

Val rolled off him, caught her breath.

"It feels like that."

A slow motion replay naturally extends the action, but it can also turn fairly simple actions into complicated exposition. In reality, a kick is a simple action made of up of dozens of complex submovements. In fiction, *Tom hits Sam, then Sam kicks Tom* is easy. However, the slow-motion verbal replay of each character's movements, body language, and twists and turns is difficult. You may find it helpful to draw out a time line of the small submovements and actions that make up each character's action and reaction.

Remember, too, that actions such as *Tom hits Sam, then Sam kicks Tom* are more overlapping than sequential. That is, as Tom gets ready to hit Sam, Sam may see it coming and flinch. As Tom's fist flies from feet to inches away from Sam, Sam may already be setting up his kick. And as Sam kicks Tom, Tom may be pulling his fist back to give Sam another smack.

Extend your action scenes by replaying that scene in slow motion. Include those many critical, small actions that make up a complex movement, and include them so they represent the nonlinear nature of human interaction. You'll find your action is more engaging to your reader and more exciting to write.

Describing action is a challenge. Describing people, places, and things is a challenge as well. Learn how to meet that challenge in your next mission.

RELATED DRILLS

Drill 16: Know the Terrain
Drill 21: Forge Your Setting
Drill 72: Find the Devil in the Details
Drill 79: Zoom In and Out
Drill 90: Make an Action Pass

MISSION IX

UTILIZE STEALTH TECHNIQUES

A good soldier knows how to use the terrain to his advantage. Soldiers use stealth techniques to keep from being observed until they can get close enough to have an impact—usually a deadly one. New recruits learn to camouflage themselves, how to blend in with the surrounding landscape so as not to betray their presence or intentions, and how to quietly get close to their objective while remaining undiscovered. Their target won't see the shooter, but it will feel the impact of the shot.

As a novelist, you have the mission of describing the people, places, and things in your story to the reader. But you don't want to be too obvious about it. Your goal is to keep your description from being observed, while still allowing it to have a powerful impact. You can use your senses, along with a variety of techniques provided in this section, to secretly, quietly, and stealthily get close to your reader.

This section offers several drills that will enhance your ability to describe people, places, and things. You may think of yourself as a camera, presenting snapshots of scenes in your book to the reader. Taking these mental pictures is a good, basic way to think about description, but it's only a start. To get the most from description, go beyond the camera concept and, as the drills later in this mission explain, modify that picture to suit a particular need. Then add to that modified picture by using your other senses. The result will be description that truly shows—with all the senses—instead of tells. Then you can be proud of your description because it will allow you to accomplish your mission as a writer just as effectively as stealth techniques help a soldier to accomplish his mission.

DRILL 74

DO MORE WITH DESCRIPTION

An experienced soldier knows how to make one tool perform several functions. For example, a soldier's poncho keeps the water off, makes a good sunshade in the desert, will snap closed to sleep in, and can be made into a raft to float gear across a stream.

Description works the same way. Although description's number-one job is to enhance the emotional content of a scene, description can serve several other purposes.

1. Description can set time and place. Need to signal to your reader that your story is set in nineteenth-century England? Then your description of a deserted street would include street lanterns instead of street lights, cobblestone paving instead of asphalt, and the distant clomp of a horse's hooves instead of the roar of an engine.

2. Description can set genre. Your description of the deserted street will be much different if you're writing a war novel instead of a romance. If your heroine is a female werewolf stalked by demons from the netherworlds, the long, vacant block will require yet a different description.

3. Description can set worldview. Suppose your main character has a cynical, negative, and generally suspicious view of the world. That worldview will color everything she sees, hears, and touches, and it will also shade your description. For example, as your protagonist looks down the street and sees a mother shooing her children inside, she might wonder where the father is. If one of the children has a cut, bump, or bruise, your character might see the small wounds as marks of abuse. When the father arrives a few seconds later, your character might look for signs of guilt on his face and wonder if those signs signal that his lateness is do to a secret affair.

Whatever point of view you choose for your novel, that narrator's views and understanding of the world should flavor how she describes what happens around her.

4. Description can foreshadow coming events. Your description can hint at what's unseen but looming around the corner. Put a happy couple on a deserted beach, then put heavy, dark clouds in the distance, and you'll clue in the reader to the fact that, despite the present serenity, something ominous is just a short time away.

5. Description can assist in characterization. Character markers are those details of clothing, appearance, mannerism, and speech that activate your reader's preconceived understandings and signal what kind of person a character is. Your description of a character's clothing, for instance, can help the reader quickly understand the nature of the character. Details are crucial here. If you put a middle-aged man in a rumpled corduroy jacket with leather patches on the elbows and give him a pipe, you have a college professor. Put the same man in an oil-stained leather biker jacket and give him a single skull-and-crossbones earring, and your reader will have a completely different understanding of the character.

6. Description can set point of view. Description can also signal your reader that a point-of-view shift has taken place, and so eliminate the potential for reader confusion. Imagine you're writing a scene in which a villain pursues his victim through the passages of a deserted castle, and you want to alternate back and forth between the points of view of the villain and the victim. Your reader would see the villain's determination, the victim's terror, the villain's increasing confidence as he closes in, the victim's increasing panic and desperation as she runs out of options, and so on. You'll want to do this back-and-forth movement with as little attribution as possible in order to keep the pace fast and the tension level high.

Each of these two characters sees the same castle walls, floors, ceilings, and stairs; feels the same cold, damp air; hears the same rats scurrying and the same thunder outside; and smells the same musty odors. Yet each will react to these stimuli differently, and how you describe those reactions will tell the reader that she's reading the victim's story, then the villain's, then the victim's.

7. Description can establish credibility and authenticity. While your reader is turning the pages of your novel, you want her to feel like she's in the world you've constructed. Is your story set in Baghdad in 1405? If so, you'll want to salt your story with critical details unique to that time and place in order to lend the setting authenticity. If you want your reader to believe your police procedural, you can describe selected technical details about arrests, jails, fingerprinting methods—anything that puts your reader in the process of your investigation.

Keep in mind that description can be the *wrong* tool for the job. It's not the most efficient method for carrying the story forward, and it is not necessarily ideal for hooking the reader's attention. Remember, too, that overuse of any tool leads to that tool becoming dull and eventually breaking.

Any discussion of description should include a discussion of setting. You dealt with setting on a novel-wide (or macro) scale earlier. Now see what small-scale setting can do for you. Where? In the next drill.

RELATED DRILLS

Drill 7: Drill Your Way to Success
Drill 21: Forge Your Setting
Drill 52: Win the First Battle
Drill 76: Know That You Are Not a Camera
Drill 88: Make a Description and Narration Pass

DRILL 75

USE MICRO SETTING FOR MAXIMUM IMPACT

When a soldier is under fire, it doesn't matter if he's in Afghanistan or Albuquerque. What matters are his immediate surroundings—that he's in a secure, deep fighting position and not sitting on an open field.

A character's immediate surroundings also matter a great deal, so don't let these micro settings just happen. Instead, carefully select these small-scale settings to get the maximum emotional impact.

Micro settings are scene specific. Like macro settings, they have a geographic place and time frame, but they're much more limited. You can describe scene settings in your novel in the same manner that screenwriters describe the setting of a particular scene in a screenplay: interior or exterior, day or night, and the kind of space the scene fills.

Some of these spaces are more emotionally charged than others. For example, consider how the following micro settings can enhance certain effects.

Setting (Space or Location)	Effect
elevators, crowded subways, very small rooms, basements, stairwells	claustrophobia, sense of being trapped, helplessness
bedrooms, bathrooms, hotel rooms	sexual tension
well-lit living rooms, kitchens, front porches, open front yards	friendship without sexual tension, a familial feel
back porches, closed-door offices, old bars	scheming, underhandedness, deception
large apartments or lofts in tall buildings, spacious offices in skyscrapers, elegant houses with extra-large, mostly empty rooms	wealth, splendor, opulence, greed, overindulgence

In general, the more confining the micro setting, the more tension the setting introduces. However, cars and generic bars and restaurants do little to add to a scene, so get your characters out of vehicles and eateries.

In the following example from Alice Sebold's best-selling debut novel *The Lovely Bones*, the fourteen-year-old narrator, Suzie, describes the underground hole built by her neighbor, Mr. Harvey, with ominous precision.

> I can still see the hole like it was yesterday, and it was. Life is a perpetual yesterday for us. It was the size of a small room, the mud room in our house, say, where we kept our boots and slickers and where Mom had managed to fit a washer and dryer, one on top of the other. I could almost stand up in it, but Mr. Harvey had to stoop. He'd created a bench along the sides of it by the way he'd dug it out. He immediately sat down.
>
> "Look around," he said.
>
> I stared in amazement, the dug-out shelf above him where he had placed matches, a row of batteries, and a battery-powered fluorescent lamp that cast the only light in the room—an eerie light that would make his features hard to see when he was on top of me.

When you're planning your novel, use the micro level setting to maximize interest and emotional impact. Just as run-of-the-mill characters make for ho-hum reading, so does a run-of the-mill setting.

Now that you see micro setting in a different way, it's time to see description in a different way as well. No matter if your characters are in a confining elevator or designer loft on the forty-fourth floor, turn the page to the next drill.

RELATED DRILLS

Drill 30: Make Your Protagonist Act Like a Dog
Drill 69: Give Your Dialogue a Good Beat(ing)
Drill 72: Find the Devil in the Details
Drill 88: Make a Description and Narration Pass

DRILL 76

KNOW THAT YOU ARE NOT A CAMERA

In mission seven, you tossed out your civilian way of thinking about dialogue. Now it's time for you to do the same with description—stash your civilian ideas about description in your wall locker. Just as you are not simply a tape recorder when it comes to dialogue, you are not a camera when it comes to description.

Good description is not a word photo of what you see. It is different from a photograph-like word picture in two critical ways.

1. Good description is selective, much more than a snapshot of setting. Good description can't afford to be just a snapshot, because a snapshot wouldn't convey what you want your readers to hear, touch, taste, and smell. It also can't be accurate and complete, because accurate and complete reality is often boring. We see, hear, feel, taste, touch, and smell countless things in our daily lives. Most of these we ignore or promptly forget. You don't want your reader to ignore and promptly forget the description in your novel.

Good description is something you craft from the many details available in reality. Just as you cut, prune, shape, invent, and rewrite dialogue, you must carefully develop your description. When you're done with your dialogue, what you have is counterfeit speech that feels more authentic than real speech. When you're done with your description, what you have is an invented, counterfeit perception—using all the senses—of reality that feels more real than reality itself.

2. Good description has a purpose (or purposes) other than description. Description is not an end in itself; you don't write a sentence, paragraph, or passage with the single goal of providing description. The purpose of fiction is to cause the reader to have an emotional experience. Description is just one more tool for achieving that purpose and carrying out your responsibilities as an author.

Like good dialogue, good description is something you invent to enhance the reader's emotional experience of your story. Good description feels more real, more exciting, and more interesting than reality. To fake it even better, make your description personal. But when you do, remain objective about it. To see how to do both, go on to the next drill.

RELATED DRILLS

Drill 21: Forge Your Setting
Drill 69: Give Your Dialogue a Good Beat(ing)
Drill 79: Zoom In and Out
Drill 88: Make a Description and Narration Pass

DRILL 77

"STONEWALL" YOUR DESCRIPTION

Legendary Confederate general Thomas Jackson got his nickname, "Stonewall," from his troops' performance in battle—his soldiers were said to have stood like a stone wall. When you give the traits of stone walls (or other objects) to humans, you are using a powerful description technique—objectification. When you give the traits of humans to objects, you're using personification. Both of these time-tested descriptive techniques help establish an emotional connection with your reader, and both have a place in your novel.

Personification is the attribution of human qualities to an animal, object, or idea. Those qualities can be actions, thoughts, feelings, habits, or appearances: two oak trees *standing like sentries* in front of a forbidding castle; the sky *changing its mind* from sunny to cloudy and back again, then *growing angry* as thunderclouds roll in. As your protagonist struggles through a swamp at night, the thick foliage might *reach out with gnarled fingers* of roots and vines to bar his way. A once-dismissed theory of who committed your mystery's murder might *take on new life and energy, almost as if it had a mind of its own* when your protagonist uncovers new evidence.

Objectification is the act of representing an abstract idea or principle as a physical thing. Seeing only a person's physical attributes and not the person that he is inside can also be called objectification. Character markers are often used to objectify characters, especially minor ones you don't wish to spend much time or space on. A mobster's wise-guy henchman can be all bulging muscle beneath his silk jacket, and a street corner working girl could be objectified by thickly painted lips, almost-bare breasts, and a mini-skirted bottom.

As with most descriptive techniques, the overuse of personification and objectification can leave a bad taste in your reader's mouth. They are seasonings—go lightly, because a little goes a long way. When you edit your work, you may find you've added too much of these spices to the mixture of your manuscript. If so, you can simply delete the offending lines or rewrite them using the other techniques of description discussed in this section.

Don't limit yourself only to visual imagery when you use personification or objectification. Taste, touch, smell, and sound all have compelling associations and connotations. These senses are also habitually underused, so invoking them in your work offers an opportunity to create something fresh and interesting. Instead of giving a character a heart of stone, how about giving her a personality with all the warmth of fingernails on a blackboard?

Some of the most well-known uses of personification and objectification are some of the oldest clichés, and you'll want to avoid those: *cold as ice, sad skies, tired houses*. Often, you'll find that you write these clichés when you're drafting. While you want to keep making progress toward finishing your draft, take a moment to rework or update such clichés. If you get stuck, simply write the cliché, mark it, and move on. You'll rework it when you're editing.

You can also throw a few hand grenades into your work. See what these explosive devices have in common with description in the next drill—but keep your head down!

RELATED DRILLS

Drill 2: Adopt a Principled Approach
Drill 69: Give Your Dialogue a Good Beat(ing)
Drill 88: Make a Description and Narration Pass
Drill 96: Focus Your Editing and Proofreading

DRILL 78

LOB A HAND GRENADE

Today's hand grenades are modern versions of a weapon that is several hundred years old. Thrown correctly, a grenade will put a large explosion in just the right place. However, if you pull the pin and drop the grenade, it'll blow up in just the wrong place.

Similes and metaphors are like grenades—they are two of the oldest and most used descriptive techniques. They're powerful, but you must use them carefully to avoid clichés, mixed metaphors, and figures of speech that just don't work. Otherwise, they'll blow up in the wrong place—your novel.

Similes and metaphors are figures of speech that refer to one thing in terms of another in order to give the first item the literal or connotative meanings of the second. A simile expresses a resemblance between two unlike items or ideas and is formed with the word *like* or *as*. In a metaphor, a word or phrase that typically implies one thing is used in the place of another word or phrase to suggest a likeness or analogy between two items or ideas. A metaphor normally doesn't use the word *like* or *as* in its comparison.

There are two crucial points to keep in mind when creating similes and metaphors in your fiction.

1. **Writers have used these powerful figures of speech so much that they've generated several cargo ships' worth of clichés.** You may want to use similes and metaphors to send your reader on an emotional roller coaster, so you'll throw in everything but the kitchen sink, thinking that writing metaphors and similes is a piece of cake and that your reader will think you're as cool as a cucumber and that you rule the roost as a novelist. But what will really happen will be as different as night and day. Instead, you'll feel like you've been run over by a Mack truck when your reader puts your book down in disgust. You'll leave that reader hungry as a horse for fresh writing. Your reader will think

that your writing is as phony as a three-dollar bill and that you're out to lunch. You'll suffer every writer's worst nightmare and miss your window of opportunity to connect with the reader. Instead of batting a thousand, you'll strike out, go down for the count, and the writing will be on the wall. … Had enough yet? Good. You get the point, then.

2. **Be careful that the concepts in your similes and metaphors really do work together.** When the two concepts in your figure of speech don't mesh, the result is what's called a mixed metaphor. Your reader's reaction to a mixed metaphor can be laughter, confusion, or a headache. Normally you wouldn't want to mix your metaphors on purpose, but if laughter, confusion, and headaches are the reactions you're trying to elicit, mix away. (Some comedians have made memorable careers of mixing metaphors in just that way.) You can have a character mix his metaphors or pour out clichés like a waterfall to help characterize him as comedic, confused, shallow, or insincere.

When it comes to similes and metaphors, understand that these powerful tools are more complex than they look. Feel free to use clichéd similes and mixed metaphors in your draft as points of departure; but, when you begin editing, hunt them down like escaped convicts. Use similes and metaphors sparingly, because a little goes a long way.

Like grenades, similes and metaphors are powerful when used correctly and devastating when they're not. You don't want to be close to a grenade—or a metaphor—when it explodes. However, you do need to move in close and see what's ahead in the next drill. Turn the page.

RELATED DRILLS

Drill 34: Open a Window to Your Character
Drill 76: Know That You Are Not a Camera

DRILL 79

ZOOM IN AND OUT

In military boot camp, recruits are required to do things ordinary people aren't—march twelve miles in full combat gear; negotiate obstacle courses; endure hunger, thirst, and physical discomfort—all to ensure they can go beyond normal limits to accomplish the mission.

In novelist's boot camp, you have to go beyond the normal as well—at least in your description. To make a significant emotional impact on your reader, your description must go beyond what you normally see. It must show the reader your fictional world in new ways.

Sight is the sense novelists most commonly use in description, and use of that sense is almost mandatory. Showing what a person, place, or thing looks like is a minimum requirement; your reader needs you to paint a word picture of what's happening.

But visual description carries with it three problems. First, it's difficult to do much that hasn't already been done. Second, because the reader expects a visual description, that description won't stand out—simple visual description is almost taken for granted. Third, visual description lacks staying power. Studies have shown that visual impressions in the brain are generally more transitory and are more readily forgotten than input from other senses.

To make your visual description more interesting and memorable, you'll need to change how your reader sees what you're showing him by zooming in with your imaginary camera. Start by describing an object (or person, or setting) from a distance, then get closer, then get very close. How far away and how close? The degree to which you use this technique depends on the specific setting, your genre, and your plot. Kick-start your imagination with the guidelines below, but modify them to fit your own work.

The first time your character sees an object, it should be far enough away so as not to be completely distinguishable but close enough to give off the general qualities or feelings you want it to have. For example, perhaps your hero can make out the individual towers of a castle in the distance, but he can't quite tell whether it's an ominous, evil place or a beckoning city of gold.

As he gets closer, he should be able to see large items that either reinforce or contrast with the qualities suggested from a distance. A forsaken castle may be surrounded by a dark moat or tangled brambles and thorns, or perhaps its towers are crumbling and decaying. On the other hand, bright flags and banners may signal a city of wealth and good fortune.

When the object is within the personal space of the character, focus on specific, smaller details. Individual details that send a clear message should be visible. Go beyond the commonplace and zoom in to an unusual close-up of seldom-described features.

People. Faces, hair, height, and eyes; a woman's legs, mouth, or figure; a man's broad forehead or big shoulders—these are what a reader commonly sees when a novelist produces a visual description of a character. Since they're the most common, they're often commonplace. Instead, consider focusing on:

- *Hands.* A close-up of a character's hands can communicate much about that character's personality. Handshakes also telegraph information, and not just in job interviews.
- *Ears.* Ear shapes are as unique as fingerprints. Note that ears don't grow exactly the same on both sides of the head.
- *Belly, hips, and thighs.* These normally neglected areas can reveal a great deal about a character, as in this example from my first mystery, *Close to Home.*

> He had the visible ribs of fitness, while his wife wore her lack of exercise in a wide-tracking tire around her waist. On one hip she held a baby, on the other several inches of junk food cellulite. He had the slim, swiveling hips of a Casanova who was enjoying himself too much.

Places. Normally novelists provide a wide-angle shot of the general setting—houses, mountains, forests, etc.—in order to set mood and tone, foreshadow a future event, or help set genre. You can reverse this tactic for greater effect. For example, notice how Michael Shaara's mix of description and action sets a tone that is both somber and personal in this passage from *The Killer Angels*.

> A boy from Illinois climbed a tree. … [He] stared and felt his heart beating and saw movement. A blur in the mist, an unfurled flag. Then the dark figures, row on row: skirmishers. Long, long rows, like walking trees. … He had a long paralyzed moment which he would remember until the end of his life. Then he raised the rifle and laid it across the limb of the tree and aimed generally toward the breast of a tall figure in the front of the line, waited, let the cold rain fall, misting his vision, cleared his eyes, waited, prayed, and pressed the trigger.

Things. Zoom in close to see the sharp edges of a timer's digital numbers as they tick away the seconds remaining before the blast. Describe the texture of the red paper that wraps the sticks of dynamite. Perhaps the blasting cap's edges are precisely, uniformly, and almost lovingly crimped around the detonating cord.

Take your description beyond the normal way of seeing—then take that same description beyond sight. To see how, turn the page to the next drill.

RELATED DRILLS

Drill 18: Find Your Character in Events, Places, and Concepts
Drill 21: Forge Your Setting
Drill 76: Know That You Are Not a Camera
Drill 88: Make a Description and Narration Pass

DRILL 80

LEVERAGE THE INTIMACY OF THE SENSES

"I love the smell of napalm in the morning. It smells like victory." If you don't know who said that and in what movie, do push-ups. Lots and lots of push-ups.

To get your novel beyond everyday mediocrity, show; don't tell. This standard advice means going beyond sight to take full advantage of *all* the senses—including hearing, smell, touch, and taste. *How* you go beyond sight can make a difference as well. As you use description to build that emotional connection between your reader and your story, consider carefully which sense you want to use. Some senses are more intimate—more personal, closer, more private—than others. Using the more intimate senses can make your description more emotionally powerful.

Sight. Sight is the most passive of the senses. Our eyes are always open and we need do nothing to see an object, so there's very little involvement and the object remains external. Visual images are also easy to interrupt; we simply close our eyes or look away. Although you can maximize the power of visual description using the drills in this mission, description using only sight is still the least intimate—not only is seeing passive, what we see remains outside the body.

Sound. More intimate than sight, sound causes a physical change in the body—the vibration of the eardrum. It takes more effort to block out sound than it does sight. Sounds are also more easily remembered, especially when they are repeated in a rhythmic fashion. Just think of Edgar Allan Poe's famous short story "The Tell-Tale Heart" and the thunderous "louder! louder! louder! louder!" of the heart beneath the floor. This is why we can remember childhood rhymes long after we've grown up and commercial jingles long after we've grown tired of the product. Description that evokes sounds is more memorable and more intimate than description that relies only on visual images. Sound, however, is still generally passive—the stimulation can come from a distance.

Touch. Touch sits squarely in the middle of the senses' spectrum of intimacy. Touch is easily remembered—much more so than visual imagery—and touch memory is stored in a different part of the brain than sight or sound. Touch can be either active or passive—our characters can both touch and be touched. Distance is important—whatever is stimulating the sense of touch must obviously be close. Touch can also be used as an intimate character marker—a character's leathered, roughened hands signal something significant, as does cool, smooth, fatty skin. But whatever is stimulating the sense of touch most often remains outside the body, making description that uses this sense more intimate than description using only sight or sound but less intimate than description using the remaining senses.

Smell. Smell would not seem like an intimate sense, yet the human brain's neural connections tie certain smells to certain primeval instincts and emotions, making it one of the most intimate of senses. Smells can produce strong, emotional reactions even when very faint. There is some truth to the cliché that a ghostly whiff of perfume can bring a powerful man to a dead halt. Smells must be taken into the body—that is, some tiny particle of what

you're smelling has to enter the nose and come in contact with the olfactory receptors. Smells have strong associations: Warm cookies might evoke Grandma's house, pipe tobacco might bring good old Uncle Billy to mind, and the piney odor of disinfectant might take you back to a grade-school locker room. Sex has its own smell, as do honky-tonk bars, new cars, and well-worn leather. It has even been suggested that certain people can smell another's fear or excitement. To have a more powerful, more intimate effect on your reader, use the sense of smell in your description.

Taste. Taste is the most intimate of the senses. The taste buds, mouth, and gums provide fast-track access to the body and to parts of the brain. Sensations that originate in the mouth can cause very powerful, very emotional reactions almost instantly. (Perhaps partly because so much of the way something tastes depends on the way it smells.) In order to activate the sense of taste, a stimulant must enter through open lips. In other words, the person must—voluntarily or not—take something into his body by opening up to it. There are also tastes that reflect emotions—for example, fear—that are even more intimate, since they originate from inside. Whether your character tastes the agony of defeat or the sweetness of a lover's kiss or the coppery taste of his own blood, description using the sense of taste can be the most intimate of all.

So do you think you can successfully use description to have an emotional effect on your reader? Be careful—more is not always better. See why in the next drill.

RELATED DRILLS

Drill 18: Find Your Character in Events, Places, and Concepts
Drill 88: Make a Description and Narration Pass
Drill 96: Focus Your Editing and Proofreading

DRILL 81

ELIMINATE DEADLY MODIFIER BUILDUP

Historically, disease has put more soldiers in the hospital than bullets and bombs have. One key to keeping a military force functioning at full capacity is to keep the troops healthy. Some writers have characterized the novel and the sentences in it as organic—as living, breathing organisms. If this is the case, it's your job as a novelist to keep your novel healthy. That may mean you'll need to call the medics to eliminate a potentially fatal condition known as deadly modifier buildup (DMBU).

DMBU usually occurs when you don't feel confident you've adequately communicated the emotion, mood, tone, or genre of the scene. In other words, you're afraid that the reader won't "get it." To make yourself feel better, you pile on adjectives and adverbs so there will be no mistaking what emotion the thick-headed reader is supposed to feel. This results in too many modifiers. The modifiers become too heavy, and the weight in the reader's hands causes her to put the book down.

How many modifiers are too many, and how much is too much? There is no set maximum or minimum; many, one, or none may be the right amount, depending upon the style, scene, and genre. However, you *can* tell when there are too many—or, rather, your reader can. If the reader notices the use of the modifiers and not the emotion you want the modifiers to produce, then there are too many. When your reader notices the technique and not the story, it's time to scale back. If you do get the signal that you need to put your sentences on a modifier diet, there are several techniques that can effectively help your prose get to the right weight.

1. **Spread your modifiers across several sentences.** Instead of using *dark*, *sticky*, *warm*, *coppery-smelling*, *thick*, and *red* in one sentence, make the blood dark in one sentence, move to some action, hit temperature in another sentence, and so on.

2. **Set artificial limits.** Allow yourself no more than one modifier per sentence, two per paragraph. Use these limits as guides to force yourself to select only the most powerful modifiers for your work.

3. **Cut them one by one.** Read your work aloud, then trust what you hear. Find a sentence with several stacked, built-up modifiers. Cut one. Read the new sentence aloud. Cut another. Read it again. Cut again. Repeat until your ear tells you the sentence is right.

As you're drafting, you may find that several of your sentences are too heavy with adjectives and adverbs. Although you can mark these, then rework and rewrite them while editing your manuscript, it's more efficient to take a stack of modifiers as a signal that you need to build some variety into your description right away. To find out how to build variety, turn to the next drill.

RELATED DRILLS

Drill 2: Adopt a Principled Approach
Drill 30: Make Your Protagonist Act Like a Dog
Drill 82: Mix It Up
Drill: 88: Make a Description and Narration Pass

DRILL 82

MIX IT UP

In combat, it takes a variety of tactics to seize an objective. Do the same thing over and over again and your enemy will anticipate you.

In your novel, it takes a variety of techniques to effectively show (instead of tell)—and to keep your reader from anticipating your tactics. Description, if not varied, can become tedious and predictable. Use a combination of descriptive techniques to clearly and powerfully show your reader the people, places, and things in your novel, as well as the mood or tone of your novel. In addition, you should intermix description with dialogue, action, and narration, which is essentially crucial summary information, to keep your writing interesting and involving.

There are several ways you can mix it up to give your reader a richer, more interesting experience, but those methods boil down to the three below (and variations on them). The method or combination of methods you use depends on your writing style, the genre, and the nature of the scene.

1. Intermix different kinds of description. You may use an adjective for description in one sentence, then use a colorful verb in the next sentence, then use a simile or metaphor in the next. In the following passage from Michael Shaara's *The Killer Angels*, several types of description are used to convey General Lee's mood.

> Lee moved off into the dark pasture. Now in motion he was aware of stiffness, of weakness, of a suspended fear. He moved as if his body was filled with cold cement that was slowly hardening, and there was something inside bright and hot and fearful, as if something somewhere could break at any moment, as if a rock in his chest was teetering and could come crashing down.

2. Intersperse description with sentences that contain action and narration. The summary information provided in narration, combined with action, can enhance the intensity of any descriptive passage. In the example from *The Killer Angels* below, a paragraph of action and description in the middle of an otherwise lazy dialogue emphasizes the immediacy of the coming battle and the danger it brings.

> Chamberlain ... strode to the prisoners.
>
> "Any of you fellas care to join us?"
>
> "The Rebs really coming?" The man said it wistfully, cautiously, not quite convinced.
>
> "They're really comin'."
>
> One man, bearded, stretched and yawned. "Well, be kind of dull sittin' up here just a-watchin'."

So far the scene is mostly dialogue—no excitement here. Even a character is yawning. But not for long.

> He stood. The others watched. At that moment a solid shot passed through the trees above them, tore through the leaves, ripped away a branch, caromed out into the dark over the line.

The cannon ball's action ends the tranquility of the scene and foreshadows the coming battle. Then Shaara swiftly adds just a drop of narration.

> A shower of granite dust drifted down. The ball must have grazed a ledge above. Granite dust had salt in it.

And finally moves quickly inside Chamberlain's mind and subtly describes the taste of fear.

> Or perhaps the salt was from your own lips.

3. Intersperse description with internal or external dialogue. Description can be more powerful when mixed with internal and external dialogue. In the passage from *The Killer Angels* below, Colonel Joshua

Chamberlain, whose regiment is out of ammunition and facing a third rebel assault, watches the progress of battle.

> Once the hill went, the flank of the army went. Good God! He could see troops running; he could see the blue flood, the bloody tide.
>
> Kilrain: "Colonel, they're coming."
>
> Chamberlain marveled. But we're not so bad ourselves. One recourse: Can't go back. Can't stay where we are. Result: inevitable.
>
> The idea formed.
>
> "Let's fix bayonets," Chamberlain said.

In battle, no one tactic is best; in your novel, no one method of description is best. Use a variety of description techniques, then intermix description with action and dialogue to gain and keep your reader's attention.

But just mixing it up isn't enough. To make sure you keep your reader entertained, throw something new into your draft's descriptive mix. To find out what that new thing might be, turn to the next drill.

RELATED DRILLS

Drill 7: Drill Your Way to Success
Drill 71: Make Your Characters Try, Try Again
Drill 72: Find the Devil in the Details
Drill 81: Eliminate Deadly Modifier Buildup
Drill 88: Make a Description and Narration Pass

DRILL 83

TRY A NEW TECHNIQUE

Sometimes soldiers find new ways of using old equipment—just ask the soldiers who got close air support from the supposedly obsolete A-10 Thunderbolt "Warthog" ground-attack aircraft.

Similarly, a good writer should always look for new ways to use language. Sometimes this means getting some extra mileage out of weaker parts of speech. Adjectives are considered one of the weakest forms of description, but there are ways you can be creative with adjectives to increase their strength and impact. While verbs normally provide the strongest description of a person, place, thing, or action (for example, what a character does says much about who he is), adjectives can serve you and your reader in new and interesting ways.

1. Attach an emotion to an adjective. For example, choose an emotion based on your character's personality points, then attach that emotion to a body part. The result might be *hateful red lips*, *timid red lips*, or *angry red lips*. You may find that attaching an emotion also causes you to reconsider your adjective. For example, you might change *timid red lips* to *timid pink lips*, since pink is a more muted color.

2. Use a hyphenated adjective to make a shortcut metaphor. Remember that a metaphor posits a similarity between dissimilar things but normally doesn't use the words *like* or *as* in its comparison. You're probably familiar with some clichéd examples of metaphor in description, such as *autumn-gold hair* or *ice-blue eyes*. Your challenge is to use this old technique in a new way: Push the metaphor to the extreme. Suppose your character is something of a dashing rogue and has green eyes that immediately tell this tale. You might construct the hyphenated shortcut metaphor *pirate-green eyes*. You wouldn't normally associate *pirate* and *green*, but when put in the context of your character's personality points, the technique works.

3. Use a noun as an adjective. A well-known version of this technique is the phrase *New York minute.* We associate a strong sense of rushing and hurriedness with New York City; thus a New York minute is only a few seconds long. One old soldiers' marching song tells of a girl across the ocean who has *battleship thighs.* Your tall, lanky character might have an *ostrich neck*, and if his bravery is mostly bravado, he might have *cardboard courage.* To avoid confusing your reader, keep the connection between the noun and what it modifies clear—the more abstract the connection, the more your reader is likely to trip over it.

4. Mismatch the senses. Measure or describe a sense (taste, touch, smell, sight, sound) in terms normally used to measure or describe a different sense. You can describe smells in terms of weight, taste in terms of touch, and so on. For example, an innocent victim hiding in the basement might hear the *heavy sounds* of her pursuer's footsteps. She might escape outside, only to lose her way in the *bitter darkness*. However, the *dull odors* of a dying campfire might lead her to safety. Finding the right mismatch of the senses is a matter of trial and error, so experiment.

5. Fragment the description. Your eighth-grade grammar teacher may foam at the mouth and rant and rave, but you *can* break the rules of grammar to enhance description. You can use a series of short, descriptive sentence fragments to give your reader a mood-appropriate view of the person, place, thing, or action you're describing. Let's say your detective enters a bedroom that is also a crime scene. You could use a series of sentence fragments to mimic the way the sights, sounds, tastes, and smells of the scene rush at him when he first enters.

> Blood spatter, chest high, far wall. Greasy ceiling. Dirty brown walls. Peeling paint.

This rapid-fire burst of description has a powerful effect, but use it judiciously. Overuse can jolt a reader.

Adjectives, those familiar elements of speech often considered one of the weaker methods of description, can serve you and your reader in new and interesting ways—if you try new techniques when you use them.

Dialogue, description, action, raising the stakes—you'll likely use all of these techniques several times as you prepare your first draft. Then, one day you'll reach those two words you've been chasing for months—*The End.*

Congratulations—now your real work begins. See why and how when you turn the page to the next mission.

RELATED DRILLS

Drill 7: Drill Your Way to Success
Drill 30: Make Your Protagonist Act Like a Dog
Drill 71: Make Your Characters Try, Try Again
Drill 78: Lob a Hand Grenade
Drill 81: Eliminate Deadly Modifier Buildup
Drill 88: Make a Description and Narration Pass

BATTLE PLAN ECHO

REVISION AND REWRITING

MISSION X: ADVANCE TO CONTACT 247
Drill 84: Triage Your Scenes 249
Drill 85: Make a Character Pass 253
Drill 86: Make an Objective Pass 256
Drill 87: Make a Dialogue Pass 259
Drill 88: Make a Description and Narration Pass 262
Drill 89: Go on the Narration Diet 264
Drill 90: Make an Action Pass 266
Drill 91: Make a Logic Pass 268
Drill 92: Circle Back for the Miscellaneous Pass 271
Drill 93: Stop Hearing Voices and Get One 273
Drill 94: Conduct the Final Assault: Rewriting 276
Drill 95: Stop Having Hallucinations Along the Way 279

MISSION X

ADVANCE TO CONTACT

Trainees spend the first few weeks of boot camp learning basic drills and skills. About two-thirds of the way, they master these basics. Then comes a very challenging test or series of tests, and when they pass those tests, many think they've got it down. But what they don't know is that with the basics mastered, boot camp has only just begun. Now comes the real work of applying their skills in more complex training.

It's that time for your manuscript as well. You've done the mental preparation and invention, and you've passed the challenging test of completing a quality draft. Now it's time for the revision phase of your battle plan. In this phase, you'll do what many writers call the real work of writing—revising and rewriting your manuscript.

In the civilian world, revision can be unfocused and confusing as you try to adhere to the vague advice to look at your manuscript, characters, plot, and organization in a new light and from a different perspective. The individual who originally coined that advice should spend the rest of his life doing push-ups.

In the novelist's boot camp battle plan, your revision and rewriting phase has three concrete stages.

Stage 1. Perform scene triage. Conduct a scene-level evaluation of your work, placing each scene into one of three categories:

1. cut
2. rework
3. improve

Stage 2. Execute seven revision passes. Read through your manuscript seven times, focusing on a different story element with each pass. You'll look at:

1. character
2. objectives
3. dialogue
4. narration and description
5. action
6. logic
7. miscellaneous items

Stage 3. Rewrite. In this final stage of revision, you'll follow your notes from the triage and revision passes and make the necessary changes by rewriting your work line by line, scene by scene.

Leverage what you've learned in earlier missions and drills, and you'll be able to make a thorough and complete assessment of your work. That assessment will lead you to build a better manuscript. Expect to do much rewriting and expect to see significant improvements.

Congratulations on making it this far. Now get to work.

DRILL 84

TRIAGE YOUR SCENES

Triage is a medical term for sorting wartime casualties on the basis of need or the likelihood that treatment will help. It's a hard-hearted technique that comes from the battlefield, where combat medical personnel need a system to most effectively allocate scarce medical resources and attention. The method they used then—and still use today—was to sort the wounded into three categories: (1) those who can't be helped, (2) those who need immediate help, and (3) those who are relatively stable and can wait for help.

Scene triage, the first stage in the revision process, resembles a combat doctor's triage in that it is a systematic but rapid way to make difficult decisions about your scenes and to ration your most precious and limited asset—time.

The key to triage is to do it quickly. Now is not the time for an extended, detailed inspection of character, action, description, dialogue, and so on. You'll do that very methodical, more precise inspection later in your revision passes. For now, move fast and make informed "gut calls." How fast? Done yet? No? Drop and give me twenty! How do you triage your novel? Follow the three steps below.

1. Prep. Print out your master story summary. Next, make a backup copy of your manuscript, a working copy that you'll use from this point forward.

2. Assess. Quickly check each scene for key indicators, which we'll discuss shortly. Read fast and be decisive in your evaluation of each scene—no fence-sitting! Then record your assessment on your master story summary, which includes your scene list and scene summaries. Mark or label each scene *cut*, *rework*, or *improve*, depending on your evaluation.

- *Cut.* Scenes marked *cut* need to come out of the work. Many authors create a special file for these deleted scenes. Making a separate file safeguards your information and eases the pain of removing passages to which you've committed time and energy.

- *Rework.* These are scenes that need major surgery and require more time and effort on your part. Problems become apparent when you perform the three tests outlined below, but cutting these scenes is not practicable and leaving them as is will seriously weaken your story. Your only option is to rework them.

- *Improve.* This category is for scenes that meet your evaluative criteria satisfactorily. While you still want to include them in your revision passes, you know that these scenes are already in pretty good shape and will require relatively less time and energy.

Use a triage checklist like the one below to decide if the scene should be marked *cut*, *rework*, or *improve*. This checklist includes three primary tests. You can remember these indicators by remembering the following: *who*; *doing what*; and *why*.

WHO?

Is/are the …

… main character present?

… window character present?

… villain present?

… minions/other opposition present?

If you get *no* answers to all of the above, mark the scene (on your master story summary!) as a cut. Note that *present* can mean the character is being discussed.

DOING WHAT?

Is …

… the protagonist, opponent, window character, or minion taking action?

… the protagonist, opponent, window character or minion having an external conflict?

Two *no* answers to these questions mean you should mark this scene as a cut. A *no* to just one question makes this scene a rework. A *yes* to both means you should label the scene *improve.*

WHY?

Is/are …

… one or more characters pursuing his/their story objectives?

… one or more characters pursuing his/their personal objectives?

If you get *no* answers to all the above questions, mark the scene to cut. A *no* to just one question makes the scene a rework. A *yes* to both means you label the scene as one to improve. Again, if the scene receives all *nos*, plan on cutting it. Never mind how wonderful its description, how clever the language, or how necessary the detail. Scenes with all *nos* are terminal.

3. Treat. Pull out your master story summary and cross out those scenes marked *cut.* Then go to the working copy of your full manuscript and actually remove the scenes. Remember to save the deleted scenes in an separate file just in case you need them later. Should you print out a new copy of your manuscript or just cross out deleted scenes and pages on your current printout? Give yourself a break: Print out a clean copy.

Those scenes you've marked *improve* you can leave alone; you'll deal with them later. Those you've marked *rework* require a judgment call on your part. You may choose to address some major issues now by rewriting the scene, or you may choose to wait until later, after you've executed the next eight drills. Ask yourself, just as that combat doc does, *How bad is it?* If it's really bad, don't wait—perform emergency surgery (rewrite the scene). At least get the scene in good enough shape that it will last through revision.

Also note that you can use this same three-step process mentally as you conduct each revision pass. That is, you can *prepare* by reviewing your notes and documents, *assess* by reading quickly and marking the subject of your revision pass on your master story summary, and *treat* by cutting or rewriting.

With the "wounded" scenes cared for and a triaged draft in hand, you can get to the detailed business of revising. To do so, get to the next drill by turning the page.

RELATED DRILLS

Drill 2: Adopt a Principled Approach
Drill 16: Know the Terrain
Drill 45: Put Your Book on an Index Card
Drill 46: Build Your Master Story Summary

DRILL 85

MAKE A CHARACTER PASS

Military ceremonies, with troops lined up on the parade fields, bands, and flags, are powerful spectacles. Near the end of most military parades comes the command *Pass in Review*, and the troops march smartly past a dignitary-filled reviewing stand.

You need to make your novel's characters pass in review for you—by making a character revision pass. From the reviewing stand of your writer's chair, go over each scene, looking solely at how well your characters are giving the reader an emotional experience, playing out the roles you've designed for them, and demonstrating their personality points. Of the seven revision passes you'll make, this is the first, the most critical, and the most complex.

This pass begins with a review of your character cards and character backgrounds. As you review your notes, think back to your initial vision of your characters. While it's likely the finished characters aren't exactly what you intended—characters have a tendency to evolve during the writing process—your notes should remind you of your basic goals and direction.

Then, as you read your manuscript, look for places where you can make each character's personality points, backstory, current situation, and character traits more intense and even larger and more pronounced. Is your character bright? If so, increase her intensity by making her brilliant. Is she pretty? Make her gorgeous. Does she have the seeds of bravery? Make her heroically courageous. Was her childhood challenging? Make it incredibly tough. It's not likely you'll overdo it but take a moment to compare your characters to those in other works in the genre. This will give you a feel for whether you're on track or whether you have pushed the character too far, to comic book level.

Working with one scene at a time, ask the following questions.

☐ **Does everyone get on stage quickly?** Within the first twenty or so pages, your reader should have met each major character. Ideally, your reader should see your protagonist in action, pursuing her objectives, within the first few pages.

☐ **Is your protagonist in the scene?** Remember, your story is about your main character. The most powerful scenes are those in which the main character is pursuing her objectives. If your scene contains other characters, such as your opponent, minions, window character, or victim, they should be talking about or otherwise referencing the protagonist. Still, scenes without your main character are not as strong as those with her physically present. Examine these scenes to see how you might get your protagonist more into the action.

☐ **Is each character pursuing her objectives?** If a character is doing something other than directly pursuing her objectives, the scene is a good candidate for cutting or extensive rewriting.

☐ **Is each character consistent?** That is, how well is each character demonstrating, acting in accordance with, and acting out her personality points? Are the character details consistent? Look at each appearance of that character. If your character is left-handed, she should consistently use her left hand to shoot, write, and so on. If she breaks her hand in a scene, make sure she doesn't miraculously regain full functionality of that hand just a few scenes later without the passage of time.

☐ **Is each character growing?** Each character has a personal objective. What progress is she making towards accomplishing that objective, and is that progress incremental?

☐ **Where can you trim your cast?** Where can you consolidate or eliminate characters? A smaller cast size is easier for you and your reader to work with.

☐ **Are your characters rehearsing or playing their parts?** Your characters should perform at maximum intensity from the moment you bring them on stage. Forget the scene that came before or the one that comes after—your characters must be putting out 100 percent toward achieving their objectives in each moment of each scene.

☐ **Are the bit players stealing the show?** If you find that your window character, opponent, or minions are more interesting and compelling than your protagonist, stop. The problem is not that these characters are too strong; the problem is that your protagonist needs to be stronger—much stronger. Go back to your main character's biography and personality points and dramatically increase her intensity.

☐ **Is the point of view consistent?** Can readers easily and readily tell through whose eyes they're seeing the story? If you shift the POV, is the change clearly marked? Any hint of head-hopping should be marked as a definite problem requiring attention. Eliminate slips or shifts in POV where a character sees or knows what she can't or shouldn't.

It's usually best not to start rewriting (emergency surgery after scene triage excepted) until you have completed all seven passes, as each pass ultimately influences the next. The changes you make in how your characters think, feel, speak, and act will impact every other part of your story.

Once you've completed your character pass, it's time to give yourself a new objective. Turn the page to see what that objective is.

RELATED DRILLS

Drill 33: Give Your Protagonist a Pointed Personality
Drill 39: Use a Character Matrix
Drill 47: Plan Your Characters' Development
Drill 58: Make It More Personal

DRILL 86

MAKE AN OBJECTIVE PASS

The objective drives everything in a military mission; all individuals and all efforts are focused on achieving it. There may be one major objective, intermediate objectives to secure along the way, and/or objectives for subordinate or supporting units. The enemy has an objective as well, and often, denying the enemy his objective is a part of the friendly force's larger objective.

You invented and developed objectives for your characters in previous phases of your battle plan. Your characters' stories and personal objectives drive their thoughts, feelings, actions, and dialogue—or at least they should. In your second revision pass, return to your manuscript printout and check each scene to ensure that these objectives truly are driving your story. Work through your story one scene at time and ask the following questions.

- ☐ **Are the objectives clearly visible in the beginning?** Can your reader clearly tell what your characters want? In general, during the first twenty pages or so your reader should be able to tell what the story and personal objectives are for your protagonist, antagonist, window character, and minions.

- ☐ **Are the objectives clearly visible in each scene?** Your scenes should be about characters doing whatever they can to get what they want. Is the scene about achieving an objective or achieving something that will enable the character—preferably your protagonist or antagonist— to make progress in achieving that objective?

- ☐ **Are the characters taking action to achieve those objectives?** Your characters must be active—they must *do* something, *deal with* an event, *discover* something, or *decide* something and take action based on that decision. (If this doesn't sound familiar, fall back to

drill 42.) All these actions must be objective-oriented. If not, why are those actions in your story? If you used these actions to show something, you've just earned yourself KP duty for a month. You should never use dialogue just to show what kind of person a character is, and you should never have a character take an action simply to show a character trait. Instead, have him take an action to make progress toward an objective; make the *kind* of action he takes and the *way* he takes that action show his personality points.

- ☐ **Are objectives in conflict with each other?** Your protagonist and antagonist should play a zero-sum, win-or-lose game. Remember that the objectives of your two main characters should be mutually exclusive.

- ☐ **Can you track the progress as you go along?** Use your character matrix to make sure your character's objectives are present in every scene. Compare the objectives on the matrix with the characters in the scene. You should be able to tell where each character is in his pursuit of those objectives.

- ☐ **In what ways can you raise the stakes?** To make the objective more important, consider revising the scene to increase the potential losses if the objective isn't obtained. Note that if you do, you'll likely have some adjusting to do throughout the rest of the book. The best way to keep track of these adjustments is to annotate your scene list from your master story summary.

- ☐ **Do the objectives get resolved in the end?** Look carefully at your closing ten to twenty pages. In those pages, do your main characters' objectives get achieved, denied, changed, or resolved in some other manner? Again, your character matrix can be a helpful checklist. Look at the objectives listed on it—are all of them addressed in some manner?

Keeping your scenes focused on your characters' objectives keeps your story consistently moving in one direction. To keep your revision phase moving, you'll need to complete a beginning-to-end objective pass. Then move on to the next pass and the next drill.

RELATED DRILLS

Drill 14: Go Beyond *What If?*
Drill 38: Define, Objectify, and Personify the Objective
Drill 42: Take Three Steps to Story Line
Drill 45: Put Your Book on an Index Card
Drill 90: Make an Action Pass

DRILL 87

MAKE A DIALOGUE PASS

If you've been around soldiers for a while, especially troops training in the field, you know there are a few things soldiers never skip. They don't skip mail call, hot chow, a few minutes' rest, or a shower and a clean change of uniform.

Readers never skip dialogue. A reader may zoom through descriptive passages and might even hop over a page full of action, but for reasons unknown to scientists, soothsayers, or even drill sergeants, that reader just won't skip the dialogue.

That's fine; neither will you. It's in your third revision pass that you'll inspect your dialogue. As with all revision passes, you'll go scene by scene. If you used the drills in mission XII as a basis for the dialogue in your draft, then your dialogue should be solid, and this pass will only strengthen it. If you didn't use those drills, your punishment won't be push-ups but extensive rewriting.

Now, take out your working copy of the manuscript, turn to the first use of dialogue, and ask the following questions.

- ☐ **Are your characters using words as weapons?** Dialogue can, of course, contribute to a story in many ways, but your cast members should be using dialogue primarily as a tool to achieve their objectives.

- ☐ **Is the dialogue only there to show something?** If so, do push-ups—lots of push-ups. Do not write dialogue just to show the reader something. Instead, write dialogue that furthers a character's pursuit of her objectives. The way in which the character speaks—how she uses her words—will show the reader her personality points, emotions, etc.

- ☐ **How could this dialogue more strongly reveal the characters?** Does the dialogue convey what kind of people the characters in the scene are—does it complement and expand on their personality points, feelings, moods, and fears?
- ☐ **How could the dialogue work harder?** Dialogue can help to set mood or tone—is the dialogue in the scene working hard to do so?
- ☐ **Is the speaker's identity clear?** Is it easy to separate the internal dialogue from the external dialogue? Are the attributions used only for clarity and nothing else?
- ☐ **Does the dialogue contain beats to punctuate it?** Are the beats physical demonstrations of a character's personality points? Do the beats convey the character's emotional state? Are the beats unspoken ways of fighting for what a character wants?
- ☐ **Is there a better arrangement?** Can the dialogue be rearranged to break up the flow of description and action?

- ☐ **Does the dialogue fit?** Is the dialogue consistent with the setting in time and with genre? Check to make sure you haven't included throwaway words or phrases (*well, uh*) or yes-or-no questions. Are there direct replies that can be made more evasive, thereby heightening conflict?

- ☐ **Does it feel real?** Does your dialogue sound exactly like real speech? If so, back to doing push-ups. Make your dialogue feel more real than real (boring) speech.

Close attention to your dialogue can increase and sharpen conflict, bring out a character's traits and emotions, increase suspense, and intensify the mood or tone of a scene. Perform this pass carefully from your first scene to your last, and your dialogue will show something—a high level of craftsmanship.

Now to show you how to perform the next pass, I'll ask you to turn the page.

RELATED DRILLS

Drill 3: No Sniveling Allowed
Drill 63: Learn How to Fake It
Drill 65: Make Your Dialogue Multitask
Drill 66: Aim for the Gut

DRILL 88

MAKE A DESCRIPTION AND NARRATION PASS

Just as terrain and weather affect the strategy, execution, and even the success of a military mission, so, too, does good description and narration affect what's happening in your story. When done well, good description—from the broad brush of setting to the microscopic details of forensic evidence at the scene of a crime—can contribute a unique richness to your novel. When done poorly, description becomes a clunky anchor that can drag your story along the bottom of Lake Boredom. The same is true of narration. Done well, it gives critical information in a concentrated dose. Done poorly, and you risk flooding your story with dull and unnecessary details.

To keep from having to send a Navy scuba team to rescue your work from the deep, conduct a fourth revision pass, looking specifically at description (discussed below), and narration (addressed in the next drill). For each descriptive passage you come across, ask the following questions.

☐ **What description can be cut?** Most novelists have a tendency to over-describe. When in doubt, take it out.

☐ **Does the description do its job?** Does it contribute to the reader's emotional experience; help to set time, place, genre; convey necessary details; or make another specific contribution?

☐ **Does the description convey a mood?** If there any passages containing emotionally neutral descriptions of people, places, or things, mark those passages for revision.

☐ **How can more variety be introduced?** Can you improve the description by presenting people, places, things, or actions from a different perspective, distance, or angle?

- ☐ **Is it a part of the scene?** How well is the description integrated with the action and dialogue in the scene? How relevant is the description to what is happening to the characters in the scene? What specific details can be substituted for generalized description? You shouldn't find a laundry list of items; replace heavy description with a few specific, powerful details.

- ☐ **Is there a better arrangement?** It's much tougher to establish an emotional connection with description than it is with dialogue or action. If description opens a chapter or scene, can it be moved so that dialogue or action opens the passage instead? If there are long blocks of description, can they be chopped up and interspersed with dialogue and action?

As you've seen in this and previous drills, description and narration are powerful tools. Used wisely and well, they'll contribute much to your novel.

However, too much of a good thing can lead to an overweight manuscript. Before your novel becomes weighed down with excessive narration, you may want to sign it up for the narration diet. The enrollment form is in the next drill.

RELATED DRILLS

Drill 21: Forge Your Setting
Drill 74: Do More With Description
Drill 81: Eliminate Deadly Modifier Buildup
Drill 90: Make an Action Pass

DRILL 89

GO ON THE NARRATION DIET

There's a reason a new recruit gets up before dawn to do physical training—he needs to be lean and strong to make it as a soldier. When it comes to showing instead of telling, your novel needs that same kind of leanness and strength.

As part of your fourth revision pass (the pass that evaluates description), look for occurrences of narration, exposition, overview, and summary: These are all terms for *telling the reader what happened.* Done correctly, narration can be excellent vehicle for:

- accounting for stretches of time you don't want to write about but must be acknowledged
- summing up crucial details that a character needs to know to solve a specific challenge in front of him
- capturing the essence of complex information
- giving snapshots of background information

At the same time, understand that for many new novelists there is a tendency to over-narrate. Your job as a novelist is to show, not tell. As you revise, make your novel leaner and stronger by putting your text on the narration diet.

☐ **Seek out excess summarizations.** Look for passages or sentences in which you've given an overview, or in which you've summed up or directly stated what the character felt physically or emotionally. Then rewrite them so that they engage your reader instead of boring him. While this kind of extra weight can accumulate anywhere, you're most likely to find it at the beginning or ending of a chapter or scene, at changes in point of view, and when significant events (also known as plot points, turning points, decisions, discoveries, and events) occur. You should also look for passages in which a character reflects on what he has seen, heard, done, or come to understand. Those are the times when you're most likely to add unnecessary extra weight to make sure the reader understands what's going on.

- ☐ **Use word-level cues to help you identify extra narration weight.** Look for adverbs (*he crept carefully*), forms of the verb *to feel* (*Dan felt sad*), and past progressive forms of the verb *to be* (*they had been thinking of* ...). These are clues that the passage may well be doing more telling than showing.

If you have any sense at all that a passage is a bit heavy on the narration side, you're probably right. Trust your instincts. Once you've identified the passages that contain extra weight, mark them and move on. Remember, the actual rewriting comes later.

Now focus on turning to the next drill to make your next pass.

RELATED DRILLS

Drill 45: Put Your Book on an Index Card
Drill 54: Hang Your Readers Off a Cliff—Repeatedly
Drill 72: Find the Devil in the Details
Drill 90: Make an Action Pass

DRILL 90

MAKE AN ACTION PASS

There's an old saying that every Marine—whether he's a cook, radioman, or tank driver—is first an infantryman. Basic infantry skills are an essential part of each Marine's training, even if he only hits the beach while driving a truck full of kitchen equipment or spare tires.

No matter what else your character may seem to be doing in your novel, he's first and foremost trying to achieve his story and personal objectives—which means he's taking action.

Performing a fifth revision pass to evaluate your action helps you ensure that your characters are doing the right things and doing them in an emotionally engaging manner. As with previous revision passes, use your manuscript printout and go from scene to scene from the beginning to the end of your novel. As you work your way through each scene, concentrate only on the action, leaving everything else for other passes.

☐ **Is the amount and type of action appropriate for the genre?** The name of your chosen genre may give you clues as to how much action it should contain—consider the amount and type of action called for in an action-adventure novel versus that required in a cozy mystery. You can always push the limits of your genre, but be sure you have a feel for where the limits are. Remember, too, that in some genres (such as category romances), the limits are hard and fast—no pushing allowed.

☐ **Is there action on every page?** Your characters should be in constant motion. If they're sitting and talking, get them out of their chairs by adding beats to your dialogue. In general, your reader wants to see things happening and is disappointed if he doesn't. Have your characters doing something on every page.

- ☐ **Does the action have the right purpose?** If your characters are doing something other than pursuing their objectives, question why and strongly consider cutting or thoroughly rewriting the given scene. Characters don't do things just to show something to the reader—they show their personality points and emotional state in the *way* they do what they do. If you think you've heard this concept before, you're right. It's that important.
- ☐ **How well is the action recounted?** Is action incorporated to heighten the level of excitement, tension, and suspense? Is the clock running in slow motion to make the action last? Is there a focus on details?
- ☐ **Does the action grow?** The action in your novel should grow in intensity and become more personal as the novel progresses. Is there more for characters to lose as your work progresses? In the end, is there a personal, all-or-nothing one–on-one confrontation between protagonist and antagonist?

Regardless of genre, you novel should contain action. That action is the *what happens* in your story, and it's the *what happens* that keeps your reader turning pages.

What happens next is that you perform your next revision pass. Act now and turn the page.

RELATED DRILLS

Drill 45: Put Your Book on an Index Card
Drill 73: Go to Time-and-a-Half
Drill 84: Triage Your Scenes

DRILL 91

MAKE A LOGIC PASS

Sometimes the military does things for no logical reason—other than that's the way it has always been done. That way may not make much sense, but that's the way it's done. Why? Because that's the way it's done. If the military wanted you to use logic, they would have issued you some.

Your novel, on the other hand, must make sense. Your readers expect a cause-and-effect flow of actions and reactions. To help ensure this symmetry, conduct a sixth revision pass looking exclusively at the logic holding your story together.

Note that while you execute other revision passes scene by scene, during your logic pass you need to look at how your scenes fit—or don't fit—together. To get a better sense of how your scenes are connecting, use your updated master story summary to keep track of what's happening when and where. As you did during the other revision passes, you'll ask a series of questions to help ensure a logical flow from beginning to end. Note, too, that your responses to these questions can often necessitate changes that go across scenes.

- ☐ **Is the first bang big enough?** Do the characters' actions fit with the causal event—are they appropriate given the characters' backgrounds and personality points? If not, consider making the big bang of your story bigger or modifying it in a way that would drive your characters to action.

- ☐ **Is there cause and effect?** Look first at how each scene builds on the previous one—is there a logical progression? Although you linked each action with *and so*, *and then*, or *but* when you developed your book on an index card, you may have made changes as you wrote your first draft. If necessary, relist all the scene summaries to ensure you can connect each with an *and so*. If you can't,

mark those that stand out for rewriting or cutting. Then look within each scene. Is there a logical action-reaction in the scene's conflict? Your characters' words and actions should be consistent with their personality points and with their development at that stage of the story. This is not to say that a character can't appear to act illogically, but the reason for her actions must eventually be made clear, and those reasons should be consistent and logical—they can't come from nowhere.

☐ **Does logic work for the characters?** Look at the progression of events from each character's perspective. Is there a logical sequence of action (a discovery or event) and then reaction for each character? Is there cause and effect for actions, discoveries, and events? Make sure that once a character discovers information, she does not repeat the discovery later. If a character has made a discovery in one scene, is that information then acted on in a later scene?

- ☐ **Do events follow each other logically in time?** Even if you're writing a science-fiction novel and even if you include flashbacks, time is linear. You do not have to give equal amounts of time an equal number of pages, nor do you need to plot or retell your story hour by hour. Narration can help you sum up chunks of time that must be accounted for. However, if one event does follow another, or if a process happens over time, make sure you have events in the right order.

- ☐ **What are the effects of changes?** If you've raised the stakes or made other changes in an earlier revision pass, what is the outcome or effect of those changes on the scene in front of you? On the remainder of the scenes?

- ☐ **Can you work backwards?** Your resolution should be the logical outcome of the scene or scenes that come before it. And those scenes should be the outcome of the scenes that preceded them, and so on. Can you work backwards from your resolution to your causal event? If so, the logic of your work is probably strong.

When you complete your logic pass, you'll have a high degree of confidence that your novel makes sense. You'll also have only one more revision pass to go, so it makes sense for you to turn the page.

RELATED DRILLS

Drill 5: See Your Target
Drill 41: Change the World
Drill 43: Turn on Your Turning Points
Drill 45: Put Your Book on an Index Card
Drill 47: Plan Your Characters' Development

CIRCLE BACK FOR THE MISCELLANEOUS PASS

If you look at an inventory of equipment packaged for shipment to troops overseas, you'll notice one category stands out as the largest overall. It's neither ammunition, nor weapons, nor even toilet paper.

It's the *miscellaneous* category.

Your miscellaneous pass—the seventh and final revision pass—is the largest overall. There are a whole series of items to check scene by scene, and you may well throw in some of your own.

- ☐ **Are genre considerations addressed?** Are genre markers present? Are characters, action, dialogue, description, and narration consistent with genre expectations?

- ☐ **Are the technical details correct?** No matter what genre you write in, expect the readers of that genre to be savvy. Now's a good time to pull out your research notes and double-check the technical details of each scene. Are the technology, speech patterns, character mannerisms and manners, food, geography (and so on) accurate?

- ☐ **Visually examine the pages for signs of weakness in your writing.** While the way your text looks double-spaced on paper will be different from how it looks when printed in book format, what you see on your draft pages can be telling. Print out five or ten pages and lay them side-by-side on your desk or simply resize them on your monitor until you can view several pages at once. With your pages displayed, look for the following three indicators—they signal there's room for improvement.

- *Too Much Black.* Do the lines of text seem to run from margin to margin solidly down the page, without the white space of paragraph indents? Does any one paragraph run more than half a page? In a group of pages, does there seem to be too much black? Conditions like these may signal excessive description or narration, or an imbalance of action, dialogue, and description.
- *Too Much White.* Does each page seem to be an endless series of white paragraph indents? Do you see a staccato series of paragraphs that runs on for several pages? Sure, dialogue and action sequences may necessitate a sequence of shorter paragraphs, but you shouldn't see this on every page. Excessive paragraphing may indicate that some paragraphs should be combined, that action or description should be mixed in with dialogue, or that long exchanges should be broken up and moved.
- *Too Much of the Same.* Do your pages all seem to look the same? Does each one seem to have the same mix of long and short blocks of text? If so, your text may be telling you that you need greater variety in your mix of dialogue, description, and action.

Using your text as a visual indicator of needed revision is an unscientific method, but it's unlikely your eyes will lie. If you see something that doesn't look right, odds are it isn't.

Once you finish your miscellaneous pass, it's time to start the actual process of rewriting your manuscript. But before you start, think about how you're going to *sound* doing it—and to hear what I mean by that, read the next drill.

RELATED DRILLS

Drill 16: Know the Terrain

DRILL 93

STOP HEARING VOICES AND GET ONE

As mentioned in an earlier drill, military manuals encourage leaders to develop a command voice and a leadership style. You need to develop your own voice and style for your writing as well. The revision phase is the best place to work on your style and voice, because most writers have their hands full figuring out *what* to say during their drafting phase; only in revision is there a real opportunity to figure out *how* to say it.

You're about to do some serious rewriting, guided by your notes from your revision passes. Now's the time to think about style and voice. First though, note that there's a subtle differences between *authorial voice, style,* and the elusive *overall voice.*

Authorial voice is normally understood as the author's voice, as opposed to the voice of a character. If you use a third-person narrator, you might have a voice that uses neutral language—much as a newscaster uses. This voice would not be clouded by the outlook, agenda, or emotions of a given character.

When Tom Clancy uses a third-person narrator, that narrator gives us information that seems factual, even if the narrator is telling us what is going on inside Jack Ryan's mind or showing us the world through Ryan's eyes. It's a fact, the authorial voice signals us, that Ryan understands the world in a certain way, even if that understanding is mistaken; the fact is, that's the way he understands it.

You can complicate the issue of these differences in authorial voice, character's voice, and overall voice by noting that often a third-person narrator, either deliberately or unconsciously, introduces elements of the author's personality into the story and so becomes a character. You can also confuse the issue by saying that characters' voices are created by an author and so must be elements of authorial voice as well. However, in the interest of actually accomplishing your writing mission rather than discussing time-wasting minutia, it's well to remember to KISS and leave these esoteric debates for the classroom rather than your writing workroom.

Style describes the way you put words together. Like art, it's hard to define—but you know it when you see it. You can often tell a certain style by its ability to be imitated. Hemingway and Faulkner are good examples of very different styles. One author is famous for his terse, compact sentences; the other for flowing prose that often tossed the rules of punctuation into the trash. Both are imitated (farcically) in contests to this day.

Then there's voice—as opposed to authorial voice—a quality so slippery that even some of the best professional editors and literary agents can't agree on what it is. Things get further confused when we read of new voices or fresh voices.

If you listen to conventional (civilian) writing wisdom, a beginning novelist and apprentice author doesn't know enough to develop her own voice. Your personal style and the voice in your work will come, a budding novelist is told, when it comes. It will be ready in its time, and not before. Just relax; keep writing, and your style will reveal itself to you.

This is just nonsense. In no other craft would you develop a skill by deliberately and consciously *not* practicing it. Like other apprentices set on becoming master craftsmen, you must follow certain steps to develop your own voice.

1. **Watch (read) the masters.** Find the best writers in your genre, and of those, the ones you're most attracted to. Immerse yourself in their work.

2. **Analyze what they do.** Isolate the elements that make up each author's particular style. Look at sentence and paragraph length and variety. Note the setting, the way in which the master describes the world around the characters, and what kind of language she uses.

3. **Find what you like and dislike.** What techniques and styles appeal most to you? Which leave you cold? As you begin to acknowledge your style preferences, you'll begin to make them

yours. Your selection will reflect your own tastes, and so take you beyond slavish imitation.

4. **Practice.** Once you have your list of preferences, practice incorporating them into your own writing. Where? You should have a marked-up manuscript from your revision passes; the first sentence you have to rewrite is a good place to start.

5. **Be open to change and growth.** Your practice of a specific set of techniques will likely lead you to discoveries about what you truly like or dislike and compel you to make changes. Embrace them.

6. **Write big.** Don't be timid in approaching your style. Mediocrity is not memorable. Commit yourself to your own style and keep practicing, even as it evolves.

As you decide on and develop characters, action, and subject matter, as you pinpoint your likes and dislikes and practice your version of a certain style, you come that much closer to solidifying your own unique voice. You can't help but do so.

While you may not make a formal revision pass for style and voice, the rewriting you'll do as part of your revision phase is the place to consciously develop them. To get started on that rewriting, turn the page to the next drill.

RELATED DRILLS

Drill 5: See Your Target
Drill 16: Know the Terrain

DRILL 94

CONDUCT THE FINAL ASSAULT: REWRITING

After all the preparation, crossing the line of departure into enemy territory, finding and locating the opposing force, and closing in, there comes a time when a military unit has to get up close and personal and go hand-to-hand with the opposing force. It's a make-or-break time; time to conduct the final assault.

It's that time for you now, too. Time to rewrite.

The rewriting stage is the last stage of the revision process. In each of your seven revision passes, you identified and marked the work you need to do. Using the following guidelines, it's time to get that work done.

- ☐ **Plan your time.** Your first step is to map out your plan of attack. As with previous phases, give yourself goals and deadlines to regulate your workflow and your creative energy. Be specific. *Work on chapter five for eight hours this week* is too general. What exactly will you work on and what will you accomplish by the end of those eight hours? Instead, work at the scene level. Assign yourself daily tasks and concrete goals. For example: *Complete the rewrites for three scenes on Tuesday, three on Wednesday, two on Thursday, and one on Friday*, or *Complete all rewrites for one scene every day this week.*

- ☐ **Make a backup copy of your manuscript.** Before you began the triage process, you saved a backup copy of your first draft and created a working copy of that draft. Then you cut scenes from that copy and printed it out again. You probably made notes on this copy as you completed your revision passes. Now that it's time for rewriting, save a backup copy of the draft as it exists now and create a new working copy to use during the revision process. Make all your changes in this new working copy, and (of course) exercise good computer discipline and save often.

- ☐ **Review your master story summary.** Even though you finished a logic revision pass just a few drills ago, review your post-triage master story summary one last time. This will give you an overall feel for your work and serve as verification that each scene builds from the scenes that precede it and sets up the scenes that follow.
- ☐ **Work one scene at a time.** Keep your focus at the scene level and, as a general rule, finish the rewrites on one scene before moving on to the next. Look over the scene to get a comprehensive understanding of the nature of the changes you've marked. You'll likely notice some trends in your comments that will help shape the focus of your rewriting efforts for that scene. If you decided to move or delete parts of a scene, do that first.
- ☐ **Do a line edit.** Next, work your way through the manuscript one scene at a time going line by line. Focus on a single task, such as rewriting a certain character's description, until you're finished with it. This minimizes your back-and-forth movement so that you don't find yourself going in circles.

You'll likely get additional ideas on how to improve each scene as you make your changes. Go with them—the very act of improving a sentence, passage, paragraph, or scene will cause your imagination to work harder.

Expect the first few scenes to be a challenge. After all, this is a new skill and a new process to you. However, after you've rewritten ten to twelve scenes or so, you'll probably find yourself falling into a rhythm. On the other hand, if you get stuck and can't determine a way to accomplish what your revision notes direct, try deliberately using techniques from the drafting missions in this book to jump-start your creativity.

When you've finished rewriting a scene, check your work against your marked-up manuscript. Have you addressed all your notes? How well? Again, you'll likely notice opportunities for additional improvement. Now's your chance.

Rewriting is, to many novelists, the heart and soul of writing. It can take many days or weeks, and it's an exhausting process. Sometimes, in their exhaustion, novelists begin to see things that aren't there—they hallucinate. For the causes and cures of these hallucinations, turn the page to the next drill.

RELATED DRILLS

Drill 4: Control Your Calendar
Drill 5: See Your Target
Drill 46: Build Your Master Story Summary

MISSION X

DRILL 95

STOP HAVING HALLUCINATIONS ALONG THE WAY

Hallucinations on the battlefield aren't uncommon—ask any soldier who faced the enemy across a dark no-man's-land if he didn't ever hallucinate that the bushes were moving. Combat is intense and produces intense emotions—and, sometimes, hallucinations.

Storytelling is an intensely creative act. Sometimes the creative power needed to write a novel can have unforeseen side effects. If you're not careful, several kinds of detrimental delusions can find their way into your draft. As you revise your manuscript, look for and eliminate these three kinds of story-halting hallucinations.

1. You hallucinate that your characters are real. This happens when a novelist sees his characters as real people and begins to write as if those same characters act like real people. Your characters may seem or feel real to you—that's fine—but should characters act real? No. They must be believable, driven, compelling, and interesting. They must move your reader's emotions and demand his attention.

Real people can act illogically. Real people can be standoffish, never making emotional connections with anyone. Real people can be stagnant and inactive—they'll do anything except decide on a goal and take action in pursuit of it. And real people can be boring and can do boring things.

If your characters were to act like real people, they wouldn't have larger-than-life problems; wouldn't move heaven, earth, and Fort Benning to solve them; and wouldn't risk everything they have and all that they are to achieve their objectives. Like many other real people, they wouldn't necessarily even have objectives. They might just get up, go to work, come home, walk the dog, and go to bed.

In other words, they'd be boring.

2. You hallucinate your book is something other than a novel. Your novel is a story of compelling characters taking actions in pursuit of objectives that mean the world—and more—to them. Regardless of genre, every chapter, scene, and page should be a recounting of those characters making discoveries, taking actions, and responding to events.

If you hallucinate that you can take a break from storytelling to paint a word picture of a scenic landscape; lecture on political, social, or moral values; describe a scientific phenomenon or complex process; or otherwise put your storyteller's duties aside, you no longer have a novel—you have a travel guide, political treatise, lecture, sermon, or textbook (unless you're John Steinbeck, and then you have a Pulitzer Prize).

3. You hallucinate that your first draft is your final copy. Finishing your draft can be exhilarating. Revision is a tough, demanding, and stressful task. You've worked hard—shouldn't that be enough? Well, sort of. Your hard work is enough—for a good start. Your novel is neither essay nor business report. No matter how good your draft, it is still a draft.

Many novelists are prone to these hallucinations, especially in the intense work of revision. In the military, hallucinations are the result of stress.

While you're writing your novel, they can be the result of stress as well. If you find yourself hallucinating, take a breather, do some push-ups, and take another look at your calendar to see if you can adjust your pace. Whatever you do, keep a close grip on the reality of the novel you're writing.

Regardless of the action you take to combat hallucinations, you need to put the final touches on your manuscript. Find out what those touches are and how to make them; turn the page to the next mission.

RELATED DRILLS

Drill 5: See Your Target
Drill 84: Triage Your Scenes
Drill 89: Go on the Narration Diet

BATTLE PLAN FOXTROT

EDITING AND PROOFREADING

MISSION XI: GIVE YOUR PROSE A SPIT SHINE . . 283

Drill 96: Focus Your Editing and Proofreading 284

Drill 97: Let It Simmer 289

Drill 98: Breach a Minefield 291

MISSION XI

GIVE YOUR PROSE A SPIT SHINE

In the military, inspections are a way of life. After all the preparation, practice, and spit and polish, there comes a time when a military unit stands at attention and puts itself under scrutiny.

Now it's your manuscript's turn to go under the microscope. In the editing and proofreading phase of your battle plan, focus on eliminating errors. Move through each scene sentence by sentence, improving each one independently so that it's the best sentence it can be. This way, each sentence receives a focused edit and proof. Then let your manuscript simmer for a while, giving your subconscious mind time to review what you've done and come up with suggestions. Finally, review the last drill in this mission to learn how to evaluate reader comments on your work. (Although you know better than to let someone close to you read your work, you'll likely do it anyway.)

This mission is no light touch-up job; you'll be doing some rubbing and buffing that will require concentration and close attention to detail. The result will be a highly professional, polished manuscript that can proudly take its place in formation.

DRILL 96

FOCUS YOUR EDITING AND PROOFREADING

Working on a manuscript is like zeroing in on a target with artillery fire. You make big shifts until you get the small marking explosions close to the target, then you make small adjustments to get a direct hit—then comes a really, really big bang. Focused editing and proofreading are those fine adjustments that help you get your sentences right on target.

Like other drills in your battle plan, this drill focuses your energy on techniques that will get you the most bang for your editing buck. You'll get good at this drill because you're going to apply it to every sentence in your manuscript.

Yes, every single sentence from page one to *The End*. Thinking about skipping some sentences you already know are good? Think you've done enough? Do push-ups until you get those thoughts out of your head. Then, for each sentence, do the following. (And because you need multiple layers of defense against errors, plan on using all of these techniques, not just one.)

1. **Use, but don't trust, your spell-checker.** Use the spell-check function of your word-processing program as a first line of defense only. Spell-check is very handy, but it's also one of the dumbest functions in a word-processing program. Spell-checkers miss most usage problems. If you accidentally type *the huskies blushed* instead *of the huskies mushed*, you could end up with a sentence that makes no sense (not to mention a pack of embarrassed sled dogs). A spell-checker will not catch your mistake if you use *your* when you should have used *you're* or when you've mixed up *there*,

their, and *they're*. Nonetheless, if your program has an option to mark spelling errors as you type, turn that option on as you write, even if you consider the squiggly lines or other markers a minor aggravation. If your word processor has a grammar-check function, turn that on as well.

2. **Kill a tree.** Proofread from a printed copy. When we read on a monitor, we tend to skim, often skipping over entire sentences. This is especially true when rereading your own work. You'll more readily skip over a typo, misspelling, incorrect word, or grammar error when reading from a screen. In one study, participants were seven times more likely to miss an error when proofing text on a computer monitor than when doing so off a printed copy. Go buy a ream of cheap paper, set your printer to a medium quality, hit print, and work from a printed copy.

3. **Work backwards with sentences.** Proofread a scene at a time (or smaller chunks, depending upon your time plan) by going from the end of the scene to its beginning one sentence at a time. This allows you to see individual words in their proper contexts while minimizing the likelihood that you'll skip over a sentence. Put a page on your desk, then slide a ruler or page-width card from the bottom of the page up one sentence at a time. This will help you isolate and focus on individual sentences. Use one of those character cards you're keeping handy. Not keeping them handy? Report to KP!

4. **Get a second set of eyes.** It's always helpful to find a detail-oriented friend or colleague who can give your manuscript the once-over for spelling and grammar. If you decide to ask a friend for help, give him your work in ten- to twenty-page chunks, which will be less intimidating than handing him your entire manuscript. (This

should not be your only correctness check, however, because in the end *you* are responsible for your work.) Be prepared to hear your proofreader's unsolicited comments on character, action, etc.

5. **Check sentence fragments.** Sentence fragments? Good. Especially in dialogue. Too many or too few? Maybe. They can make dialogue, description, or a scene really move. Fast. If noticeable, you've overdone it.

6. **Check vocabulary.** Vocabulary in fiction is about your characters, your genre, and your reader. Words that are appropriate and expected in vampire erotica will most likely be either ineffective or alarming in a cozy mystery. What words would your characters use? What are the norms of your genre? What are your audience's expectations?

7. **Check sentence complexity.** Let your characters be complex, your sentences simple. Break long, complex sentences into shorter, simpler ones. While subject-verb-object gets old if repeated too often, make it your mainstay. And it's okay to begin a sentence with a conjunction. But like any technique, don't overdo. Remember that slavish adherence to formal rules of style—such as never ending a sentence with a preposition—leads to clumsy writing up with which your reader will not put.

8. **Check for grammar gotchas.** While a novelist has some license with the rules of grammar, that license only goes so far. You can bend some rules, but break them one too many times and you'll bring your manuscript's progress and your reader's attention to a dead halt. A good grammar text will give you definitions and solutions for the following seven most common problems. Here's an example of each to give you the gist of what to look for.

RUN-ON SENTENCES

He went to stand in line to get beer for his buddies and the line was really long and he saw his old girlfriend there but she wouldn't speak to him, and he was really ticked off so he waited some more and then he finally ended the run-on sentence.

COMMA SPLICES

Henrietta loaded up her car, soon she was on the road.
(One fix: Henrietta loaded up her car. Soon, she was on the road.)

SUBJECT-VERB DISAGREEMENT

Be sure that your shirt and pants is clean.
(Should be: Be sure that your shirt and pants are clean.)

FAULTY PRONOUN REFERENCE

A student is encouraged to express their creativity.
(One fix: Students are encouraged to express their creativity.)

FAULTY PARALLELISM

She wanted expensive clothes, to race fast cars, and gourmet food.
(One fix: She wanted to buy expensive clothes, to race fast cars, and to eat gourmet food.)

FAULTY VERB-TENSE SHIFTS

Just as Sam started the car, the cat jumps on the garden gnome and knocks it over.
(One fix: Just as Sam started the car, the cat jumped on the garden gnome and knocked it over.)

MISPLACED AND DANGLING MODIFIERS

The wizard stood seven feet tall with a long beard weighing almost three hundred pounds.

Despite all your efforts, a typo or two may well creep into your manuscript. That happens—the little devils are insidious. A few minor errors in your manuscript are no big deal. No human being is perfect and no product produced by a human will be either. One or two errors a page—now that's a big deal, signaling that it's time to give the manuscript another close look.

When you're confident you've flushed out your manuscript's mechanical errors, give your conscious mind a break and put your subconscious mind to work. To become conscious of how you do that, go to the next drill.

RELATED DRILLS

Drill 4: Control Your Calendar
Drill 7: Drill Your Way to Success

DRILL 97

LET IT SIMMER

Even the toughest combat units get pulled off the line to take a break, rearm, refuel, rest, and reconstitute. During those breaks, support troops, which normally operate in the background, go to work 24/7.

After you've proofed your manuscript, you should take a break as well. Put your manuscript away for a period of time to get emotional and intellectual distance from the work. Civilians often call this *letting the manuscript simmer*. Give your conscious mind some R&R, and put your subconscious into active duty. For weeks and months, your conscious mind has been doing the heavy creative lifting—from inventing to developing, revising, editing, and proofreading. All the while, your subconscious mind has been involved only in the background. An enforced break gives your subconscious mind time to consider your work as a whole. While your manuscript simmers in your desk drawer, your story will be simmering in your subconscious.

Schedule your writing process so that your work goes into the drawer just as you leave for vacation, a business trip, or a weekend getaway. Whatever activity you have planned—or even if you haven't planned anything—let your work sit for at least a couple of weeks or (ideally) a month.

After several days or a week, you may feel the urge to break out your story and look at it again. You might well have a flash of inspiration—there might be something to improve or add. You may realize you need to change something, decide to delete a scene or character, or want to make some other revision or edit. Make notes, but leave the manuscript alone—it's not done simmering, and your subconscious mind is not done thinking about it.

When you pick up the manuscript again, take your time—no rushing. As you read, you'll likely feel a strong temptation to make notes in the margins. Yield to that temptation and mark away. Only after you've read your work from beginning to end should you act on the advice your subconscious mind has given you. Then and only then should you begin to make any improvements or modifications.

The process of writing a novel is one of focusing on your text in order to make continuous improvement. From ideation through editing, concentrate on making concepts, scenes, and sentences better. When you've finished the phases of the writing process, give your conscious mind a rest and put your subconscious mind to work. Put your manuscript away and let it simmer.

Then put your hand on the page and turn to the next drill.

RELATED DRILLS

Drill 2: Adopt a Principled Approach
Drill 5: See Your Target
Drill 13: Be More Successful

DRILL 98

BREACH A MINEFIELD

Obstacles, most military strategists will tell you, are not good things to try to go through. However, sometimes the mission or tactical situation dictates that a unit go through terrain that's filled with tank traps or barbed wire. It's dangerous ground, but with specialized tools and tactics, a unit can make it through.

Having someone read and respond to your novel is like volunteering to negotiate a minefield. When it's time to traverse this literary minefield, ensure you get focused feedback and not a face full of shrapnel by asking your early reader to respond only to the following three specific questions.

1. **At what point did you put it down?** If your reader went from beginning to end without halting, that's an indicator that your first thirty pages are doing their job of introducing the situation, characters, and stakes while holding the reader's attention. On the other hand, if your friend says that at page eight she took a break to have a root canal—well, that speaks for itself.

2. **What characters did you feel the most strongly about?** If your reader hates your protagonist's opponent (a.k.a. your villain), consider reexamining that character to give her some qualities that make her at least a little sympathetic and therefore more complex. If, however, your reader doesn't remember your protagonist's name, closely evaluate how you can make your protagonist more intense and even larger than larger than life.

3. **What parts did you skip?** The answer to this question can be a real eye-opener. Although the answer will surely differ from reader to

reader, what a reader decides not to read is important. By skipping a passage, your reader is telling you that that section of text didn't establish an emotional connection. Check these skipped passages closely—they're prime targets for rewriting or elimination.

It's usually best for your early reader to be an objective party, like a member of a critique group. However, you may decide to share your work with a friend or family member. After all, these are people who know you well, whose opinions you trust, and who want you to succeed. But to spare the strain on your friendship or relationship, make sure your reader understands that you're not asking what she, your *buddy*, thinks. Rather, you're asking what she, a *book-buying reader*, thinks. Also, it's best not to toss a five-hundred-page opus at a friend—no matter how close you are. Instead, give her just the first thirty pages and ask for responses on very specific topics. Otherwise, keep the relationship and put away the manuscript.

Maybe it's time to talk to someone other than your close friends about your writing. Maybe it's time to enter the larger writing community. To find your way out there, turn the page to the next mission.

RELATED DRILLS

Drill 5: See Your Target

Drill 10: Write What You Must

BATTLE PLAN GOLF

STAYING BATTLE READY

MISSION XII: GO BEYOND BOOT CAMP 294

Drill 99: Get the Most From Writing Groups 295

Drill 100: Scout Out Writers' Conferences 298

Drill 101: Plan Your Next Move 301

MISSION XII

GO BEYOND BOOT CAMP

There comes a time when a boot camp trainee has learned all he can learn in basic training. He's physically fit and mentally focused. He's ready to leave the training environment of boot camp, join a unit, and become part of a wider and more complex military environment and community.

There's a larger environment and community awaiting you, as well. The drills in this mission address two of the most relevant parts of that community: writing groups and writers' conferences. In addition, this mission looks at life after boot camp—at how to stay focused and dedicated to your craft long after you've mastered the drills presented here.

So, how will your book fare in its first true test of combat readiness—that is, will it survive its first encounter with a reader? There are no guarantees, save one. If you've followed the battle plan outlined here, you can have a high degree of confidence that you've produced a quality work of fiction.

Now do a few push-ups to build your courage and go see what—and who—is out there.

DRILL 99

GET THE MOST FROM WRITING GROUPS

There's an old military saying: If you have a choice, never join a unit with three or more Murphys in it.

Soldiers may not have a choice about what unit they're assigned to, but you do have a choice about what groups you join. Writing is not as solitary a pursuit as common wisdom would have us believe. By joining a writers' group, you can connect with other writers and find feedback, support, encouragement, and education in the art, craft, and business of writing.

Writing groups are a dime a dozen, so you shouldn't need to search too long or too hard to find a group of writers who regularly come together to discuss their art and craft. Communities often offer them as part of their parks and recreation services (or the equivalent).

In addition, libraries often sponsor meetings for readers who desire to write. Then there are writers' associations such as Mystery Writers of America (www.mysterywriters.org) and Romance Writers of America (www.rwanational.org), which often have local chapters with active writing groups. Some bookstores, both independents and chains, sponsor writers groups as well.

There are also a wide variety of groups on the Internet. Most major service providers have at least one writers' group (or discussion list, or forum) for each genre, and many have several. If you can't find a group locally, you're almost sure to find one virtually.

Availability of a group isn't the issue—the quality of a group is. The ultimate measure of a writing group's quality is how well and how much it contributes to your growth as a novelist and to the effectiveness of your novel. The right group should give you much in both these areas. The wrong group can be a waste of your time. Even worse, the wrong group can waste your emotional and creative energies and do damage to your work.

Telling right from wrong in a writers' group takes close observation and an investment of time. To determine if a writers' group is right for you, look at the group from both the outside and the inside.

Check it out from the outside. Look at the group's Web site (if it has one) and ask several group members the following questions.

- *What forms and genres do members of the group write in?* A group of all poets or magazine article writers might well be interesting, but a group that specializes in your genre will be able to provide more focused feedback. If several genres and forms are represented, how does the group address the needs of specific members?
- *What's the group's process and agenda?* How often does the group meet? (Once or twice a month is best.) Is there homework outside of meetings? Do guest speakers ever come? Is there a moderator or facilitator? Are there published rules or guidelines?
- *What is supposed to happen during meetings?* The group needs a plan for its meetings. Do people read their work? Distribute copies of scenes or chapters for feedback? Discuss relevant issues in writing?

Check it out from the inside. What's supposed to happen during a meeting and what actually occurs can be two entirely different things. Sit in on a meeting and pay attention to the following.

- *Who shows up and when?* Do the members follow the agenda and rules for the group? You don't want to waste time and energy on an undisciplined mob that meanders around. If the group starts very late, if it appears disorganized, and if no one lives up to the obligation to contribute, your interests are likely better served with a different group.
- *Are group members' responses valuable?* Sometimes members of the group will do nothing but mean-spiritedly eviscerate a work.

Other times, they will offer no suggestions for improvement, simply a touchy-feely declaration of *It's good—I like it.* Neither of those responses is helpful. You need professional feedback. Acidic, satirical criticism does nothing to support you. Pollyanna-ish unconditional love for your text may be good for your ego but not for improving your novel. Group members should offer comments that are framed by the vocabulary, techniques, and concepts in this book.

- *Is the group working at the right level for you?* A good writing group challenges you to rise to a higher level of craftsmanship. You'll know in two or three meetings if the group will be able to help you. It will take about the same amount of time to know whether you'll be able to make your own contribution.

While a writers' group can give you specific guidance, sometimes you need more general information, perhaps about genre or about new or different techniques. Sometimes you just need motivation, encouragement, or a different perspective. You won't find those in the next drill, but you will learn where to start looking.

RELATED DRILLS

Drill 10: Write What You Must
Drill 13: Be More Successful
Drill 93: Stop Hearing Voices and Get One

DRILL 100

SCOUT OUT WRITERS' CONFERENCES

Military history is full of tales of battles lost because of missed opportunities: the captured plans not analyzed, the concealed trail not taken, the indicators of an attack ignored, the weakness left unexploited, the advantage not pressed.

Writers' conferences aren't combat, but they are full of opportunities—which you can either take advantage of or miss. Writers' conferences can present you with multiple opportunities to enrich both your novel and your life as a novelist. That's *can*, and not *will*—like military strategists and front-line soldiers, you must be on the lookout for opportunities and be prepared to take advantage of them as they present themselves. The best way for you to get the most from opportunities at a writers' conference is to be ready, and the best way to be ready is to follow these five guidelines.

1. **Get in the right frame of mind.** Go to the conference in a positive state of mind. A writer's' conference is a celebration of the craft of writing, and genre-specific conferences are celebrations of one particular kind of writing. Additionally, see the conference as an opportunity for you to contribute—and not just to contribute your registration fee. Can you participate in a panel discussion, contribute specific knowledge, ask a good question, or offer an experience that might add to someone else's writing success? Most writers' conferences are run on shoestring budgets and good luck; can you lend a hand to make the conference a better experience for all?

2. **Set realistic goals.** No conference is perfect. There will be last-minute changes, lack of organization, glitches, lines, clam chowder instead of vichyssoise, and a dozen other fumbles. Expect them and shrug them off. The conference team is surely doing the best it can, and you came for something other than a five-star hotel vacation.

3. **Make it an event.** The conferences you do attend should be carefully chosen special events. Treat them that way. Turn off the cell phone. Deliberately forget to check your e-mail. If the conference is over a weekend and you're staying away from home, plan on missing the TV newscasts. Splurge a little on a good dinner or room service, and be sure to splurge in a way you likely will not when you return to your real life—take some time just for you, away from others, noise, and requirements.

4. **Plan on exploring.** A writers' conference is a great opportunity to get outside your writing space, genre, mind-set, and worldview. Make the most of this opportunity by investigating new authors and genres. Identify and attend one workshop or presentation well outside your area of usual interest. Take good notes when you do attend a presentation, speech, or workshop. In each event you attend, strive to learn one new item. If there is a freebie table or display with promotional items, take one of everything.

5. **Leverage the camaraderie.** Everyone at a conference shares common interests and a common desire to see others succeed. Take advantage of this bond and goodwill. Plan on meeting and greeting both new writers and published novelists. Introduce yourself to at least one new person in each workshop or event. Bring your contact information (on business cards or in some other distributable form), and carry a small notepad to get information from those people who aren't as prepared as you are. Soak in the support—everyone at the conference wants you to succeed—and note how that support makes you feel. Doing so will provide you with a reserve of emotional energy you can use when your writing turns difficult.

Writing groups and conferences can give you the opportunity to find encouragement, feedback, information on valuable new techniques, inspiration, even advice and direction. In the end, though, it's you who will have to make the decisions, especially the decision on what to do with that manuscript you've just completed. To see what your options are, it's time to execute one more drill—so turn the page.

RELATED DRILLS

Drill 4: Control Your Calendar

Drill 12: Make Peace With the Publishing Industry

Drill 13: Be More Successful

DRILL 101

PLAN YOUR NEXT MOVE

In the military, after a trainee successfully completes boot camp, the new soldier goes on to her unit or to advanced training. After completing one mission, military units refit, rearm, and prepare for new missions.

So now what for you?

Your courses of action boil down to two: put your manuscript away or publish it.

1. Put it away. Yes, you've already let your work simmer for thirty days, give or take. However, you can still bundle up those pages and lock them away in a drawer or closet. For how long? Who knows? You've accomplished what you set out to do—you've written a novel. Take pride in your accomplishment. Many people paint, make pottery, carve sculptures, or write poetry for themselves and just for themselves. There is nothing wrong with writing a novel for the sole purpose of being able to tell yourself that you did it and did it well. Unless your manuscript centers on contemporary events and is time-sensitive, you lose little by setting your manuscript aside and going on to your next creative project, whether that project is executing a battle plan for your next book or learning to ride a motorcycle. In the end, the person who's responsible for your creative efforts and the person you must answer to is the person you greet in the mirror every morning. If that person is pleased with your efforts and results, you truly need to please no one else.

It's more than likely, though, that you have a hunger to make your creative work public. If that's the case, you'll want to explore your second course of action, below.

2. Publish it. You can fill several bookshelves with how-to books on getting your work published, and it would be presumptuous to even attempt to summarize them here. There are many forms of publishing—traditional, self, independent, small-press, electronic—and each has its benefits and liabilities. While no one can make the choice for you, there are several important issues to take into consideration as you think about publishing your novel.

- *Think long-term.* Take the longest view possible. Where do you want to be—in terms of your writing—next year? In five years? In ten? Having a time frame in mind can help you shape your goals.
- *Decide whether you see writing as a business or as a hobby.* This is a critical decision and one that is often overlooked by many novelists. How you position yourself—as someone in the novel-writing business out to make a profit or as a hobbyist who writes mostly for enjoyment—has significant consequences, especially in terms of U.S. federal tax liabilities.
- *Do your homework.* You prepared thoroughly well before you drafted your first sentence. Your preparation for publishing your work should be just as extensive. You need to understand how the publishing industry works, the obstacles your manuscript must overcome, the role of agents and editors, distribution, marketing, query letters, synopsis, and much more. You also need to be aware of the legion of scam artists more than ready to separate an uninitiated novelist from her money. It's here that the writing community—found in writing groups and conferences—can be exceptionally helpful.

Whatever path you choose, know that you are already a success. While millions of people talk about writing a novel, very few ever start, and far fewer reach those two words that signal they've demonstrated the personal and creative discipline necessary to complete a book-length work of fiction: *The End.* You have. Do some push-ups—not because you have to but because you can.

Boot camp is finished. Your mission is accomplished. Now, with your manuscript in hand, you're no longer a trainee. Congratulations on completing your novel.

So, what's your next book about?

APPENDIX

TWELVE-WEEK NOVELIST'S BOOT CAMP

Military basic training (boot camp) runs from twelve to twenty-four weeks, depending on the branch of service, specialty, and other factors. Novelist's boot camp is a twelve-week program based on the six primary battle plans.

Twelve weeks is eighty-four days of hard work. In boot camp, recruits often work twelve-, fourteen-, or twenty-four-hour days. You probably can't pull that kind of shift when writing your novel—you likely have a job, a family, and other responsibilities that make claims on your time and energy.

These eighty-four days may therefore take you an entire calendar year to complete. Use the schedule below as a guide and adapt it to your own situation, needs, and activities. While you don't want your life to get in the way of your novel, you also don't want your novel to get in the way of your life. What's critical is that you allocate your time proportionally as outlined in the plan below, that you establish target dates for achieving the listed objectives, and that you follow the plan to ensure that you create an integrated, interesting work of fiction.

WEEK 1

Battle Plan Alpha: Mental Preparation and Mission Planning

Mission I: Get Your Imagination in Formation

- ☐ Develop a novelist's mind-set
- ☐ Develop calendar

Battle Plan Bravo: Invention

Mission II: Invent Your Comprehensive Concept

- ☐ Create comprehensive concept
- ☐ Choose genre
- ☐ Develop main character, opposition, macro setting
- ☐ Begin research

WEEK 2

Battle Plan Charlie: Development

Mission III: Enlist Your New Recruits

- ☐ Develop character matrix
- ☐ Write character bios
- ☐ Create character cards

WEEK 3

Battle Plan Charlie: Development

Mission IV: Devise Your Operations Order

- ☐ Create master story summary (scene list and summaries)
- ☐ Create book on an index card (BIC)

WEEK 4

Battle Plan Delta: Drafting

Mission V: Cross the Line of Departure

- ☐ Complete 25 percent of scenes on scene list

WEEK 5

Battle Plan Delta: Drafting

Mission VI: Commit Your Reserves

- ☐ Complete 45 percent of scenes on scene list

WEEK 6

Battle Plan Delta: Drafting

Mission VII: Sound Off!

- ☐ Complete 65 percent of scenes on scene list

WEEK 7

Battle Plan Delta: Drafting

Mission VIII: Execute Shock and Awe

- ☐ Complete 95 percent of scenes on scene list

WEEK 8

Battle Plan Delta: Drafting

Mission IX: Utilize Stealth Techniques

- ☐ Complete 100 percent of scenes on scene list

Battle Plan Echo: Revision and Rewriting

Mission X: Advance to Contact

- ☐ Perform triage to completed first draft

WEEK 9

Battle Plan Echo: Revision and Rewriting

Mission X: Advance to Contact

- ☐ Perform character pass
- ☐ Perform objective pass
- ☐ Perform dialogue pass
- ☐ Perform description and Narration pass
- ☐ Perform action pass
- ☐ Perform logic pass
- ☐ Mark draft with notes from the revision passes

WEEK 10

Battle Plan Echo: Revision and Rewriting

Mission X: Advance to Contact

- ☐ Perform miscellaneous pass
- ☐ Mark draft with notes from the miscellaneous revision pass
- ☐ Complete 30 percent of revisions

WEEK 11

Battle Plan Echo: Revision and Rewriting

Mission X: Advance to Contact

- ☐ Complete 100 percent of revisions

WEEK 12

Battle Plane Foxtrot: Editing and Proofreading

Mission XI: Give Your Prose a Spit Shine

- ☐ Proofread draft

INDEX

Action
  checking verbs for, 138–139
  extended by dialogue, 193
  mixed with dialogue and description, 211–213
  physical, to break up dialogue, 204–207
  stretching scenes, with description, 215–219
Adverbs, avoiding, 202–203
Alpha female, 083–085
Alpha male, 080–082, 199–200
Antagonist, 074–075. *See also* Opposition
  defined, 016
  putting face on, 107–108
Authorial voice, 273–275
Backstory, 102–104
  and feather duster scene, 190–191
  for minor characters, 158
Beginning, strong, 154–156
Body language, 086–088. *See also* Facial expressions
Book–length fiction, 016
Calendar, controlling, 013–015, 303–306
Causal event, 119–120, 130
Chabon, Michael, 205
Chapter breaks, 152
Character(s). *See also* Alpha female, Alpha male, Antagonist
  adjectives that describe, 138
  creating, 019–020
  finding, 052–056
  giving distinct markers, 089–092
  importance of establishing, 049–051
  main. *See* Protagonist
  making struggle public, 170–171
  minor, telling stories of, 157–160
  oppositional. *See* Antagonist
  rounded. *See* Personality points
  types of, 074–076
  victims, 181–183
  window, 075, 098–101
Character biography, 103–104, 107
Character cards, 115–117, 158
Character development, 073, 135–137
Characterization, and description, 222
Character matrix, 112–114
Clancy, Tom, 096, 273
Clichés, 229
Cliffhangers, 161–163
Climax, defined, 017
Clothing, 089
Concept, comprehensive, 040–043
Conferences, 298–300
Conflict
  creating, with conflicting personality points, 099–100
  defined, 017
  in dialogue, 208–210
  and one–on–one confrontation, 127
  starting with, 156
Confrontation, one-on-one, 127, 131
Crais, Robert, 041, 131–132
Creativity, disciplined, 004
Critique, 291–292
Danger, physical, 178–180
Deadlines, setting, 013–014
Deadly Decisions, 121–124, 162–163
DeMille, Nelson, 179
Demolition Angel, 041, 131–132
Denouement, 017, 129
Description
  character markers, 089–092
  and dialogue, 194
  fragmenting, 245

mixed with action and dialogue, 211–213, 240–242
purposes of, 221–223, 226–227
sensual, 235–237
stretching action with, 215–219
zooming in and out, 232–234
Details, 091–092
Development phase, 073
Dialogue, 188–189. *See also* Speech patterns
alpha male, 199–200
asking questions, 196–198
in beats, with action, 204–207
mixed with action and description, 211–213
multifunctional, 193–195
tags, 201–203
Dickens, Charles, 135–136
Directives, following, 011–012
Discipline, 004–006, 009–010
Drafting
and character cards, 117
unwritten rules for, 145–147
*D*s, four, 121–122, 131, 139
Editing
and character cards, 117
focused, 284–288
line, 277
Editor, internal, 145
Ending, developing strategy for, 127–129
Ensign, Georgianne, 156
Facial expressions, 204
Feather duster scene, 190–191
Fiction
defined, 016
hallucinating about, 279–281
trends in, 029–031
types of. *See* Genre
versus reality, 061–062
First-person POV, 148–149
Foil, defined, 017
Foreshadowing, through description, 222
Genre, 044–046
and beginning, 154
choosing, 019–020
and comprehensive concept, 042
and description, 221
meeting and exceeding expectations of, 125–126
and point of view, 149
Grammar, 286–287
Griffin, W.E.B., 056, 199, 211–213
Hammett, Dashiell, 111, 128
Hosseini, Khaled, 205–206
Literary terms, defined, 016–018
Macro setting, and comprehensive concept, 042
Mannerisms, 091
Manuscript
letting simmer, 289–290, 301
publishing, 301–302
Metaphors, 230–231
Micro settings, 224–225
Minions, defined, 017
Modifiers, limiting, 238–239
Motivation. *See also* Objectives
alpha female character's, 083–085
alpha male character's, 080–082
Narration, revising, 264–265
Networking, writers' groups and conferences, 295–300
Note-taking, 024–025, 067
Novel in progress, talking about, 164–165
Objectification, 228–229
Objectives
and BIC format, 131
characters', 109–111
personalizing, 172–174
Opponent. *See* Antagonist
Opposites, finding character in, 055–056
Opposition
and BIC format, 130
and comprehensive concept, 042
defining, 105–106
Paragraph breaks, 153

Patterson, James, 161–163, 215–216
Personality points
antagonist's, 107
protagonist's, 095–097
window character's, 099–100
Personification, 228–229
Perspective. *See* Points of view
Plot, defined, 017
Plot points, intensifying, 125–126
Points of view
choosing, 148–150
defined, 017–018
and description, 222–223
shifting, 151–153
Process, trusting and following, 007
Progress, logging, 147
Proofreading, focused, 284–288
Protagonist, 074
and BIC format, 130
body language, 086–088
and comprehensive concept, 042
defined, 016
differentiating, from author, 077–079
eliminating weaknesses in, 093–094
personality points, 095–097, 130
Publishing, 301–302
industry realities, 034–036
scams, 026–028
Reader, getting feedback from, 291–292
Reading
disciplined, 023–025
to study genre, 047–048
Reich, Kathy, 121–124, 162–163
Research, 063–070, 116
Resolution, 017, 182–183
Revision. *See also* Editing, Rewriting
action, 266–267
and character cards, 117
character, 253–255
description, 262–263
dialogue, 259–261
logic, 268–270
miscellaneous, 271–272
narration, 264–265
objective, 256–258
scene triage, 249–252
Rewriting, 276–278
Scene
feather duster, 190–191
slow motion, 217–219
triage, 247, 249–252
Scene list, 066–067, 133
Scene summaries, 133–134
Schedule, weekly, 303–305
Sebold, Alice, 225
Second-person POV, 148
Senses, 235–237, 244
Setting, 059–060
and description, 221
defined, 017
Shaara, Michael, 172–174, 234, 240–242
Sidekicks, defined, 017
Similes, 230–231
Slow motion scenes, 217–219
Speech patterns, 089–090, 208–210
Story idea, 057–058
Story line, 019, 073, 121–124, 139
Story time, 184–185
Structure, assessing, 023
Style, 018, 273–275
Subplots, defined, 017
Success, commercial, critical, and personal, 037–038
Summary
BIC, 130–132, 139
story, 133–134
through dialogue, 194–195
Technique, studying, 023–024
Theme, 018
Third-person POV, 148–149
Time, establishing passage of, 184–185
Trends, trying to predict, 029–031
Victims, drafting, 181–183
Voice, 018, 273–275
Web sites, researching, 069–070
Workspace, 032–033
Writer's block, 166–168
Writers' groups, 295–297
Writing goals, daily, 146

ABOUT THE AUTHOR

Multiple award-winning novelist Todd A. Stone is the author of four novels in two genres, the head writer for the Web's only interactive forensic investigation site, Crime Scene www.crimescene.com, a teacher of writing, and a salaried professional communications manager.

An avid motorcyclist, Stone is a former Army Airborne/Ranger Infantry officer whose military assignments included duty as an assistant professor at the United States Military Academy at West Point.

Stone is a member of the Author's Guild, Mystery Writers of America, EPIC (the Electronically Published Internet Connection), the National Writers' Union, the Crime Writers' Guild, and is a graduate of his local Citizens Police Academy. He is a founding member of the board of the internationally renowned mystery/dark fiction conference Love Is Murder.

Stone also consults on corporate communications in Chicagoland, teaches collegiate writing workshops, and presents at writers' conferences throughout the country.

He has his undergraduate degree from Indiana University and his master's in English from Northwestern University. He lives with his family in a perfectly normal suburb outside Chicago, Illinois.